# MONDO POPEYE®

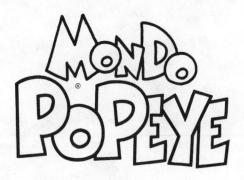

# MONDO POPEYE

**BOBBY LONDON**

St. Martin's Press   New York

First Edition

# MONDO POPEYE®

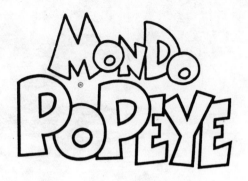

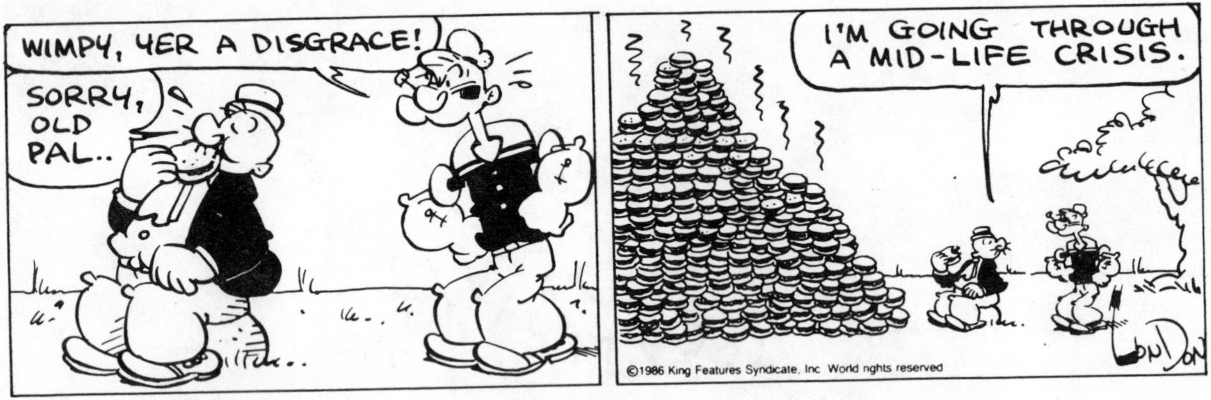
WIMPY, YER A DISGRACE!
SORRY, OLD PAL..
I'M GOING THROUGH A MID-LIFE CRISIS.
©1986 King Features Syndicate, Inc World rights reserved

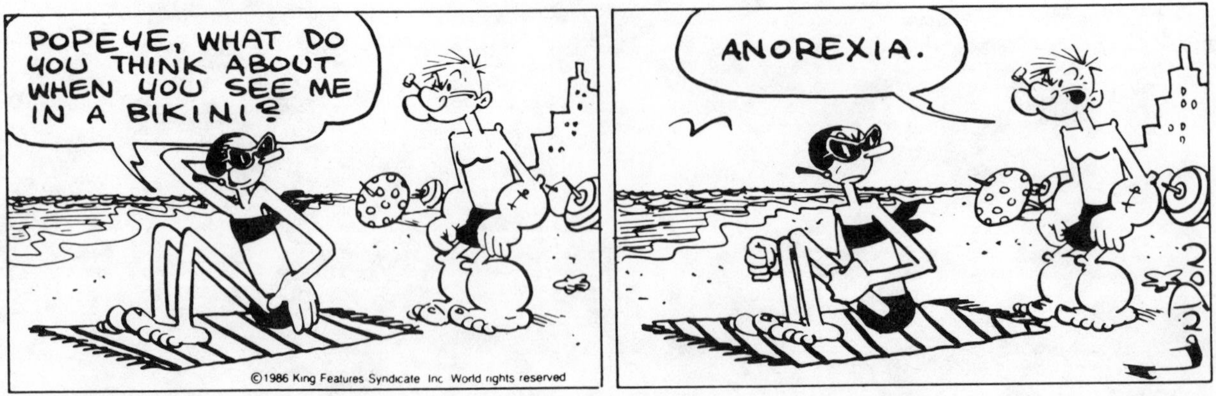
POPEYE, WHAT DO YOU THINK ABOUT WHEN YOU SEE ME IN A BIKINI?
ANOREXIA.
©1986 King Features Syndicate Inc World rights reserved

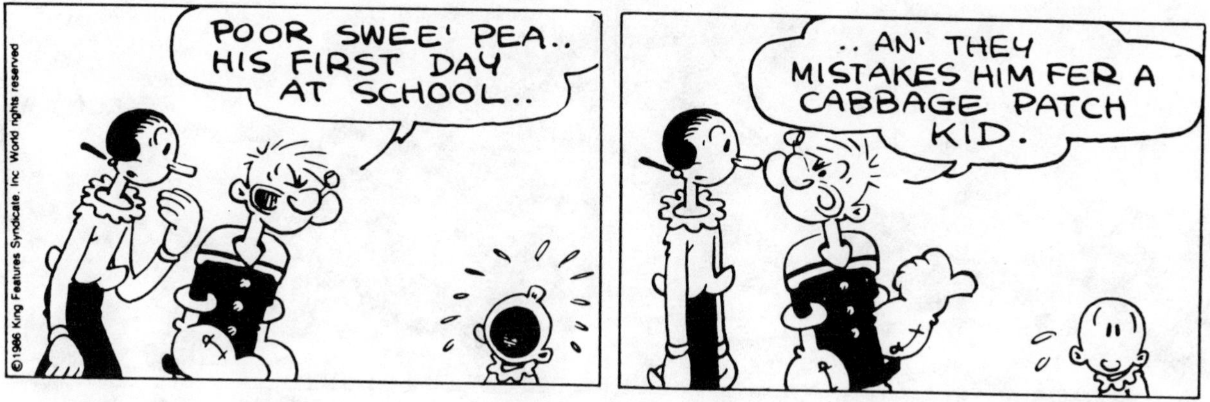
©1986 King Features Syndicate, Inc World rights reserved
POOR SWEE' PEA.. HIS FIRST DAY AT SCHOOL..
.. AN' THEY MISTAKES HIM FER A CABBAGE PATCH KID.

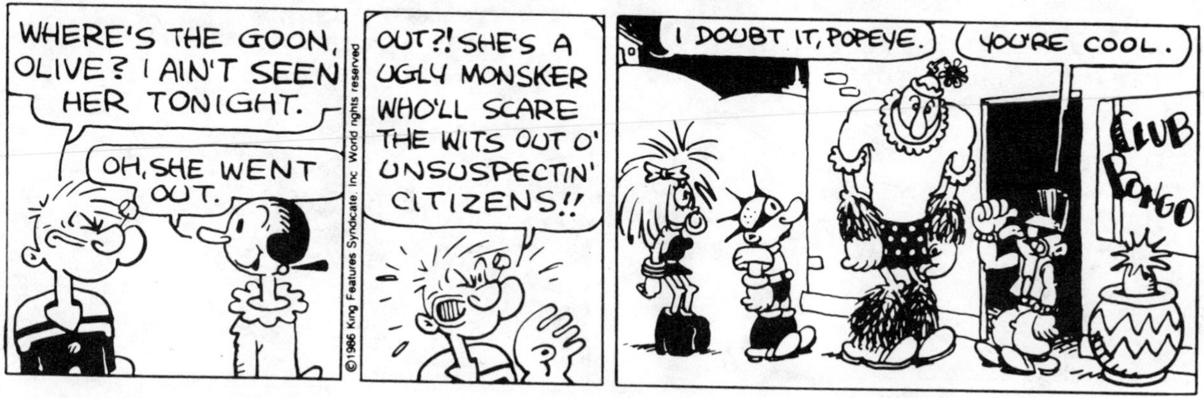
WHERE'S THE GOON, OLIVE? I AIN'T SEEN HER TONIGHT.
OH, SHE WENT OUT.
©1986 King Features Syndicate, Inc World rights reserved
OUT?! SHE'S A UGLY MONSKER WHO'LL SCARE THE WITS OUT O' UNSUSPECTIN' CITIZENS!!
I DOUBT IT, POPEYE.
YOU'RE COOL.
CLUB BONGO

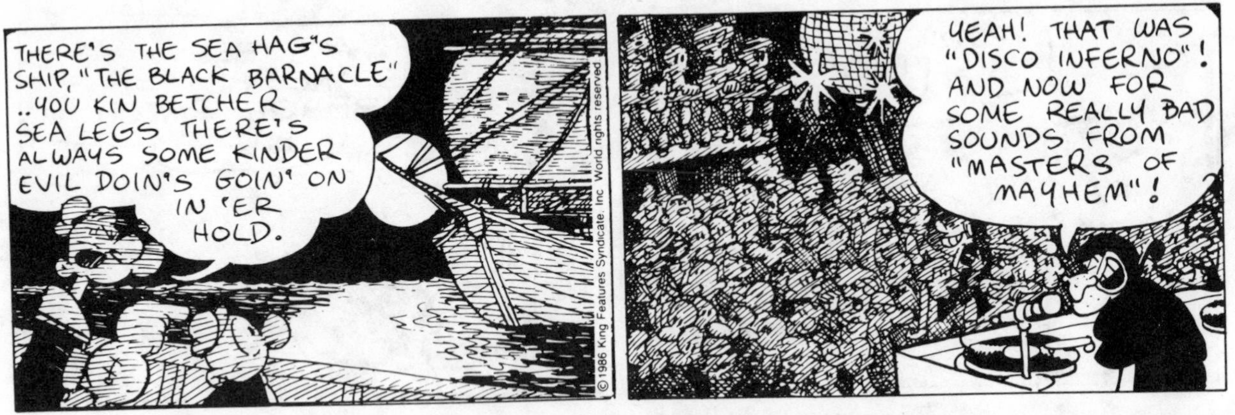
THERE'S THE SEA HAG'S SHIP, "THE BLACK BARNACLE" ..YOU KIN BETCHER SEA LEGS THERE'S ALWAYS SOME KINDER EVIL DOIN'S GOIN' ON IN 'ER HOLD.
© 1986 King Features Syndicate, Inc. World rights reserved
YEAH! THAT WAS "DISCO INFERNO"! AND NOW FOR SOME REALLY BAD SOUNDS FROM "MASTERS OF MAYHEM"!

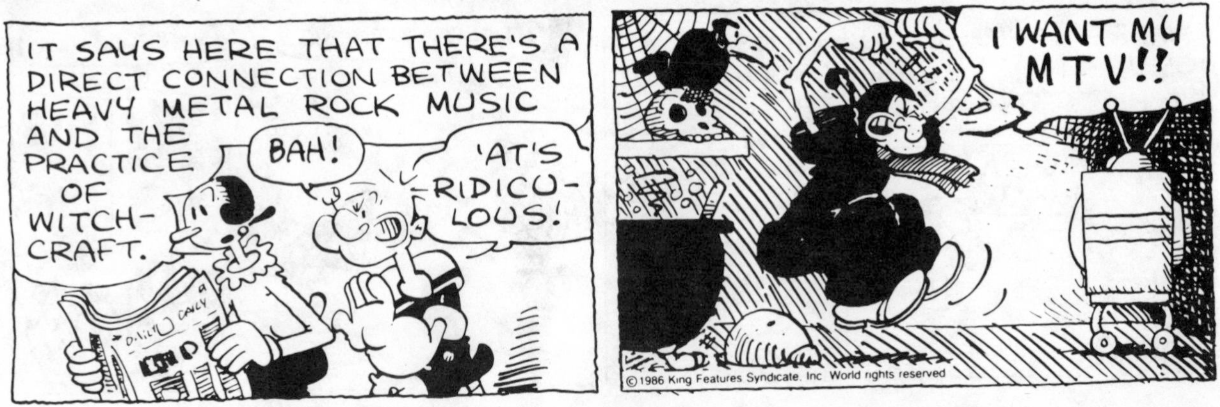
IT SAYS HERE THAT THERE'S A DIRECT CONNECTION BETWEEN HEAVY METAL ROCK MUSIC AND THE PRACTICE OF WITCH-CRAFT.
BAH!
'AT'S RIDICU-LOUS!
I WANT MY MTV!!
© 1986 King Features Syndicate, Inc. World rights reserved

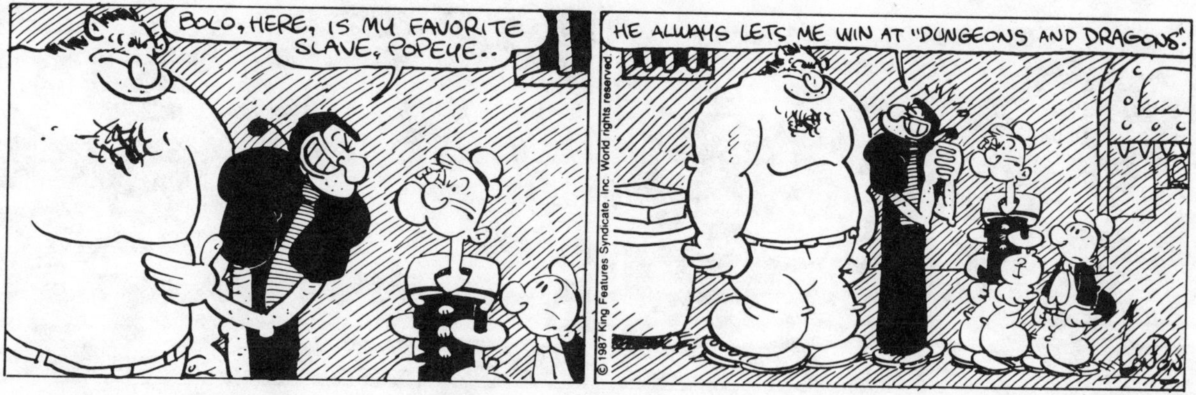
BOLO, HERE, IS MY FAVORITE SLAVE, POPEYE..
HE ALWAYS LETS ME WIN AT "DUNGEONS AND DRAGONS".
© 1987 King Features Syndicate, Inc. World rights reserved.

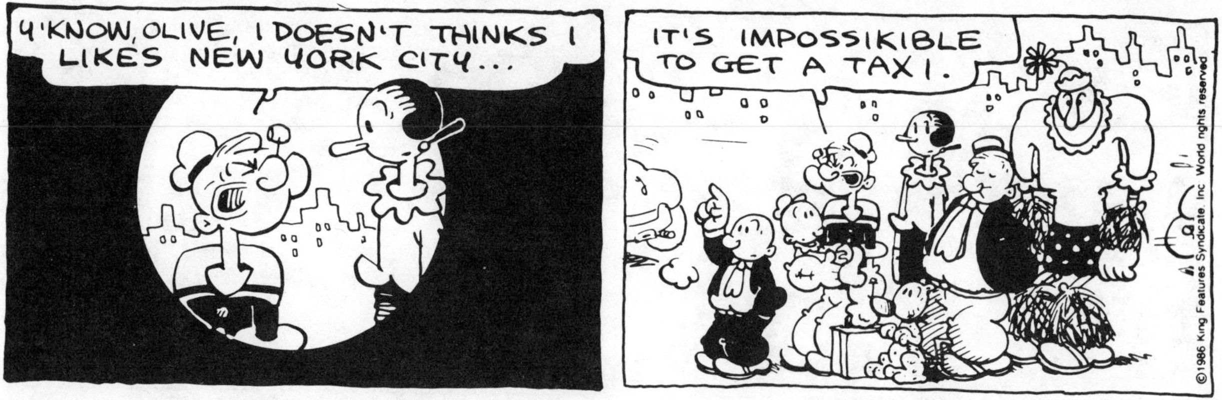
Y'KNOW, OLIVE, I DOESN'T THINKS I LIKES NEW YORK CITY...
IT'S IMPOSSIKIBLE TO GET A TAXI.
©1986 King Features Syndicate, Inc. World rights reserved

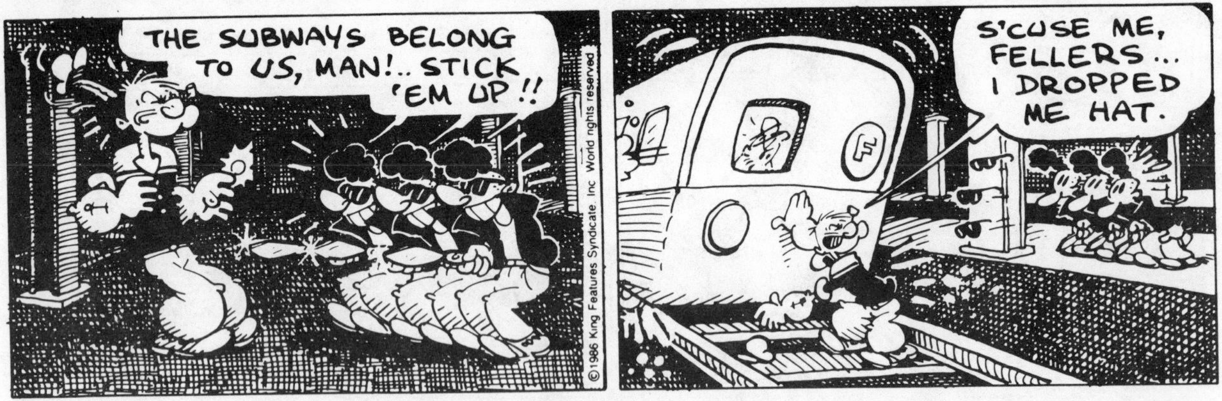
THE SUBWAYS BELONG TO US, MAN!.. STICK 'EM UP!!
©1986 King Features Syndicate, Inc World rights reserved
S'CUSE ME, FELLERS... I DROPPED ME HAT.

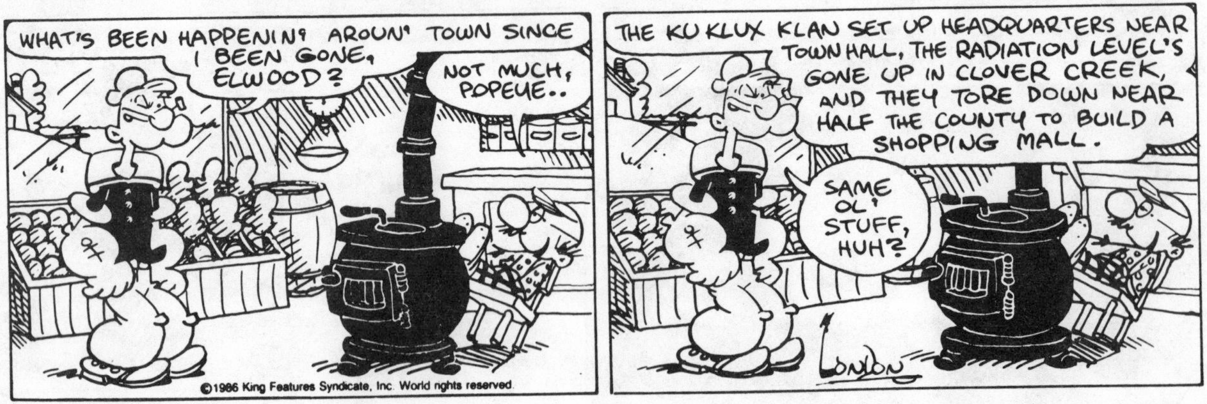
WHAT'S BEEN HAPPENIN' AROUN' TOWN SINCE I BEEN GONE, ELWOOD?
NOT MUCH, POPEYE..
THE KU KLUX KLAN SET UP HEADQUARTERS NEAR TOWN HALL, THE RADIATION LEVEL'S GONE UP IN CLOVER CREEK, AND THEY TORE DOWN NEAR HALF THE COUNTY TO BUILD A SHOPPING MALL.
SAME OL' STUFF, HUH?
LONDON
©1986 King Features Syndicate, Inc. World rights reserved.

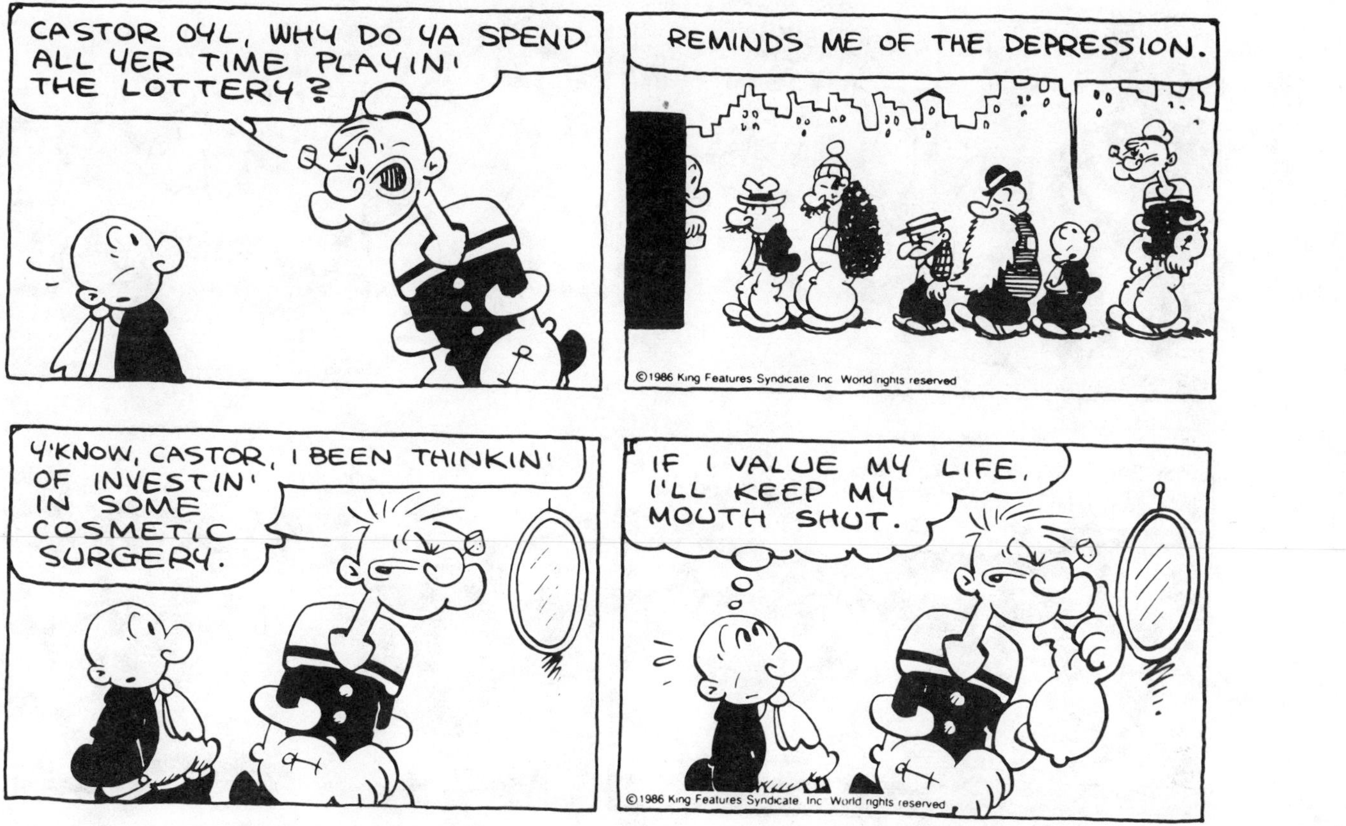
CASTOR OYL, WHY DO YA SPEND ALL YER TIME PLAYIN' THE LOTTERY?
REMINDS ME OF THE DEPRESSION.
©1986 King Features Syndicate Inc World rights reserved
Y'KNOW, CASTOR, I BEEN THINKIN' OF INVESTIN' IN SOME COSMETIC SURGERY.
IF I VALUE MY LIFE, I'LL KEEP MY MOUTH SHUT.
©1986 King Features Syndicate Inc World rights reserved

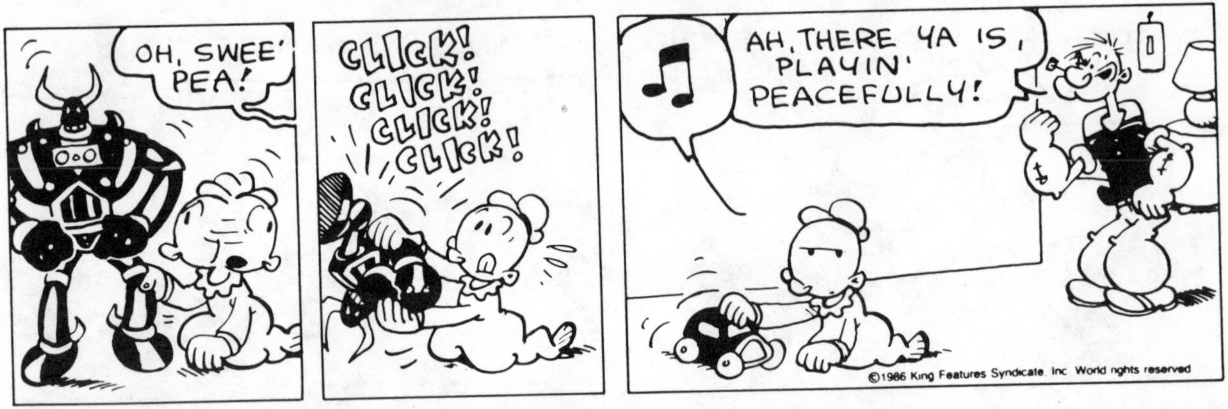
OH, SWEE' PEA!
CLICK! CLICK! CLICK! CLICK!
AH, THERE YA IS, PLAYIN' PEACEFULLY!
©1986 King Features Syndicate, Inc World rights reserved

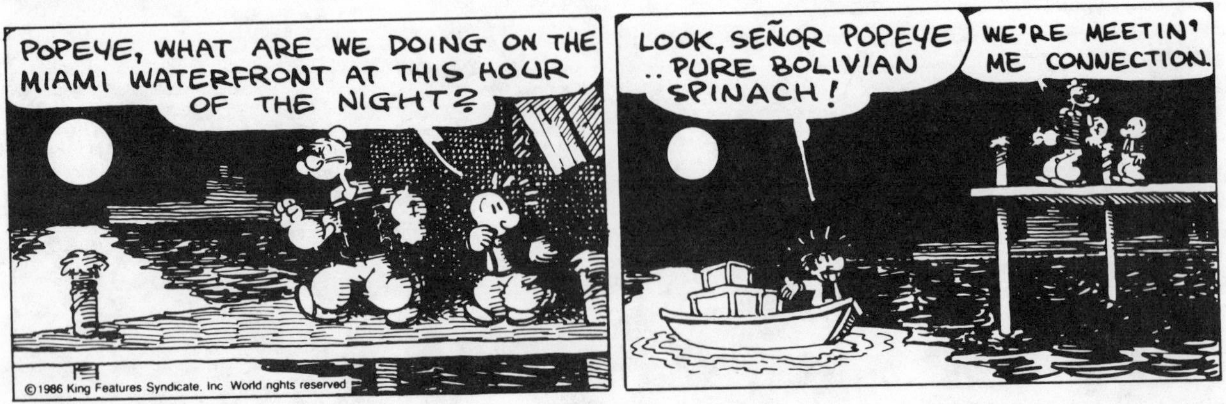
POPEYE, WHAT ARE WE DOING ON THE MIAMI WATERFRONT AT THIS HOUR OF THE NIGHT?
©1986 King Features Syndicate, Inc World rights reserved
LOOK, SEÑOR POPEYE .. PURE BOLIVIAN SPINACH!
WE'RE MEETIN' ME CONNECTION.

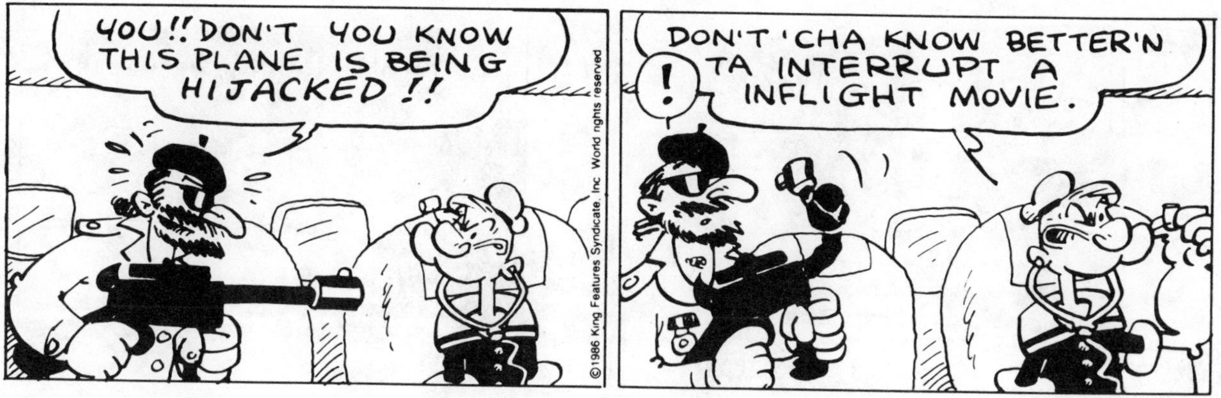
YOU!! DON'T YOU KNOW THIS PLANE IS BEING HIJACKED!!
©1986 King Features Syndicate, Inc World rights reserved
!
DON'T 'CHA KNOW BETTER'N TA INTERRUPT A INFLIGHT MOVIE.

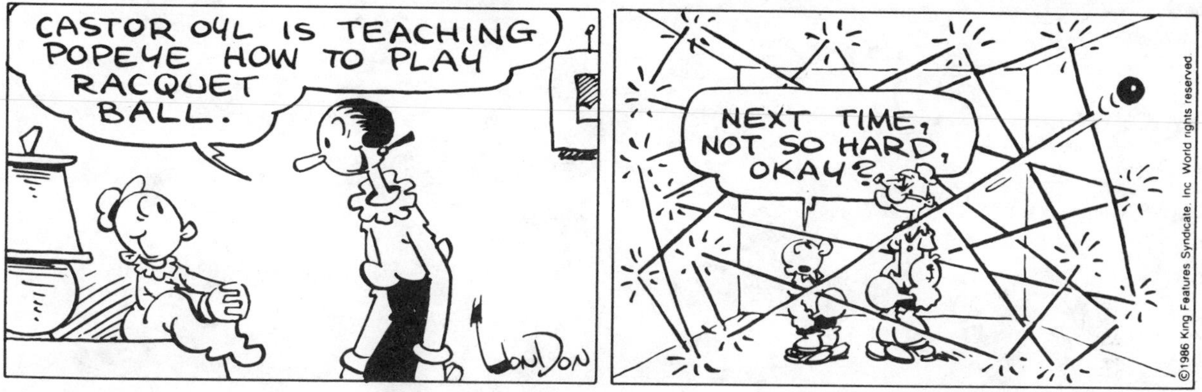
CASTOR OYL IS TEACHING POPEYE HOW TO PLAY RACQUET BALL.
NEXT TIME, NOT SO HARD, OKAY?
©1986 King Features Syndicate, Inc World rights reserved.

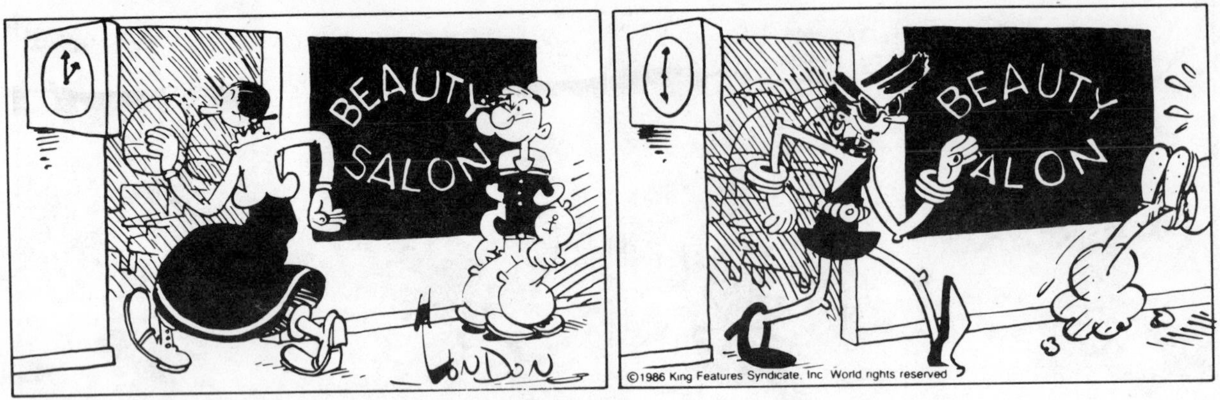
BEAUTY SALON
LONDON
BEAUTY ALON
©1986 King Features Syndicate, Inc World rights reserved

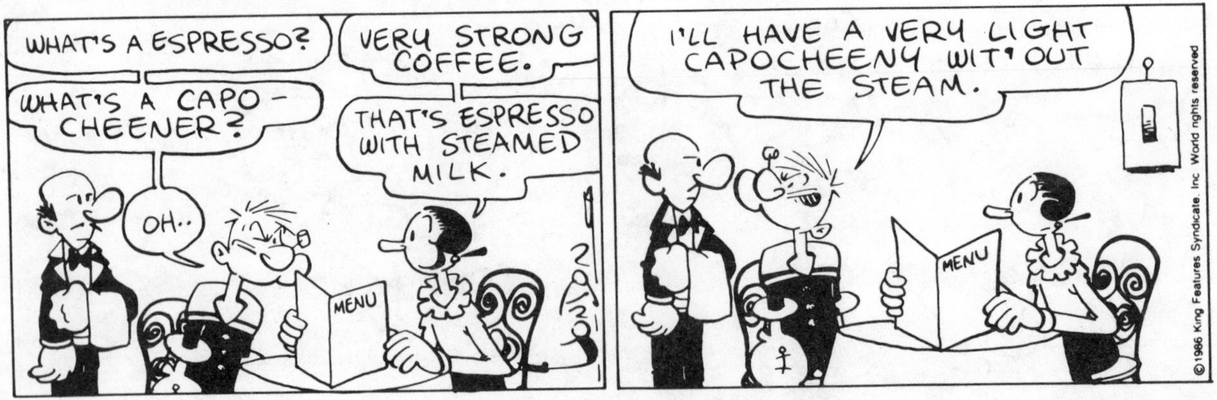
WHAT'S A ESPRESSO?
VERY STRONG COFFEE.
WHAT'S A CAPO-CHEENER?
THAT'S ESPRESSO WITH STEAMED MILK.
OH..
MENU
I'LL HAVE A VERY LIGHT CAPOCHEENY WIT'OUT THE STEAM.
MENU
©1986 King Features Syndicate, Inc World rights reserved

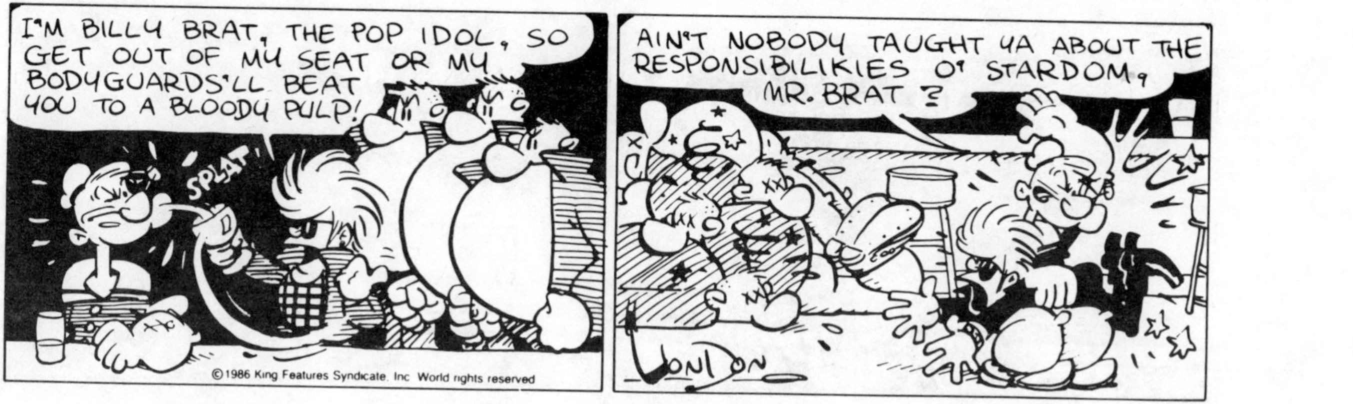
I'M BILLY BRAT, THE POP IDOL, SO GET OUT OF MY SEAT OR MY BODYGUARDS'LL BEAT YOU TO A BLOODY PULP!
SPLAT!
© 1986 King Features Syndicate, Inc World rights reserved
AIN'T NOBODY TAUGHT YA ABOUT THE RESPONSIBILIKIES O' STARDOM, MR. BRAT?
LONDON

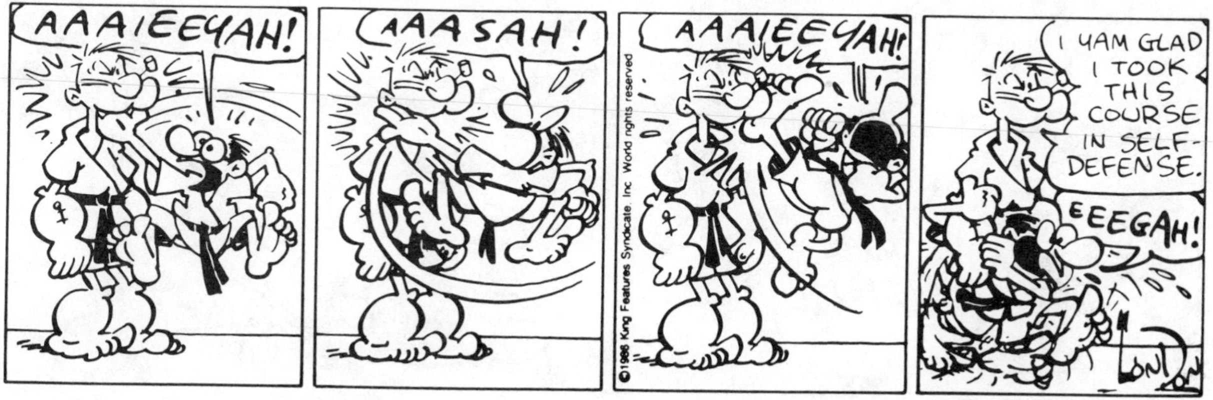
AAAIEEYAH!
AAASAH!
© 1986 King Features Syndicate, Inc World rights reserved
AAAIEEYAH!
I YAM GLAD I TOOK THIS COURSE IN SELF-DEFENSE.
EEEGAH!
LONDON

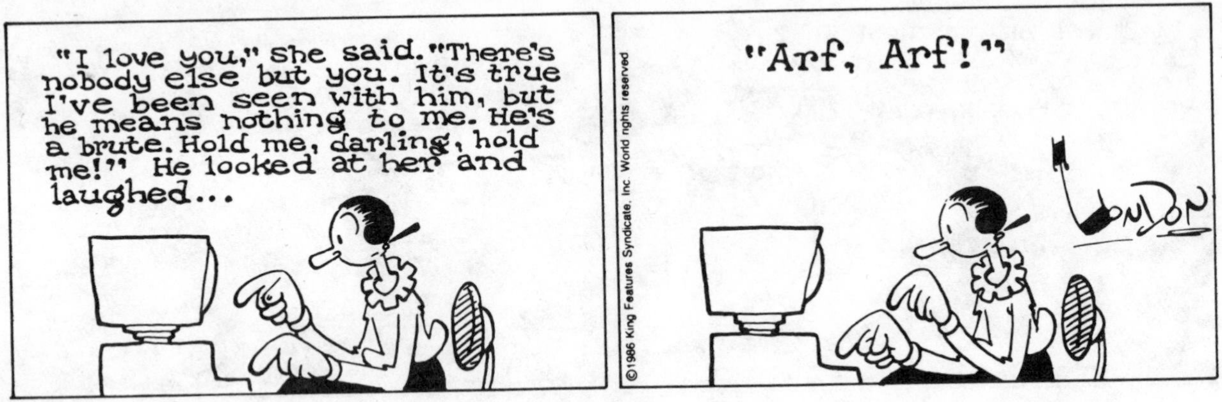
"I love you," she said. "There's nobody else but you. It's true I've been seen with him, but he means nothing to me. He's a brute. Hold me, darling, hold me!" He looked at her and laughed...
©1986 King Features Syndicate, Inc. World rights reserved
"Arf, Arf!"
LONDON

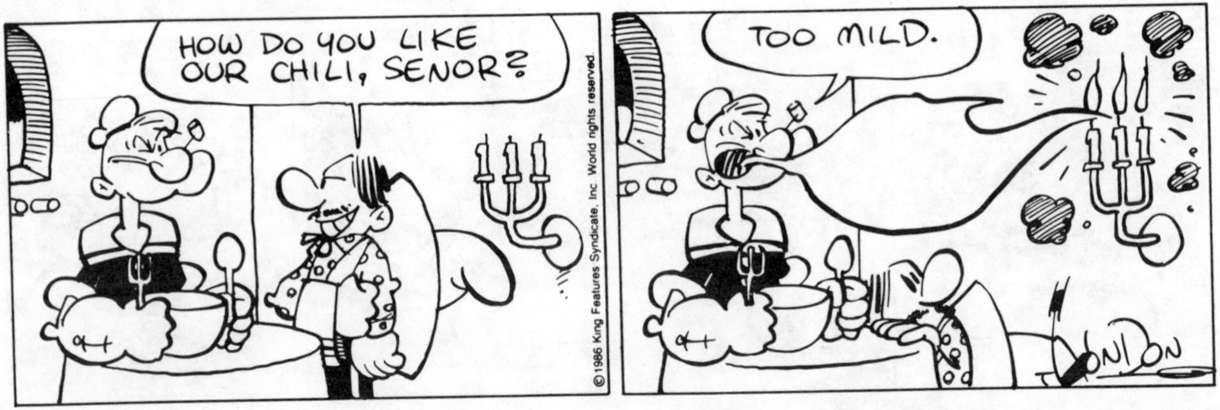
HOW DO YOU LIKE OUR CHILI, SENOR?
©1986 King Features Syndicate, Inc. World rights reserved
TOO MILD.
LONDON

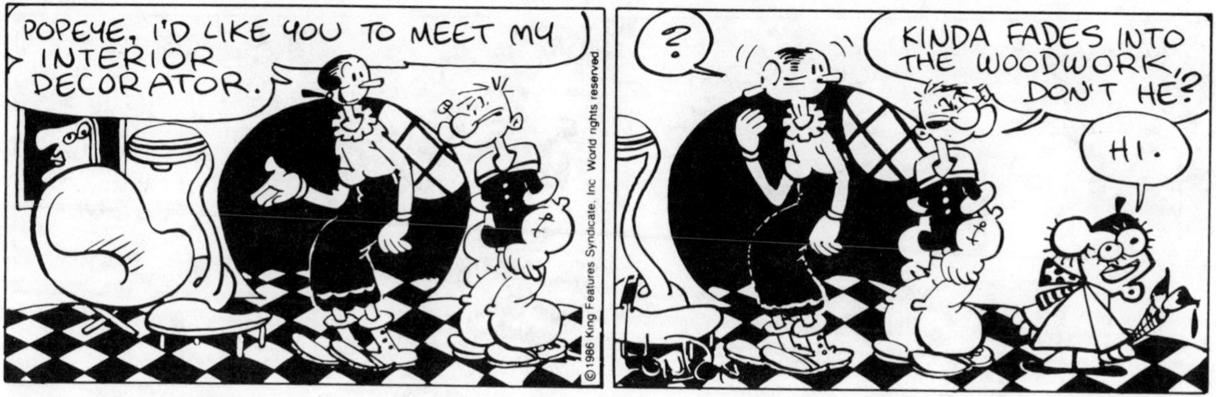
POPEYE, I'D LIKE YOU TO MEET MY INTERIOR DECORATOR.
©1986 King Features Syndicate, Inc World rights reserved
?
KINDA FADES INTO THE WOODWORK, DON'T HE?
HI.

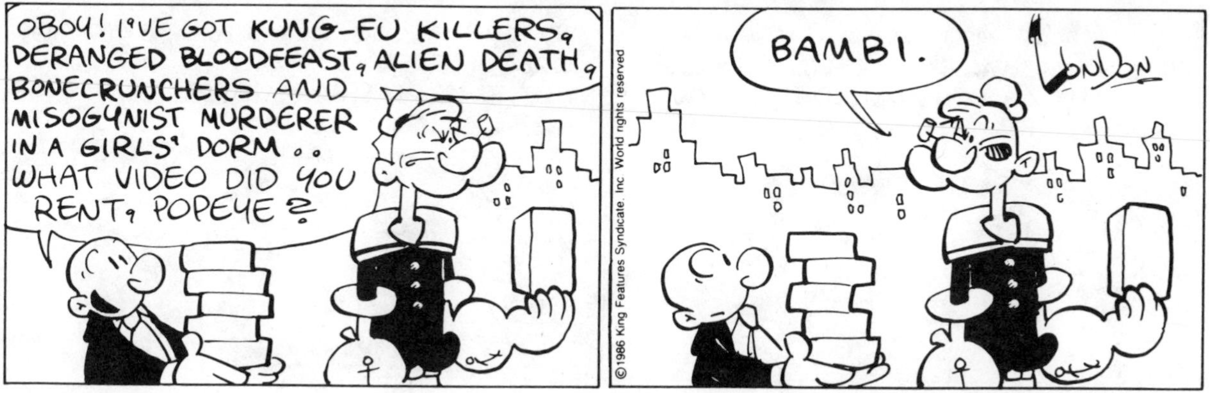
OBOY! I'VE GOT KUNG-FU KILLERS, DERANGED BLOODFEAST, ALIEN DEATH, BONECRUNCHERS AND MISOGYNIST MURDERER IN A GIRLS' DORM .. WHAT VIDEO DID YOU RENT, POPEYE?
©1986 King Features Syndicate, Inc World rights reserved
BAMBI.

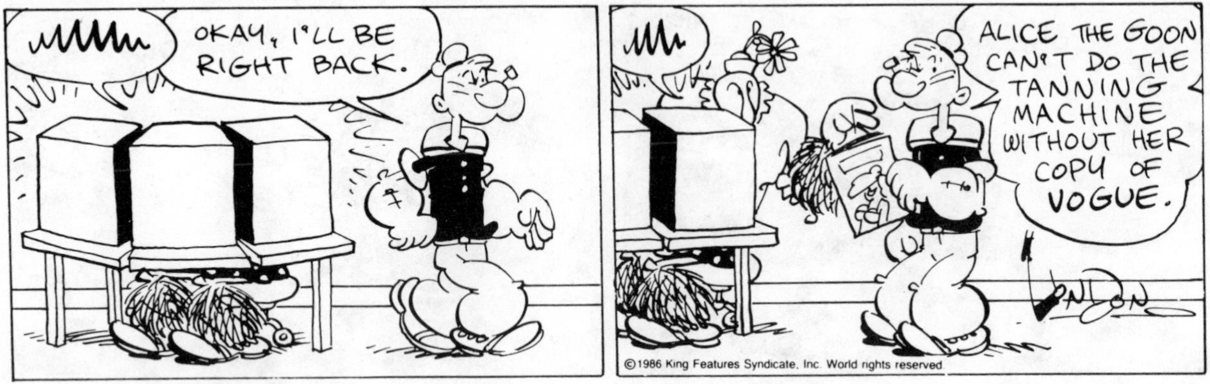
OKAY, I'LL BE RIGHT BACK.
ALICE THE GOON CAN'T DO THE TANNING MACHINE WITHOUT HER COPY OF VOGUE.
LONDON
©1986 King Features Syndicate, Inc. World rights reserved.

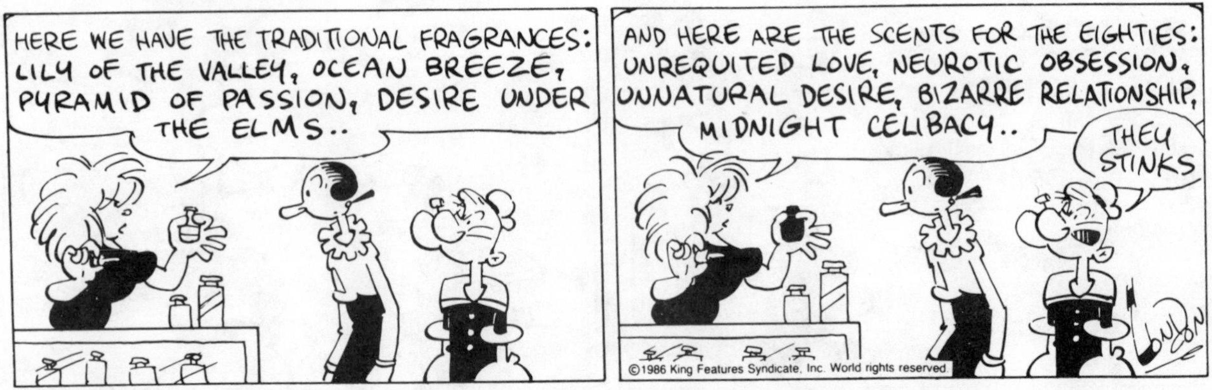
HERE WE HAVE THE TRADITIONAL FRAGRANCES: LILY OF THE VALLEY, OCEAN BREEZE, PYRAMID OF PASSION, DESIRE UNDER THE ELMS..
AND HERE ARE THE SCENTS FOR THE EIGHTIES: UNREQUITED LOVE, NEUROTIC OBSESSION, UNNATURAL DESIRE, BIZARRE RELATIONSHIP, MIDNIGHT CELIBACY..
THEY STINKS
LONDON
©1986 King Features Syndicate, Inc. World rights reserved.

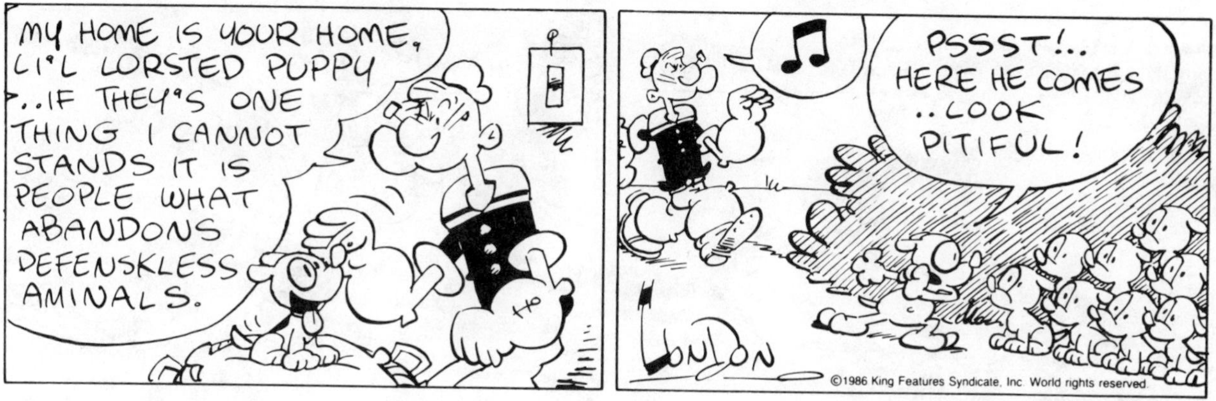
MY HOME IS YOUR HOME, LI'L LORSTED PUPPY ..IF THEY'S ONE THING I CANNOT STANDS IT IS PEOPLE WHAT ABANDONS DEFENSKLESS AMINALS.
♫
PSSST!.. HERE HE COMES ..LOOK PITIFUL!
LONDON
©1986 King Features Syndicate, Inc. World rights reserved.

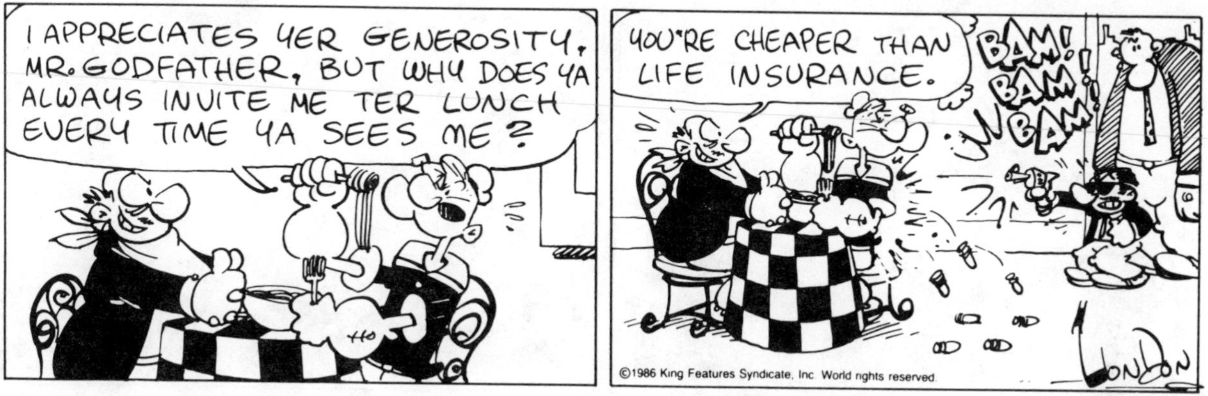
I APPRECIATES YER GENEROSITY, MR. GODFATHER, BUT WHY DOES YA ALWAYS INVITE ME TER LUNCH EVERY TIME YA SEES ME?
YOU'RE CHEAPER THAN LIFE INSURANCE.
BAM! BAM! BAM!
©1986 King Features Syndicate, Inc. World rights reserved.
LONDON

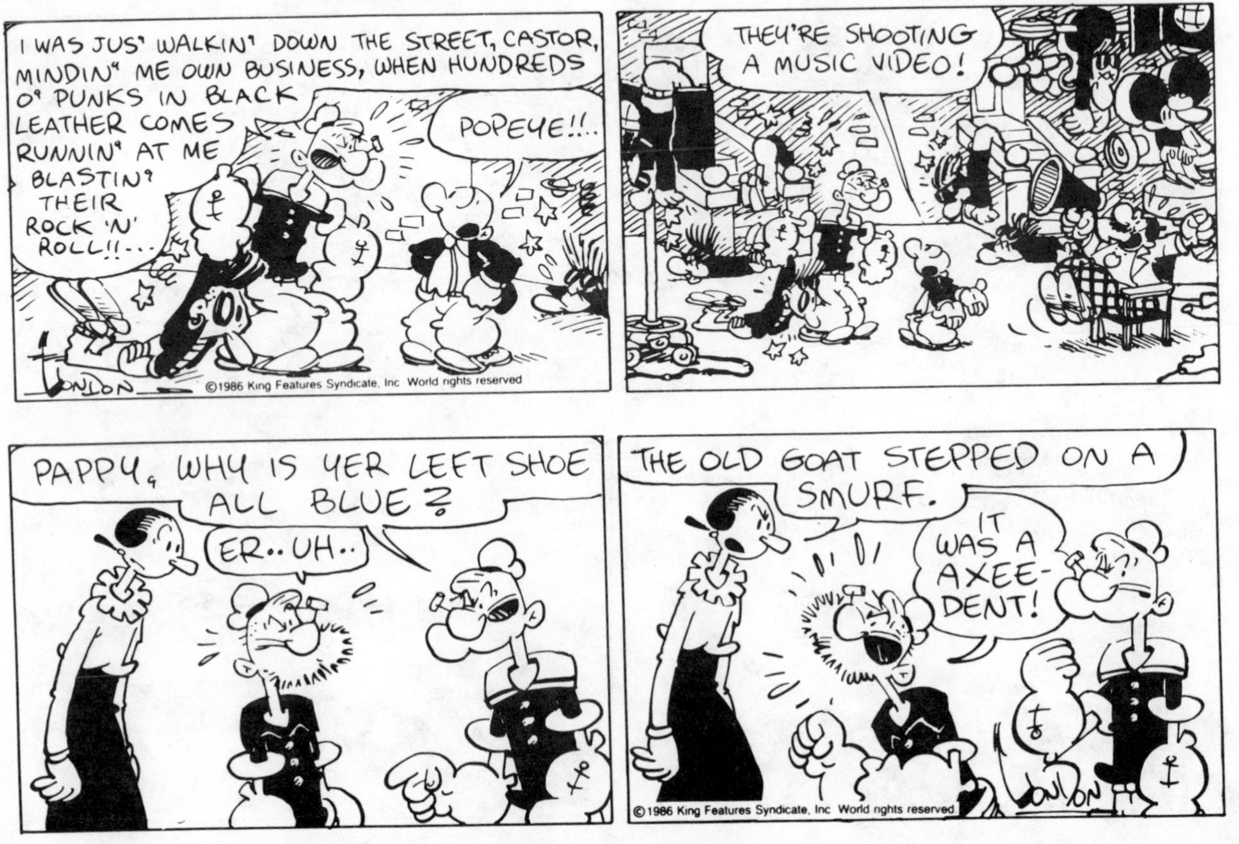
I WAS JUS' WALKIN' DOWN THE STREET, CASTOR, MINDIN' ME OWN BUSINESS, WHEN HUNDREDS O' PUNKS IN BLACK LEATHER COMES RUNNIN' AT ME BLASTIN' THEIR ROCK 'N' ROLL!!...
POPEYE!!...
©1986 King Features Syndicate, Inc World rights reserved
THEY'RE SHOOTING A MUSIC VIDEO!
PAPPY, WHY IS YER LEFT SHOE ALL BLUE?
ER.. UH..
THE OLD GOAT STEPPED ON A SMURF.
IT WAS A AXEE-DENT!
©1986 King Features Syndicate, Inc World rights reserved

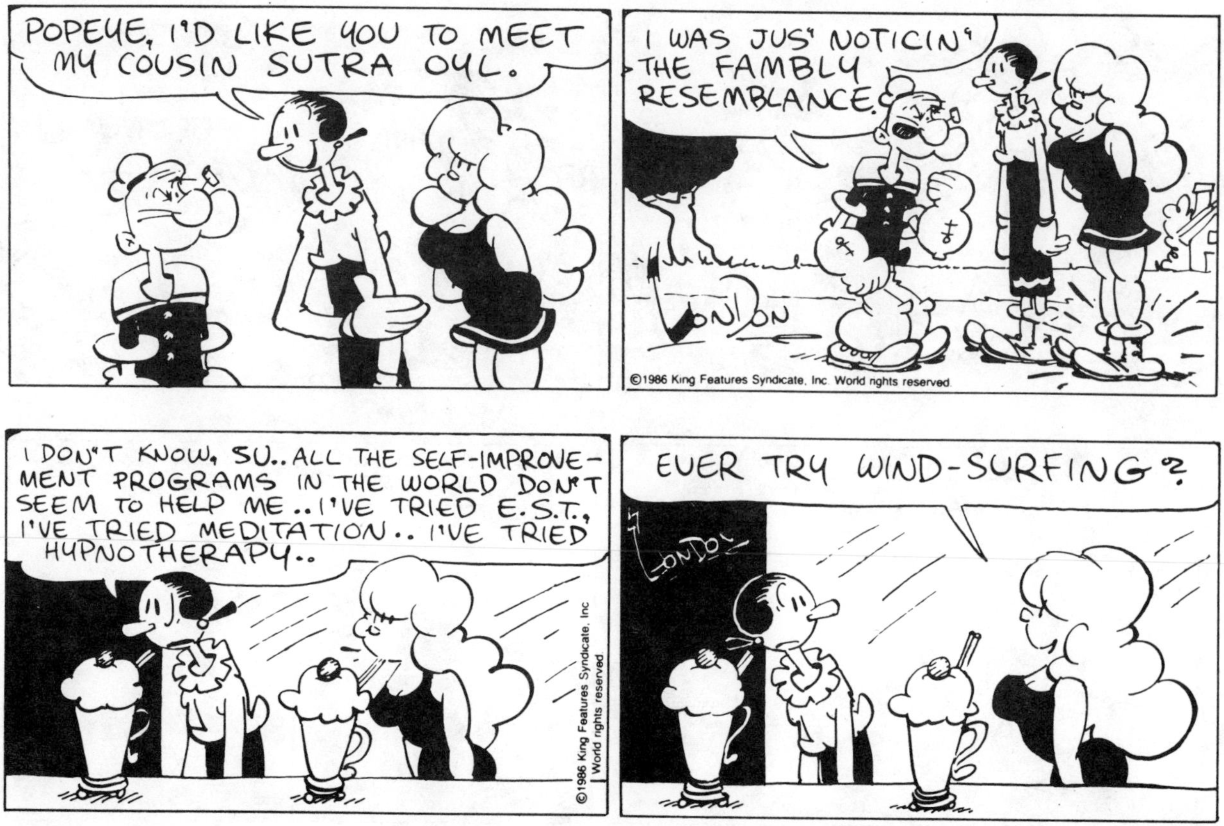

POPEYE, I'D LIKE YOU TO MEET MY COUSIN SUTRA OYL.
I WAS JUS' NOTICIN' THE FAMBLY RESEMBLANCE.
LONDON
©1986 King Features Syndicate, Inc. World rights reserved.
I DON'T KNOW, SU.. ALL THE SELF-IMPROVEMENT PROGRAMS IN THE WORLD DON'T SEEM TO HELP ME.. I'VE TRIED E.S.T., I'VE TRIED MEDITATION.. I'VE TRIED HYPNOTHERAPY..
©1986 King Features Syndicate, Inc World rights reserved.
EVER TRY WIND-SURFING?
LONDON

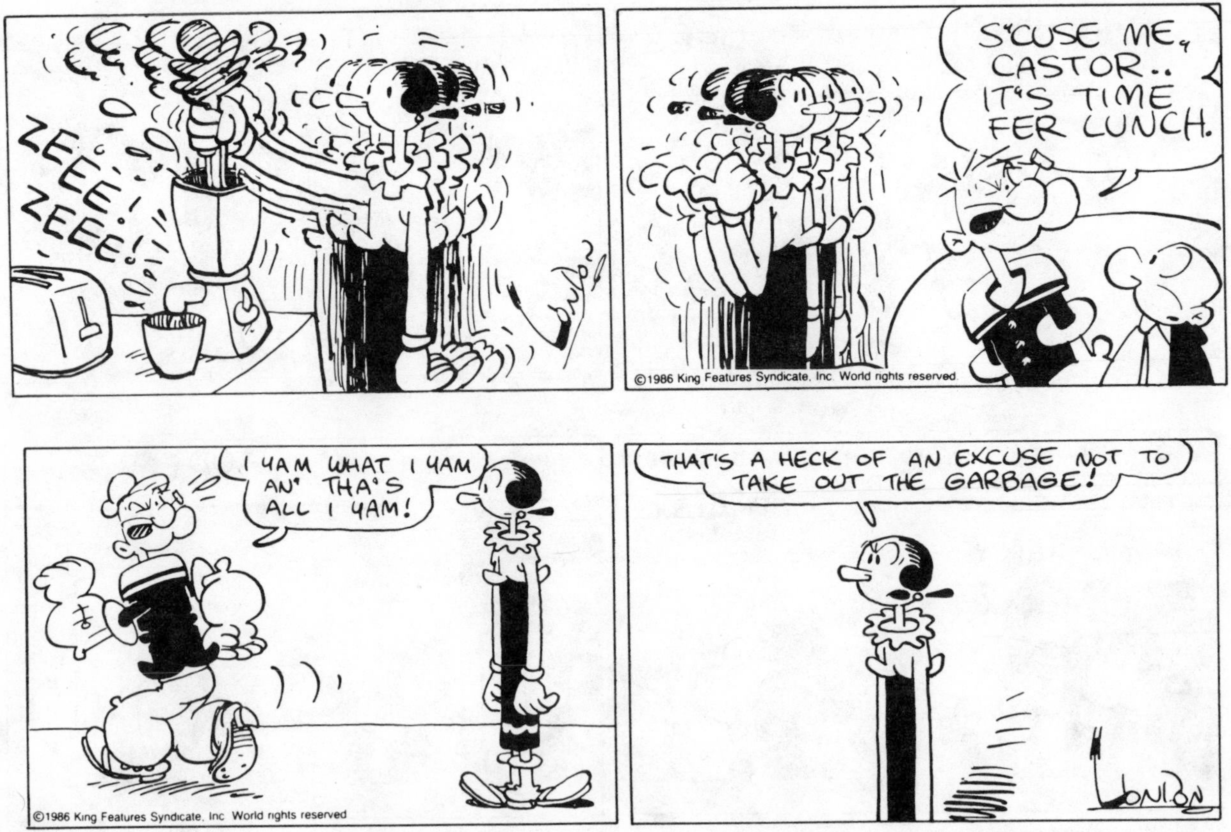
ZEEE! ZEEE!
S'CUSE ME, CASTOR.. IT'S TIME FER LUNCH.
©1986 King Features Syndicate, Inc. World rights reserved.
I YAM WHAT I YAM AN' THA'S ALL I YAM!
©1986 King Features Syndicate, Inc. World rights reserved
THAT'S A HECK OF AN EXCUSE NOT TO TAKE OUT THE GARBAGE!
LONDON

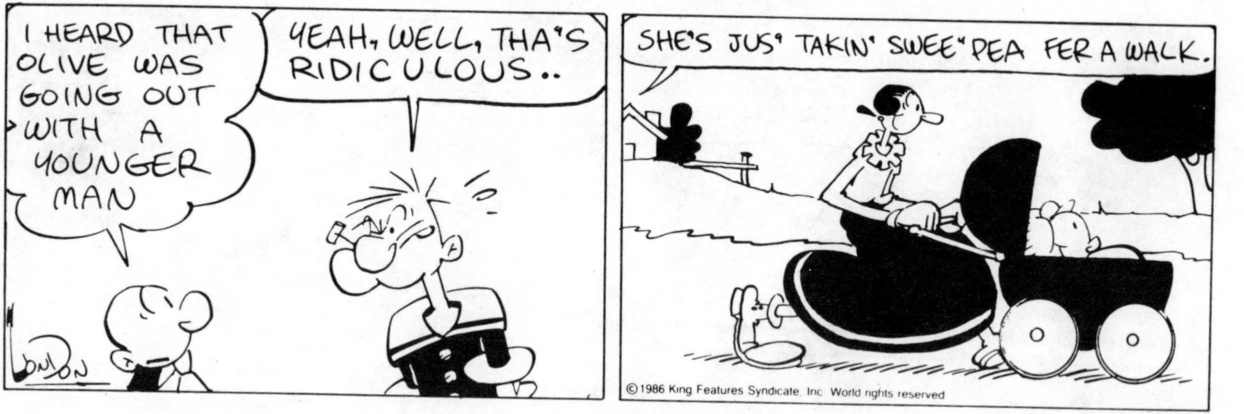
I HEARD THAT OLIVE WAS GOING OUT WITH A YOUNGER MAN
YEAH, WELL, THA'S RIDICULOUS..
SHE'S JUS' TAKIN' SWEE'PEA FER A WALK.
©1986 King Features Syndicate, Inc World rights reserved

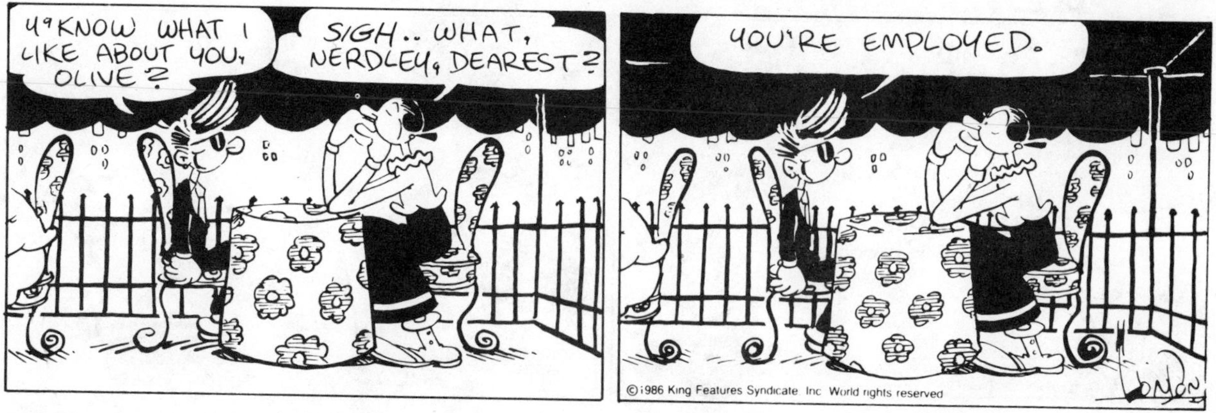
Y'KNOW WHAT I LIKE ABOUT YOU, OLIVE?
SIGH.. WHAT, NERDLEY, DEAREST?
YOU'RE EMPLOYED.
©1986 King Features Syndicate, Inc World rights reserved

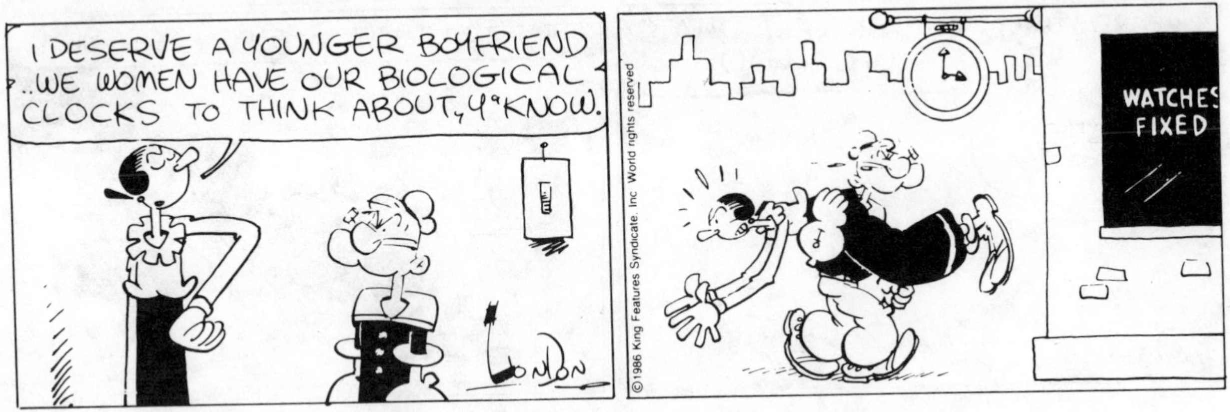
I DESERVE A YOUNGER BOYFRIEND ..WE WOMEN HAVE OUR BIOLOGICAL CLOCKS TO THINK ABOUT, Y'KNOW.
©1986 King Features Syndicate, Inc World rights reserved
WATCHES FIXED

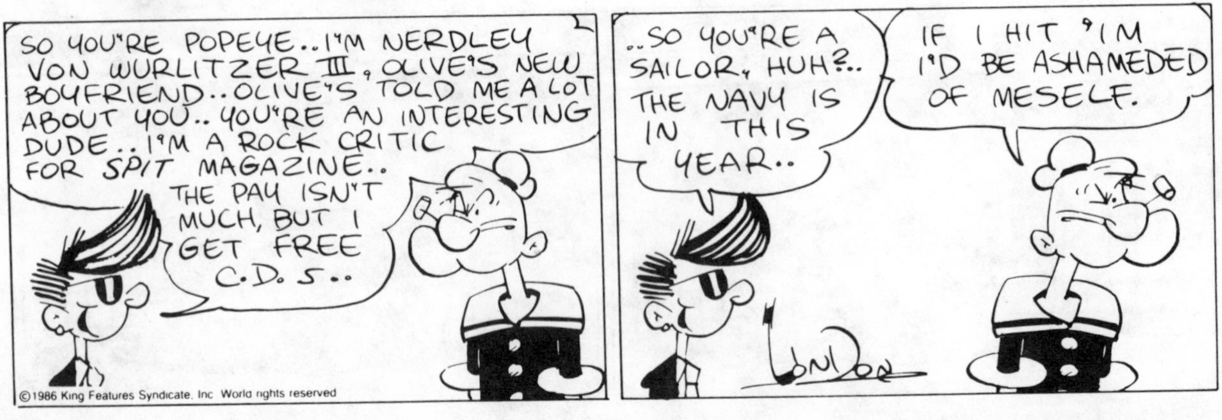
SO YOU'RE POPEYE..I'M NERDLEY VON WURLITZER III, OLIVE'S NEW BOYFRIEND..OLIVE'S TOLD ME A LOT ABOUT YOU..YOU'RE AN INTERESTING DUDE..I'M A ROCK CRITIC FOR SPIT MAGAZINE..
THE PAY ISN'T MUCH, BUT I GET FREE C.D.S..
..SO YOU'RE A SAILOR, HUH?..THE NAVY IS IN THIS YEAR..
IF I HIT 'IM I'D BE ASHAMEDED OF MESELF.
©1986 King Features Syndicate, Inc World rights reserved

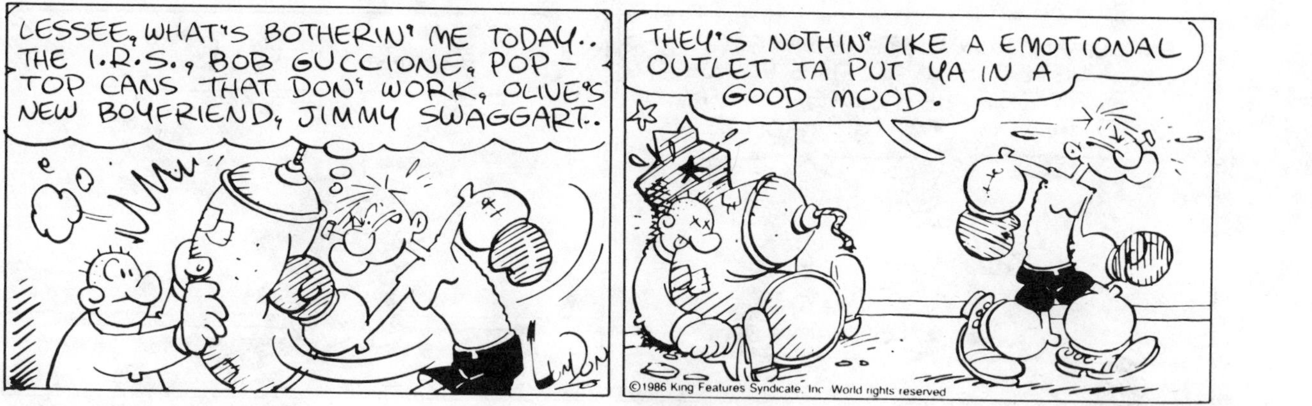
LESSEE, WHAT'S BOTHERIN' ME TODAY.. THE I.R.S., BOB GUCCIONE, POP-TOP CANS THAT DON' WORK, OLIVE'S NEW BOYFRIEND, JIMMY SWAGGART..
THEY'S NOTHIN' LIKE A EMOTIONAL OUTLET TA PUT YA IN A GOOD MOOD.
LONDON
©1986 King Features Syndicate, Inc World rights reserved

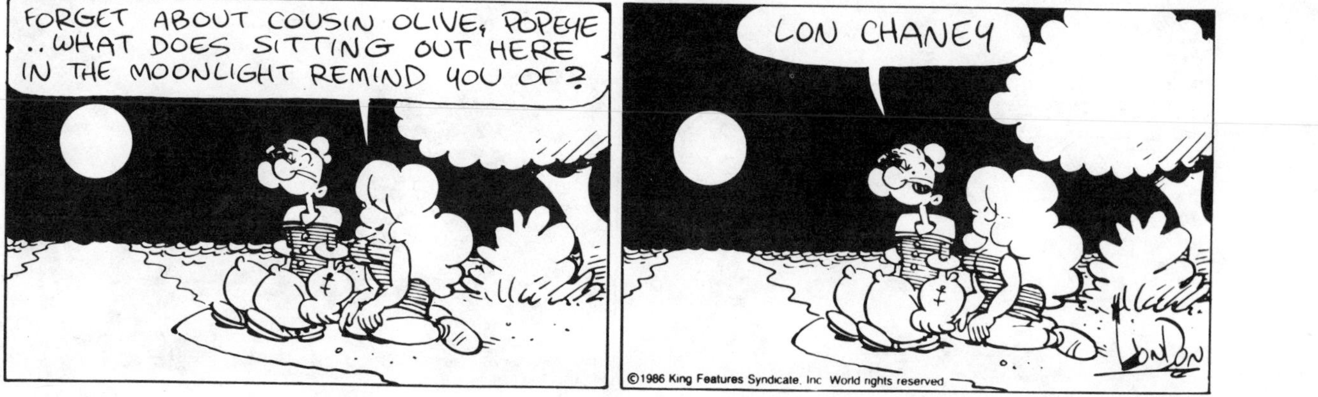
FORGET ABOUT COUSIN OLIVE, POPEYE ..WHAT DOES SITTING OUT HERE IN THE MOONLIGHT REMIND YOU OF?
LON CHANEY
LONDON
©1986 King Features Syndicate, Inc World rights reserved

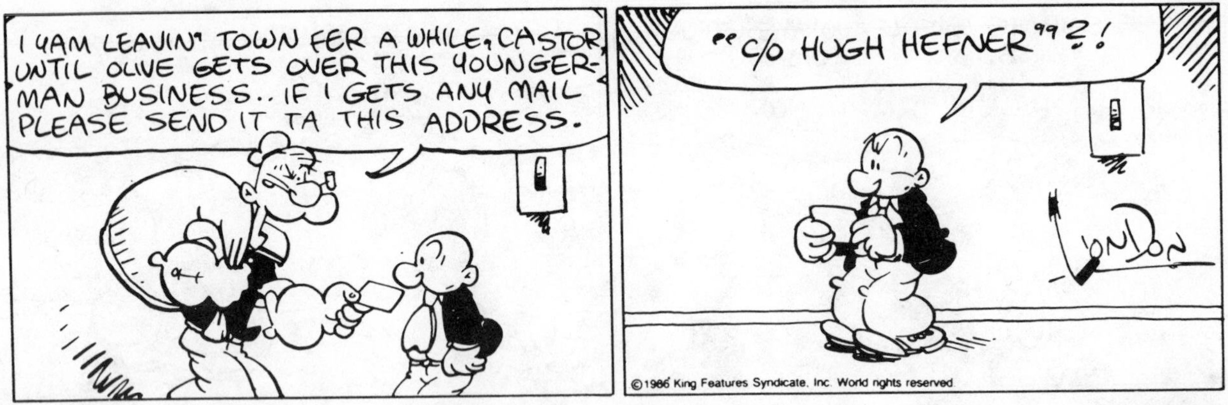
I YAM LEAVIN' TOWN FER A WHILE, CASTOR, UNTIL OLIVE GETS OVER THIS YOUNGER-MAN BUSINESS.. IF I GETS ANY MAIL PLEASE SEND IT TA THIS ADDRESS.
"C/O HUGH HEFNER"?!
LONDON
©1986 King Features Syndicate, Inc. World rights reserved.

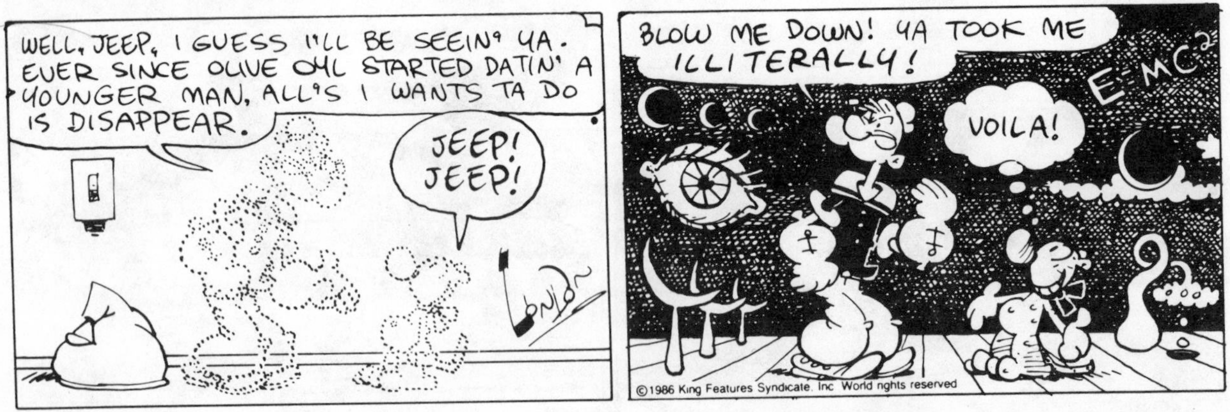
WELL, JEEP, I GUESS I'LL BE SEEIN' YA. EVER SINCE OLIVE OYL STARTED DATIN' A YOUNGER MAN, ALL'S I WANTS TA DO IS DISAPPEAR.
JEEP! JEEP!
LONDON
BLOW ME DOWN! YA TOOK ME ILLITERALLY!
$E\ MC^2$
VOILA!
©1986 King Features Syndicate, Inc. World rights reserved

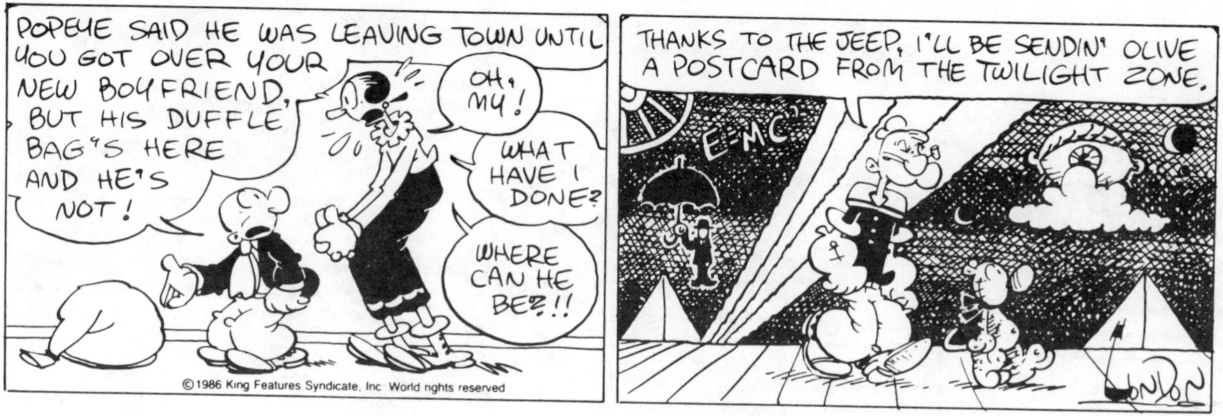
POPEYE SAID HE WAS LEAVING TOWN UNTIL YOU GOT OVER YOUR NEW BOYFRIEND, BUT HIS DUFFLE BAG'S HERE AND HE'S NOT!
OH, MY!
WHAT HAVE I DONE?
WHERE CAN HE BE?!!
THANKS TO THE JEEP, I'LL BE SENDIN' OLIVE A POSTCARD FROM THE TWILIGHT ZONE.
E=MC²


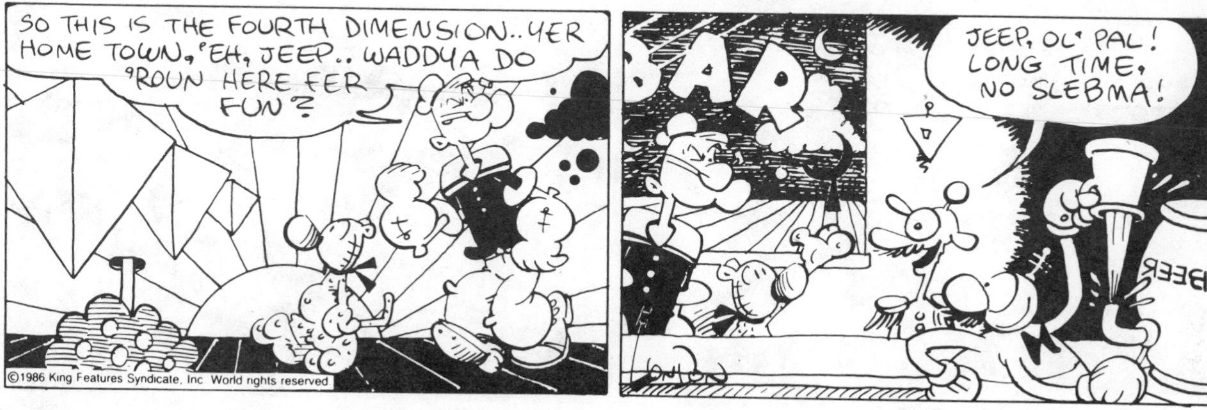
SO THIS IS THE FOURTH DIMENSION.. YER HOME TOWN, 'EH, JEEP.. WADDYA DO 'ROUN HERE FER FUN?
BAR
JEEP, OL' PAL! LONG TIME, NO SLEBMA!
BEER

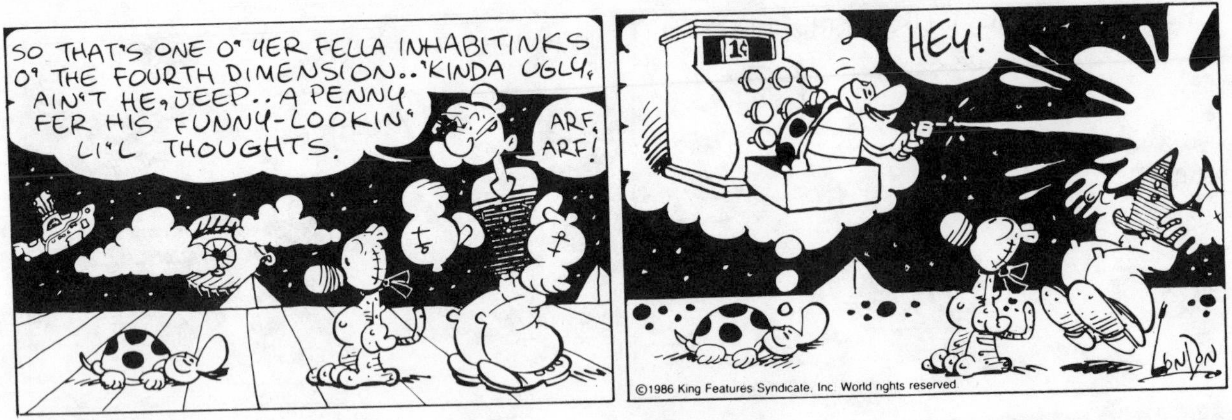
SO THAT'S ONE O' YER FELLA INHABITINKS O' THE FOURTH DIMENSION..'KINDA UGLY, AIN'T HE, JEEP.. A PENNY FER HIS FUNNY-LOOKIN' LI'L THOUGHTS.
ARF, ARF!
1¢
HEY!
LONDON
©1986 King Features Syndicate, Inc. World rights reserved.

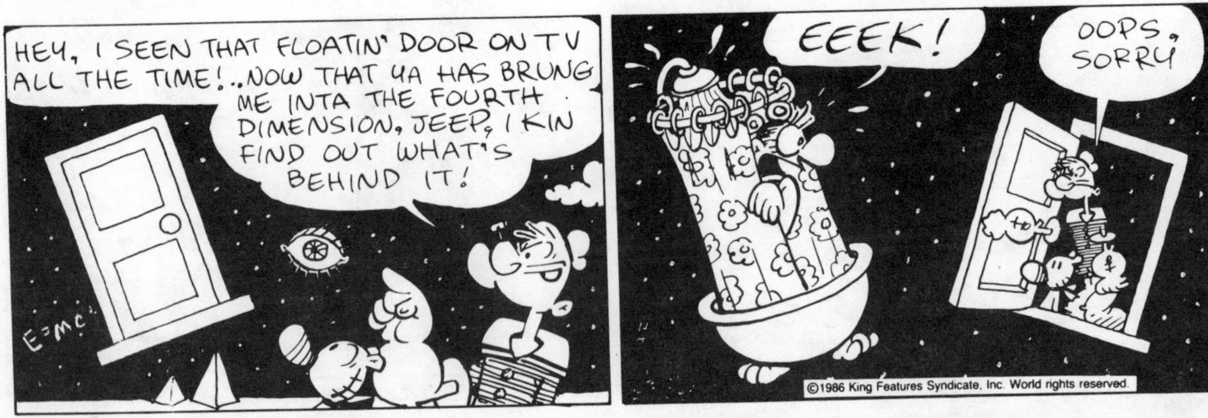
HEY, I SEEN THAT FLOATIN' DOOR ON TV ALL THE TIME!..NOW THAT YA HAS BRUNG ME INTA THE FOURTH DIMENSION, JEEP, I KIN FIND OUT WHAT'S BEHIND IT!
EEEK!
OOPS, SORRY
©1986 King Features Syndicate, Inc. World rights reserved.

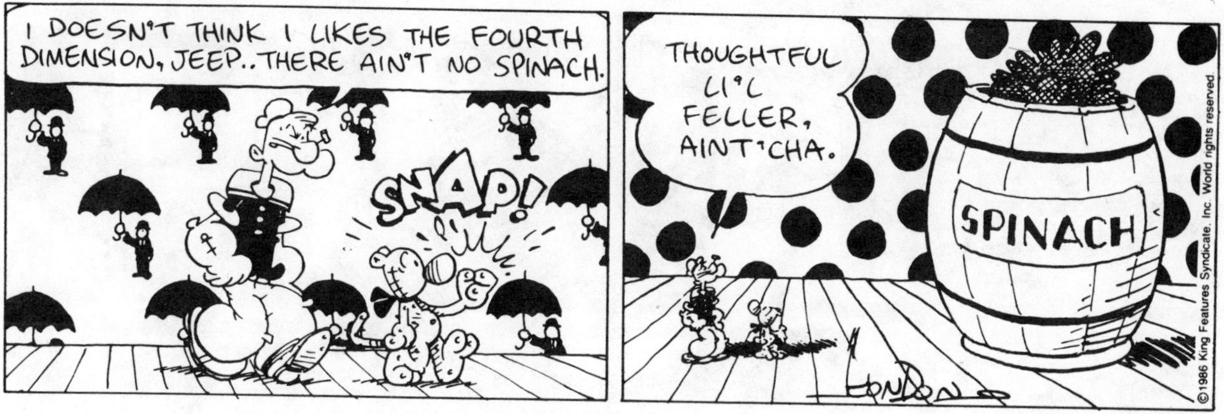
I DOESN'T THINK I LIKES THE FOURTH DIMENSION, JEEP.. THERE AIN'T NO SPINACH.
SNAP!
THOUGHTFUL LI'L FELLER, AINT'CHA.
SPINACH
©1986 King Features Syndicate, Inc. World rights reserved.

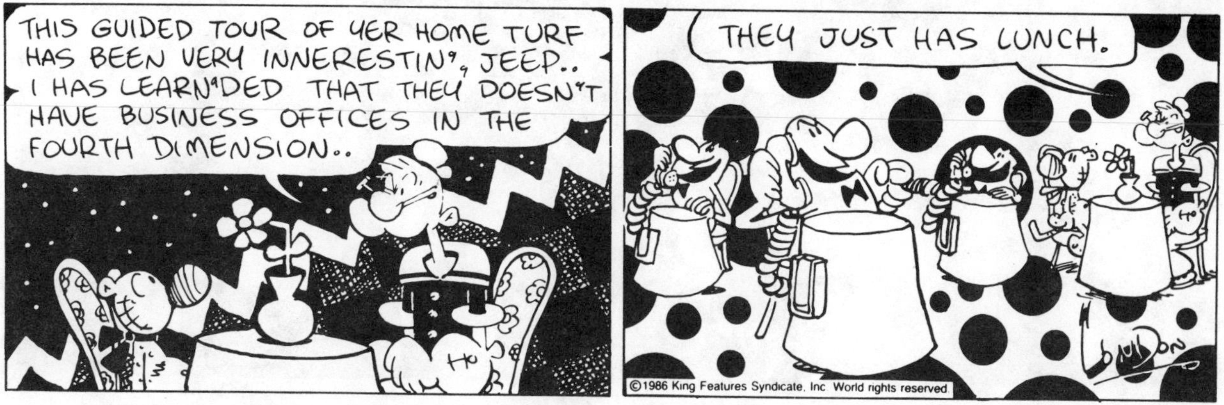
THIS GUIDED TOUR OF YER HOME TURF HAS BEEN VERY INNERESTIN', JEEP.. I HAS LEARN'DED THAT THEY DOESN'T HAVE BUSINESS OFFICES IN THE FOURTH DIMENSION..
THEY JUST HAS LUNCH.
©1986 King Features Syndicate, Inc. World rights reserved.

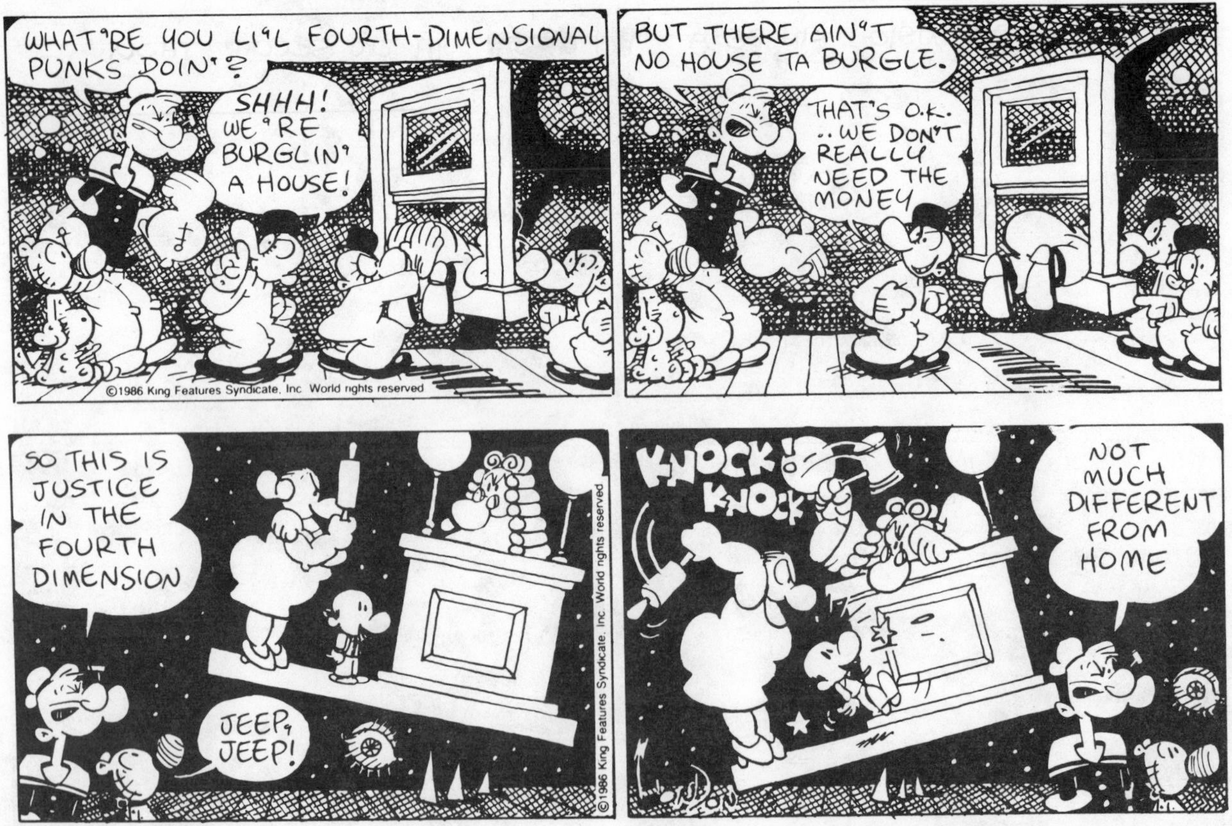
WHAT'RE YOU LI'L FOURTH-DIMENSIONAL PUNKS DOIN'?
SHHH! WE'RE BURGLIN' A HOUSE!
©1986 King Features Syndicate, Inc. World rights reserved
BUT THERE AIN'T NO HOUSE TA BURGLE.
THAT'S O.K. ..WE DON'T REALLY NEED THE MONEY
SO THIS IS JUSTICE IN THE FOURTH DIMENSION
JEEP, JEEP!
©1986 King Features Syndicate, Inc. World rights reserved
KNOCK! KNOCK
NOT MUCH DIFFERENT FROM HOME

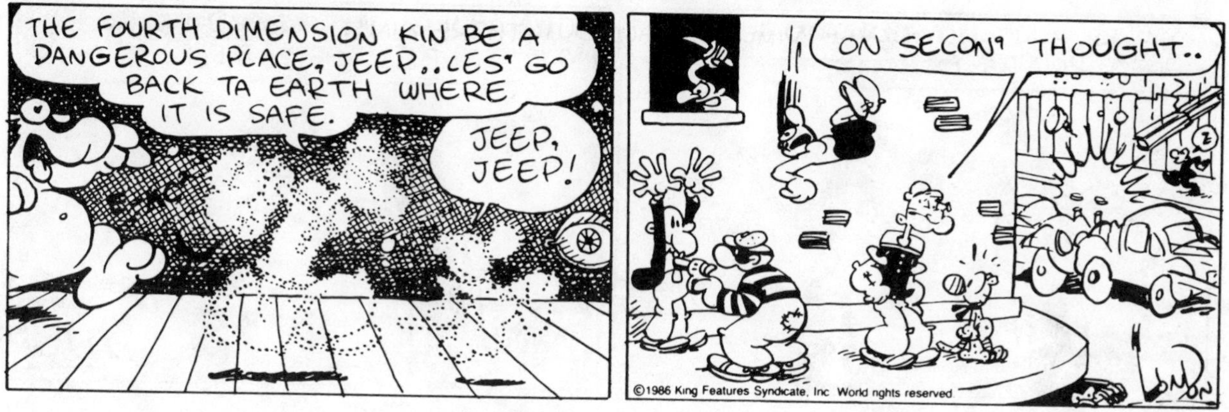
THE FOURTH DIMENSION KIN BE A DANGEROUS PLACE, JEEP..LES' GO BACK TA EARTH WHERE IT IS SAFE.
JEEP, JEEP!
ON SECON' THOUGHT..
©1986 King Features Syndicate, Inc World rights reserved
LONDON

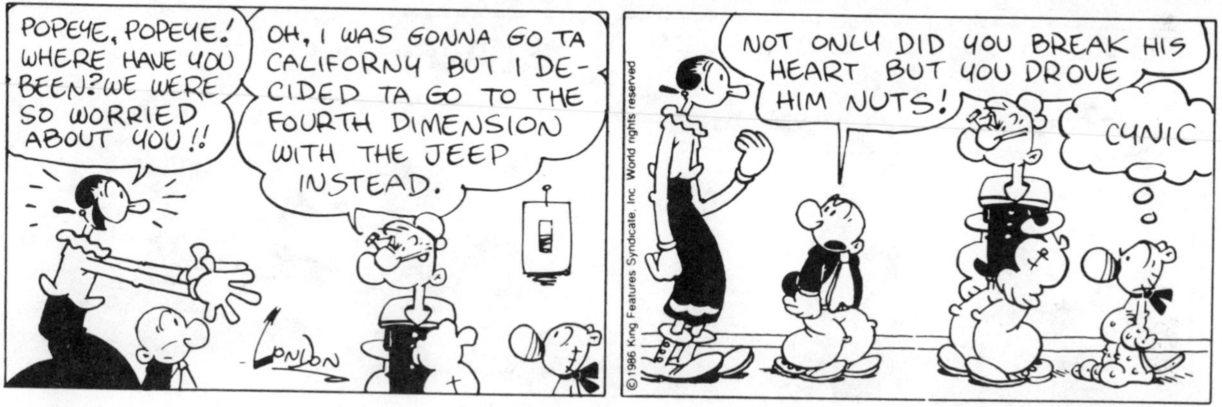
POPEYE, POPEYE! WHERE HAVE YOU BEEN? WE WERE SO WORRIED ABOUT YOU!!
OH, I WAS GONNA GO TA CALIFORNY BUT I DECIDED TA GO TO THE FOURTH DIMENSION WITH THE JEEP INSTEAD.
LONDON
NOT ONLY DID YOU BREAK HIS HEART BUT YOU DROVE HIM NUTS!
CYNIC
© 1986 King Features Syndicate, Inc World rights reserved

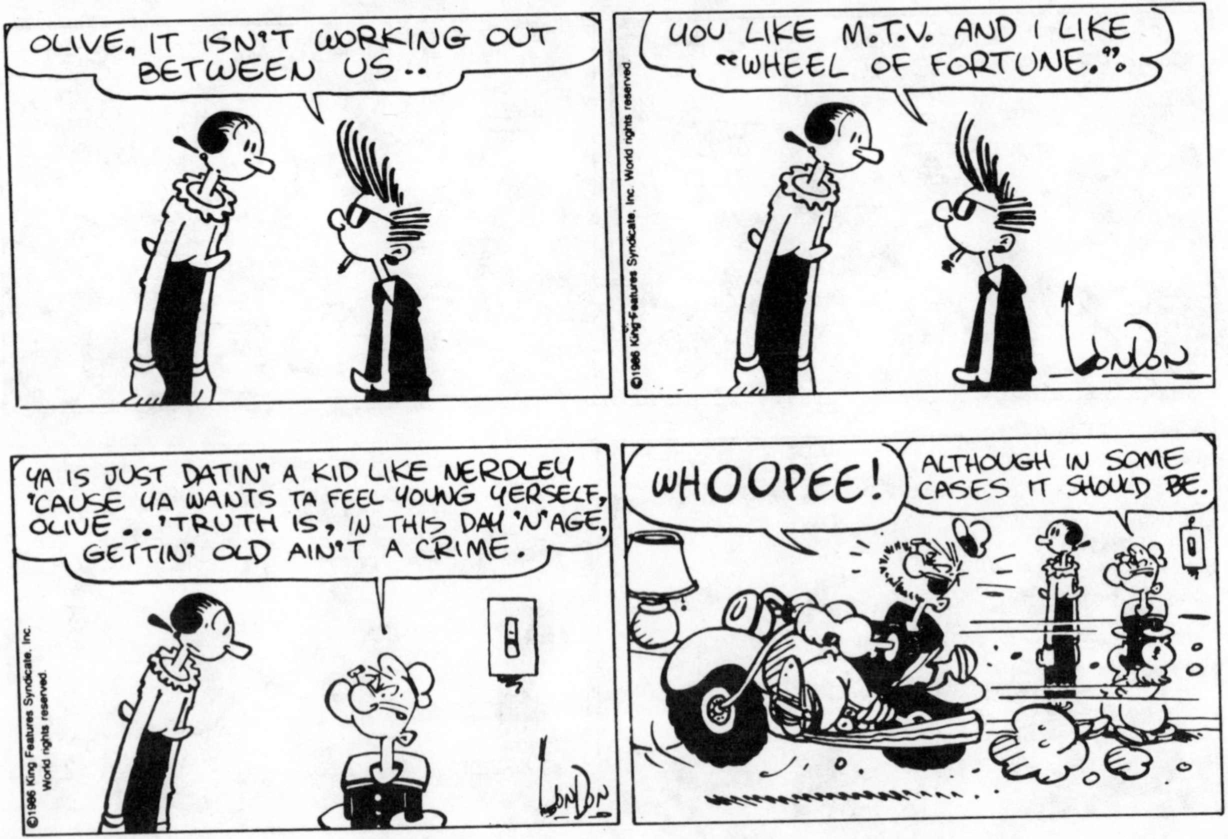
OLIVE, IT ISN'T WORKING OUT BETWEEN US..
YOU LIKE M.T.V. AND I LIKE "WHEEL OF FORTUNE."
©1986 King Features Syndicate, Inc. World rights reserved.
LONDON
YA IS JUST DATIN' A KID LIKE NERDLEY 'CAUSE YA WANTS TA FEEL YOUNG YERSELF, OLIVE..'TRUTH IS, IN THIS DAY 'N' AGE, GETTIN' OLD AIN'T A CRIME.
©1986 King Features Syndicate, Inc. World rights reserved.
LONDON
WHOOPEE!
ALTHOUGH IN SOME CASES IT SHOULD BE.

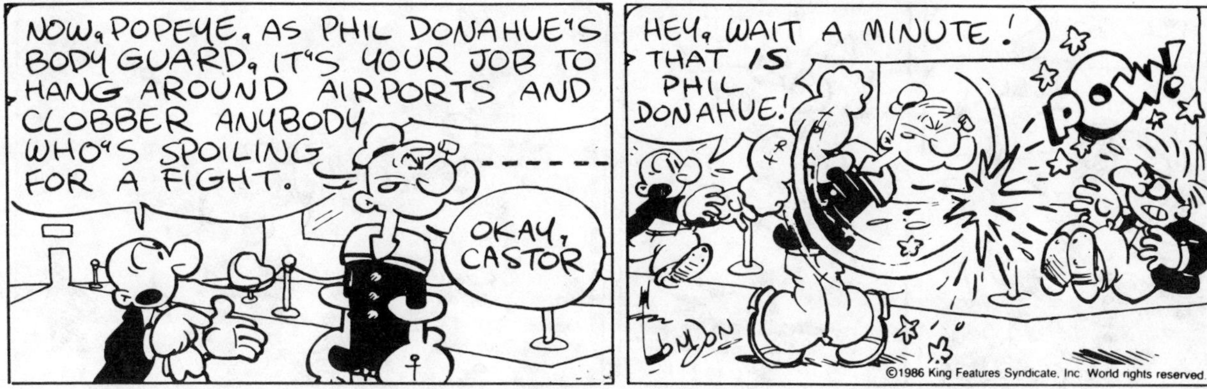
NOW, POPEYE, AS PHIL DONAHUE'S BODYGUARD, IT'S YOUR JOB TO HANG AROUND AIRPORTS AND CLOBBER ANYBODY WHO'S SPOILING FOR A FIGHT.
OKAY, CASTOR
HEY, WAIT A MINUTE! THAT IS PHIL DONAHUE!
POW!
LONDON
©1986 King Features Syndicate, Inc. World rights reserved.

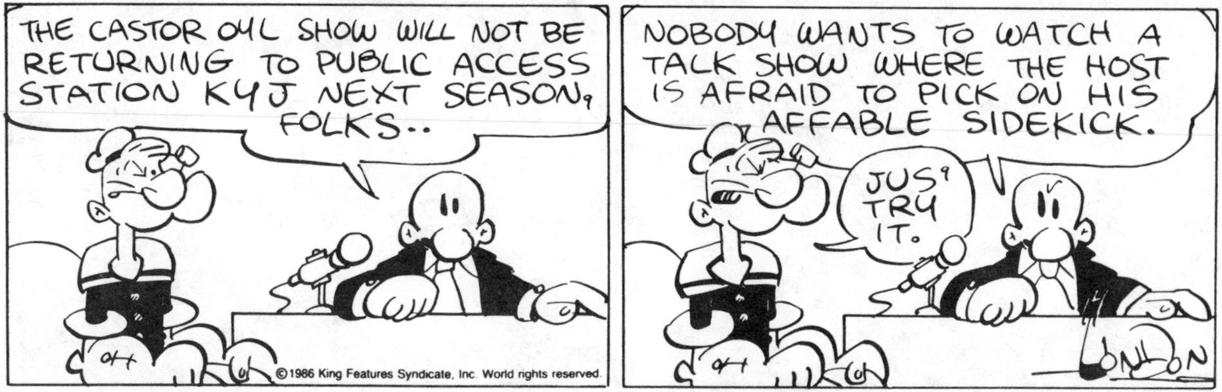
THE CASTOR OYL SHOW WILL NOT BE RETURNING TO PUBLIC ACCESS STATION KYJ NEXT SEASON, FOLKS..
©1986 King Features Syndicate, Inc. World rights reserved.
NOBODY WANTS TO WATCH A TALK SHOW WHERE THE HOST IS AFRAID TO PICK ON HIS AFFABLE SIDEKICK.
JUS' TRY IT.
LONDON

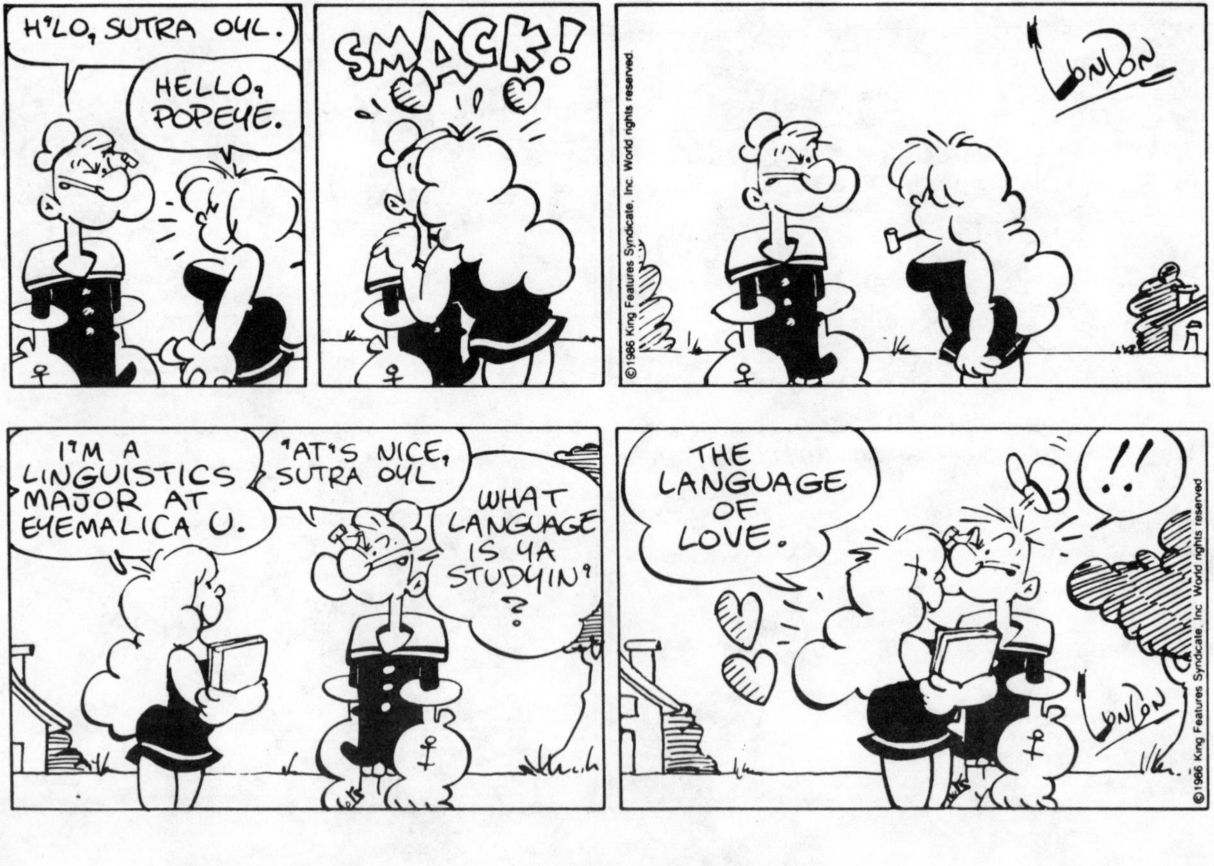
H'LO, SUTRA OYL.
HELLO, POPEYE.
SMACK!
©1986 King Features Syndicate, Inc. World rights reserved.
LONDON
I'M A LINGUISTICS MAJOR AT EYEMALICA U.
'AT'S NICE, SUTRA OYL
WHAT LANGUAGE IS YA STUDYIN'?
THE LANGUAGE OF LOVE.
!!
LONDON
©1986 King Features Syndicate, Inc. World rights reserved

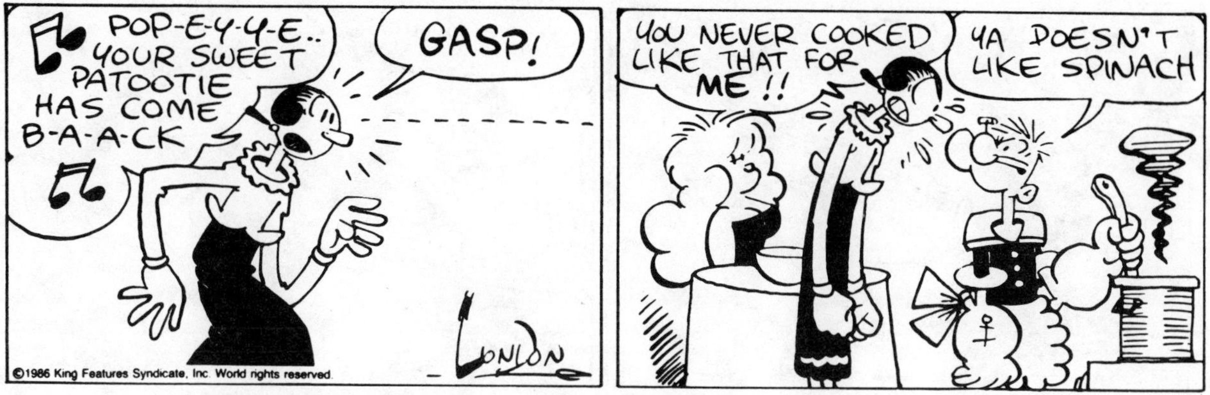
POP-E-Y-Y-E.. YOUR SWEET PATOOTIE HAS COME B-A-A-CK
GASP!
©1986 King Features Syndicate, Inc. World rights reserved.
YOU NEVER COOKED LIKE THAT FOR ME !!
YA DOESN'T LIKE SPINACH

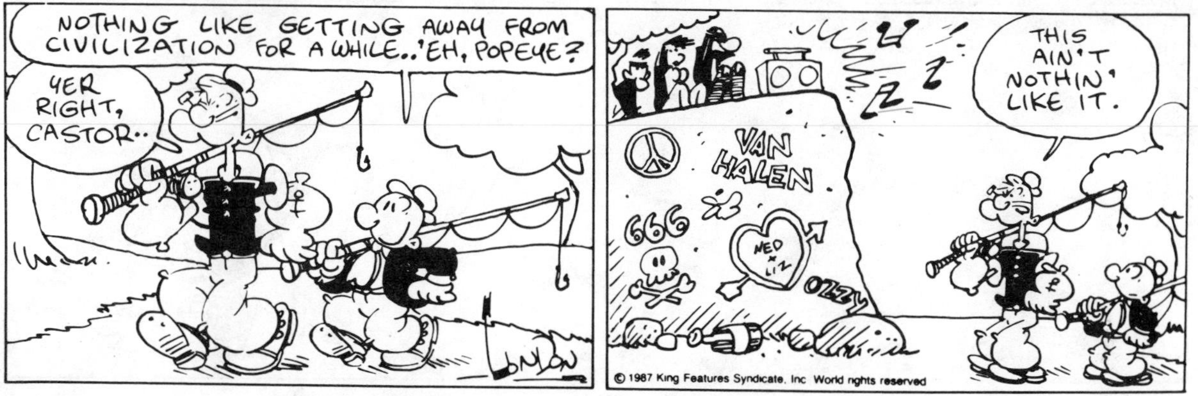
NOTHING LIKE GETTING AWAY FROM CIVILIZATION FOR A WHILE..'EH, POPEYE?
YER RIGHT, CASTOR..
VAN HALEN
666
NED + LIZ
OZZY
THIS AIN'T NOTHIN' LIKE IT.
© 1987 King Features Syndicate, Inc World rights reserved

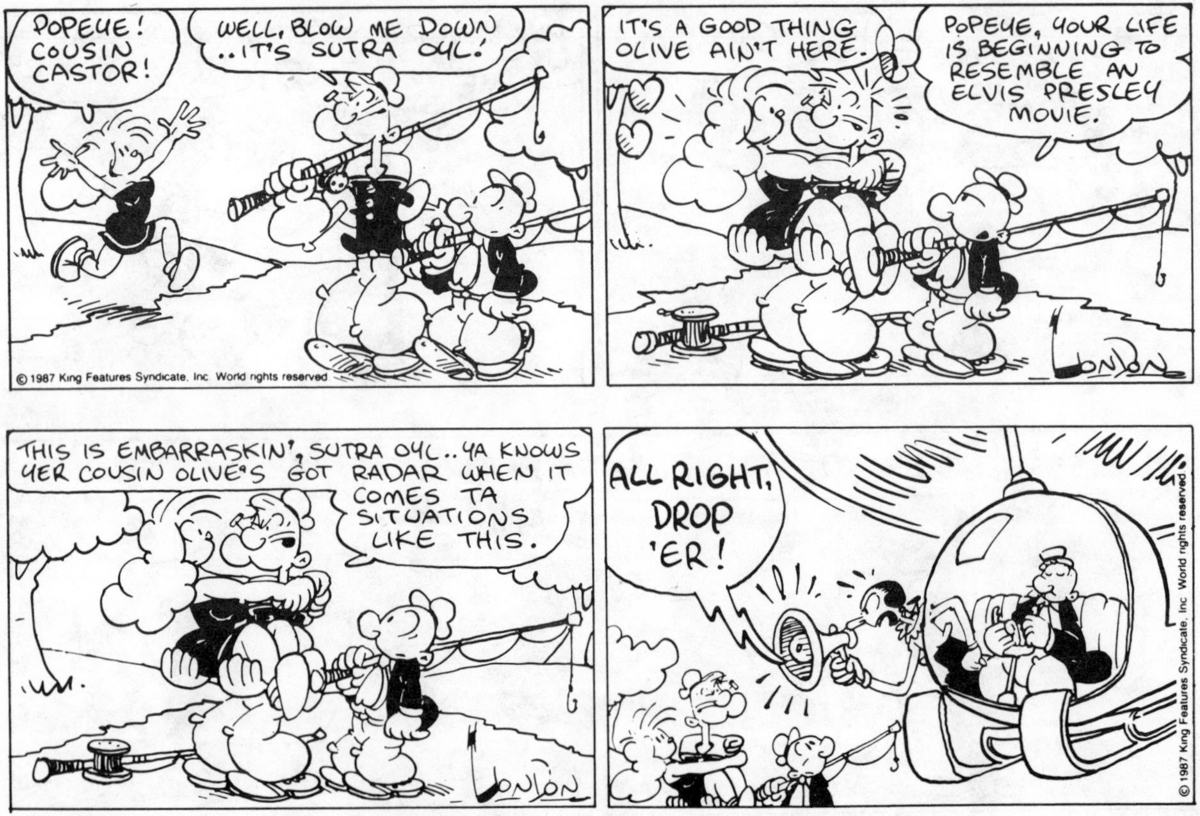
POPEYE! COUSIN CASTOR!
WELL, BLOW ME DOWN ..IT'S SUTRA OYL!
© 1987 King Features Syndicate, Inc. World rights reserved
IT'S A GOOD THING OLIVE AIN'T HERE.
POPEYE, YOUR LIFE IS BEGINNING TO RESEMBLE AN ELVIS PRESLEY MOVIE.
LONDON
THIS IS EMBARRASKIN', SUTRA OYL.. YA KNOWS YER COUSIN OLIVE'S GOT RADAR WHEN IT COMES TA SITUATIONS LIKE THIS.
LONDON
ALL RIGHT, DROP 'ER!
© 1987 King Features Syndicate, Inc. World rights reserved

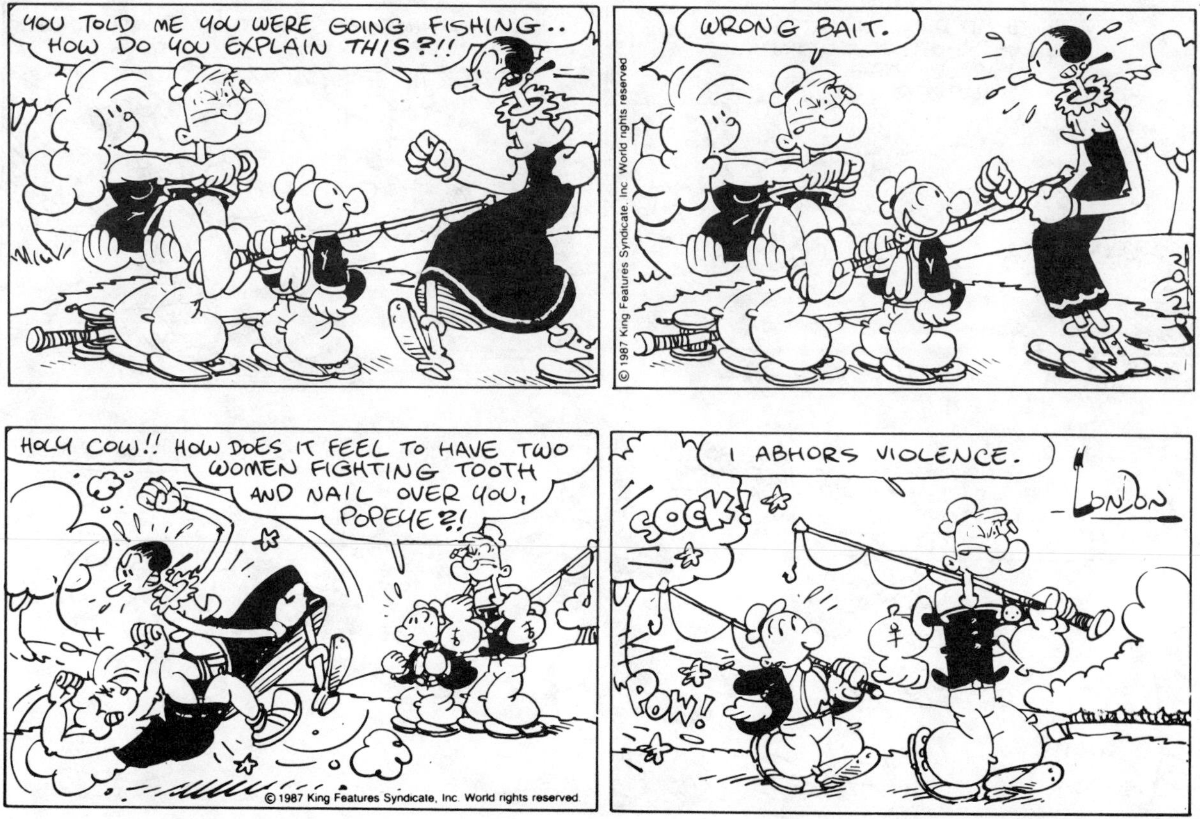
YOU TOLD ME YOU WERE GOING FISHING.. HOW DO YOU EXPLAIN THIS?!!
WRONG BAIT.
© 1987 King Features Syndicate, Inc. World rights reserved
HOLY COW!! HOW DOES IT FEEL TO HAVE TWO WOMEN FIGHTING TOOTH AND NAIL OVER YOU, POPEYE?!
© 1987 King Features Syndicate, Inc. World rights reserved.
I ABHORS VIOLENCE.
-LONDON
SOCK!
POW!

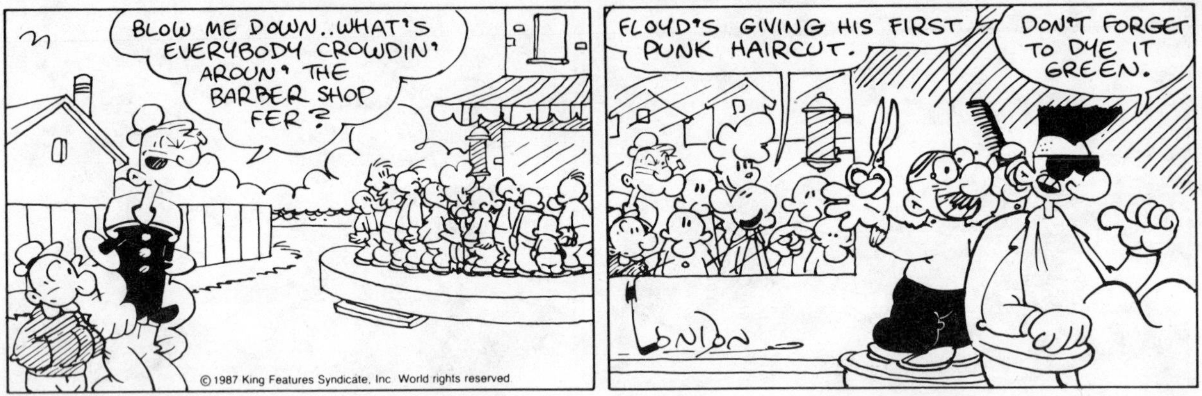
BLOW ME DOWN..WHAT'S EVERYBODY CROWDIN' AROUN' THE BARBER SHOP FER?
© 1987 King Features Syndicate, Inc. World rights reserved.
FLOYD'S GIVING HIS FIRST PUNK HAIRCUT.
DON'T FORGET TO DYE IT GREEN.

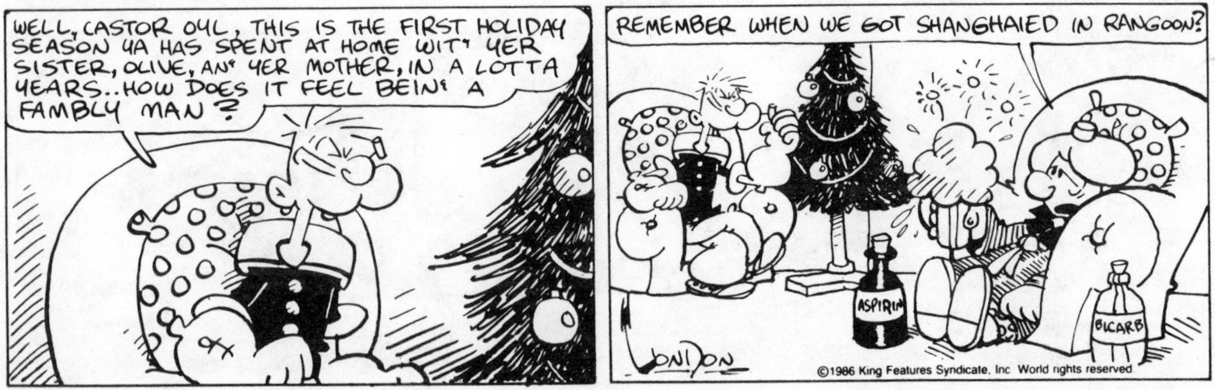
WELL, CASTOR OYL, THIS IS THE FIRST HOLIDAY SEASON YA HAS SPENT AT HOME WIT' YER SISTER, OLIVE, AN' YER MOTHER, IN A LOTTA YEARS..HOW DOES IT FEEL BEIN' A FAMBLY MAN?
REMEMBER WHEN WE GOT SHANGHAIED IN RANGOON?
ASPIRIN
BICARB
©1986 King Features Syndicate, Inc. World rights reserved.

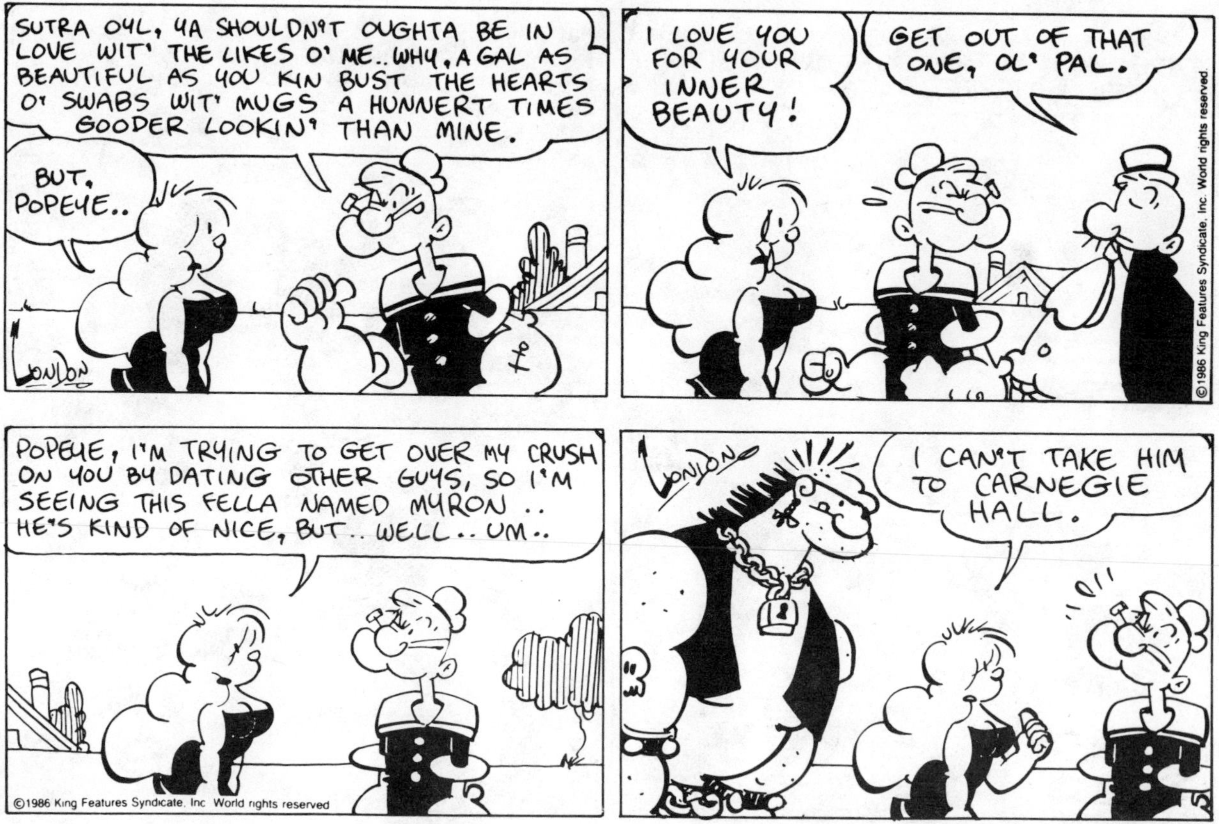

SUTRA OYL, YA SHOULDN'T OUGHTA BE IN LOVE WIT' THE LIKES O' ME.. WHY, A GAL AS BEAUTIFUL AS YOU KIN BUST THE HEARTS O' SWABS WIT' MUGS A HUNNERT TIMES GOODER LOOKIN' THAN MINE.
BUT, POPEYE..
LONDON
I LOVE YOU FOR YOUR INNER BEAUTY!
GET OUT OF THAT ONE, OL' PAL.
©1986 King Features Syndicate, Inc. World rights reserved.
POPEYE, I'M TRYING TO GET OVER MY CRUSH ON YOU BY DATING OTHER GUYS, SO I'M SEEING THIS FELLA NAMED MYRON .. HE'S KIND OF NICE, BUT.. WELL.. UM..
©1986 King Features Syndicate, Inc World rights reserved
LONDON
I CAN'T TAKE HIM TO CARNEGIE HALL.

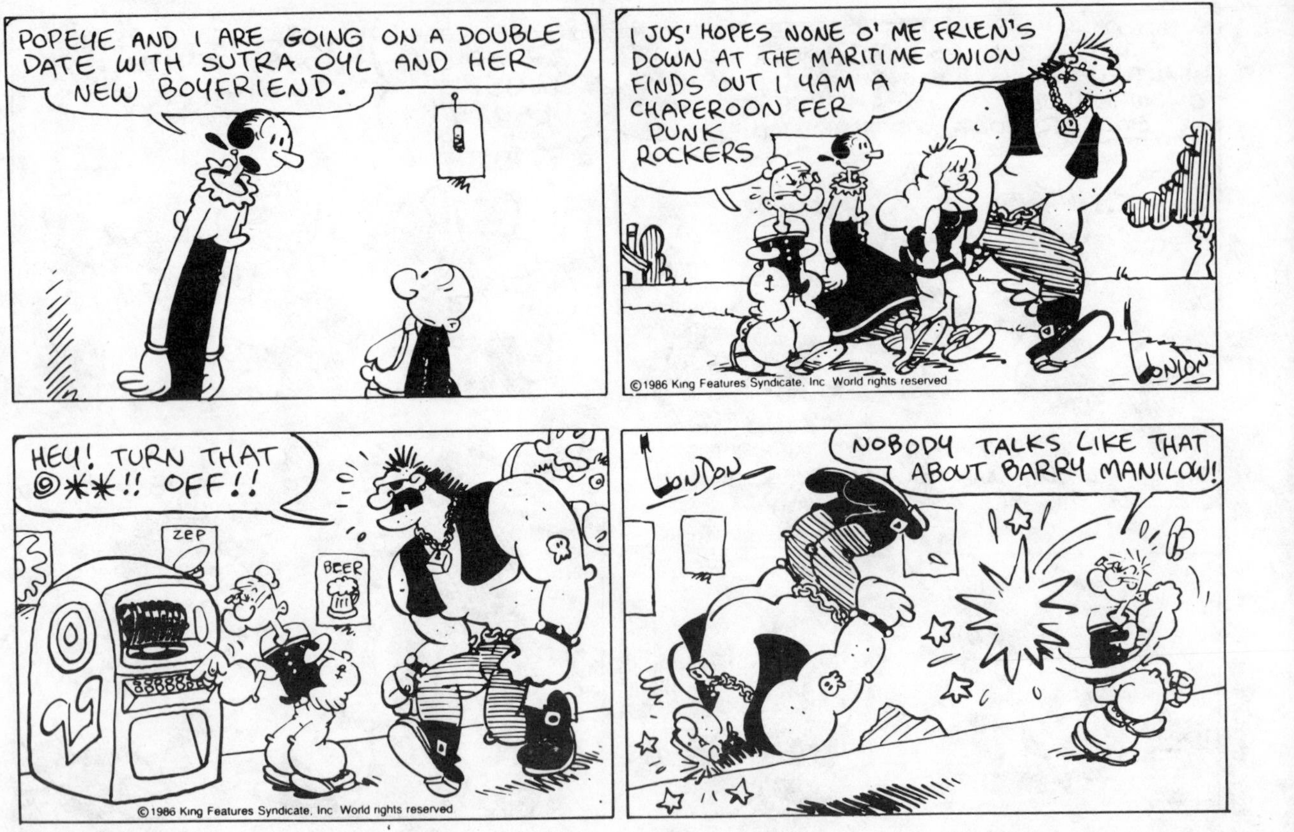
POPEYE AND I ARE GOING ON A DOUBLE DATE WITH SUTRA OYL AND HER NEW BOYFRIEND.
I JUS' HOPES NONE O' ME FRIEN'S DOWN AT THE MARITIME UNION FINDS OUT I YAM A CHAPEROON FER PUNK ROCKERS
LONDON
©1986 King Features Syndicate, Inc World rights reserved
HEY! TURN THAT @✱✱!! OFF!!
ZEP
BEER
©1986 King Features Syndicate, Inc World rights reserved
LONDON
NOBODY TALKS LIKE THAT ABOUT BARRY MANILOW!

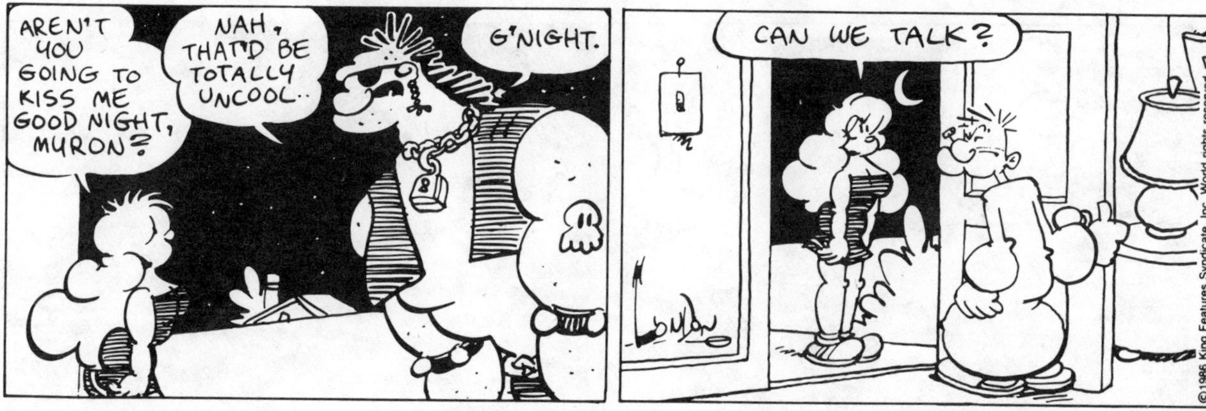
AREN'T YOU GOING TO KISS ME GOOD NIGHT, MYRON?
NAH, THAT'D BE TOTALLY UNCOOL..
G'NIGHT.
CAN WE TALK?
©1986 King Features Syndicate, Inc. World rights reserved.

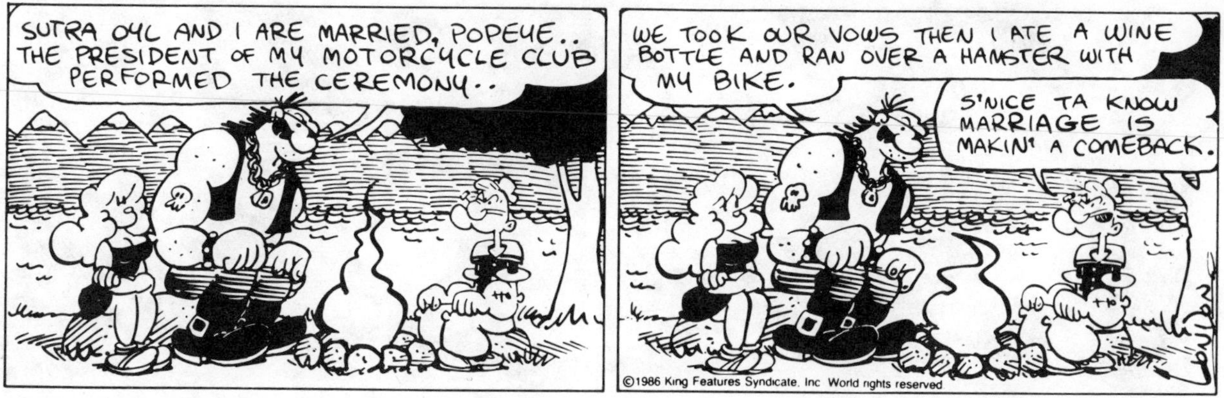
SUTRA OYL AND I ARE MARRIED, POPEYE.. THE PRESIDENT OF MY MOTORCYCLE CLUB PERFORMED THE CEREMONY..
WE TOOK OUR VOWS THEN I ATE A WINE BOTTLE AND RAN OVER A HAMSTER WITH MY BIKE.
S'NICE TA KNOW MARRIAGE IS MAKIN' A COMEBACK.
©1986 King Features Syndicate, Inc. World rights reserved.

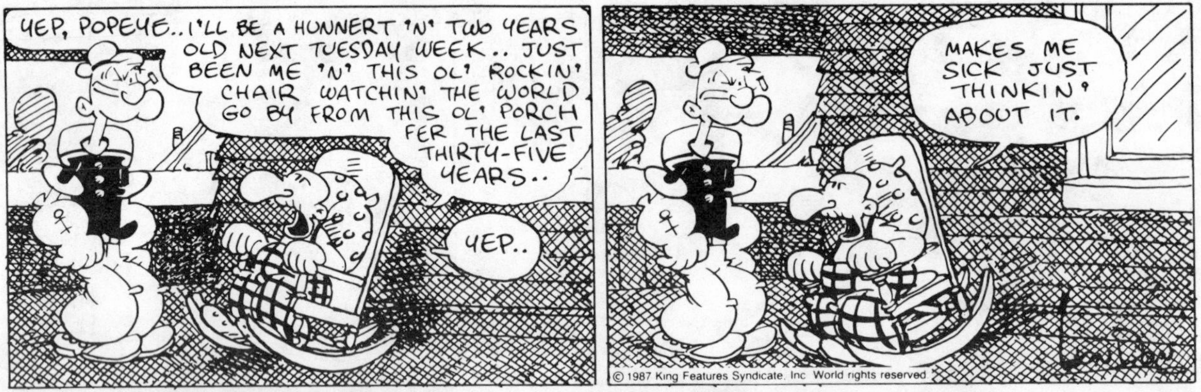
YEP, POPEYE.. I'LL BE A HUNNERT 'N' TWO YEARS OLD NEXT TUESDAY WEEK.. JUST BEEN ME 'N' THIS OL' ROCKIN' CHAIR WATCHIN' THE WORLD GO BY FROM THIS OL' PORCH FER THE LAST THIRTY-FIVE YEARS..
YEP..
MAKES ME SICK JUST THINKIN' ABOUT IT.


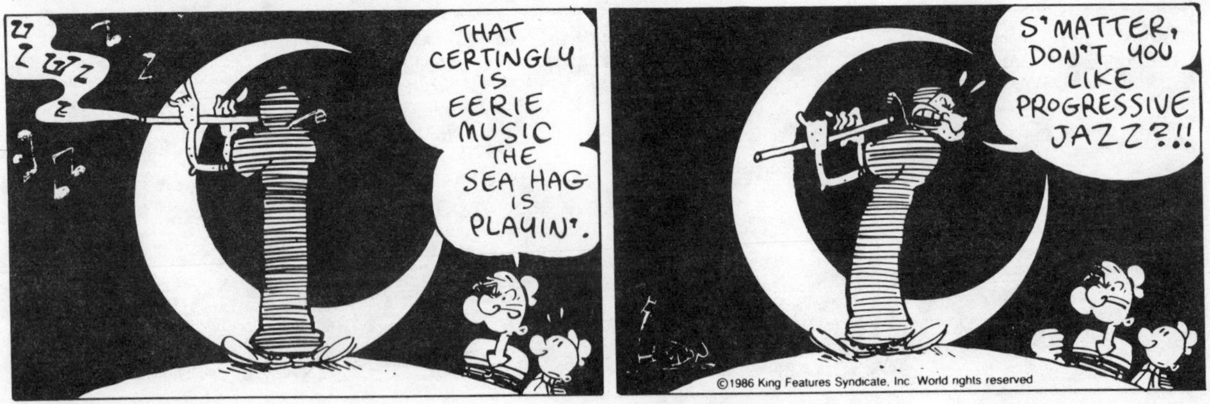
ZZ Z ZZZ Z
THAT CERTINGLY IS EERIE MUSIC THE SEA HAG IS PLAYIN'.
S'MATTER, DON'T YOU LIKE PROGRESSIVE JAZZ?!!

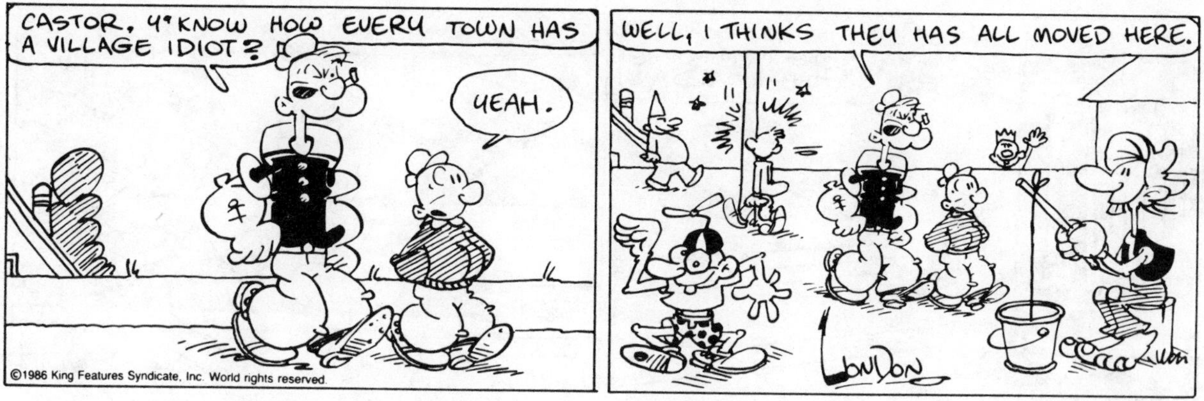
CASTOR, Y'KNOW HOW EVERY TOWN HAS A VILLAGE IDIOT?
YEAH.
WELL, I THINKS THEY HAS ALL MOVED HERE.
LONDON
©1986 King Features Syndicate, Inc. World rights reserved.

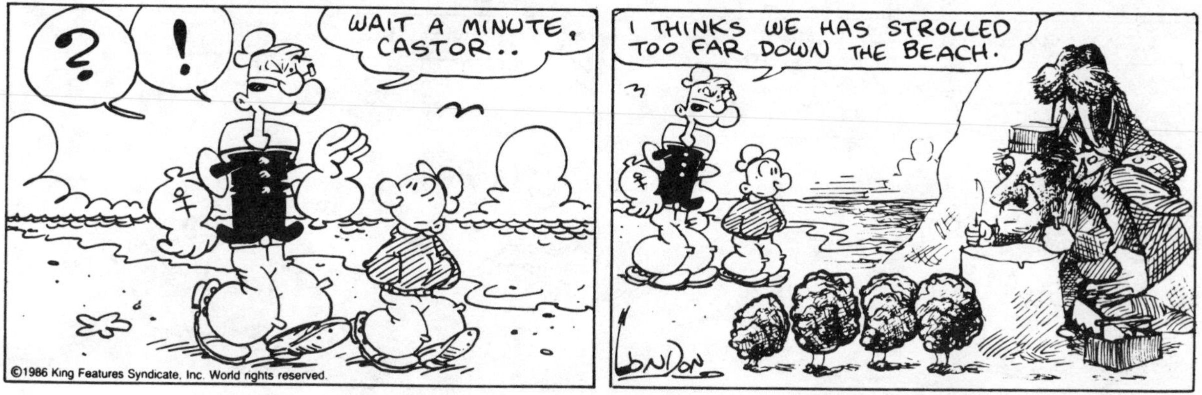
?
!
WAIT A MINUTE, CASTOR..
I THINKS WE HAS STROLLED TOO FAR DOWN THE BEACH.
LONDON
©1986 King Features Syndicate, Inc. World rights reserved.

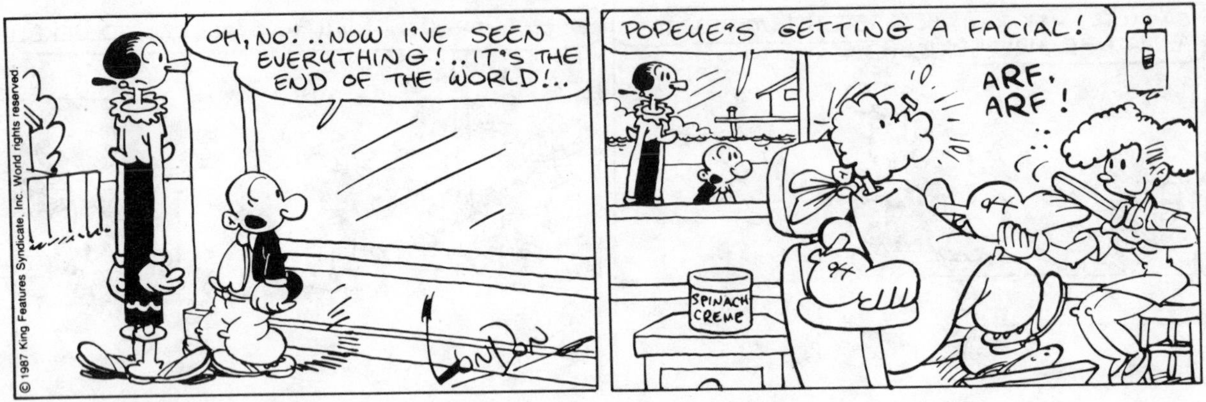
OH, NO! ..NOW I'VE SEEN EVERYTHING! ..IT'S THE END OF THE WORLD!..
POPEYE'S GETTING A FACIAL!
ARF, ARF!
SPINACH CREME
LONDON
© 1987 King Features Syndicate, Inc. World rights reserved.

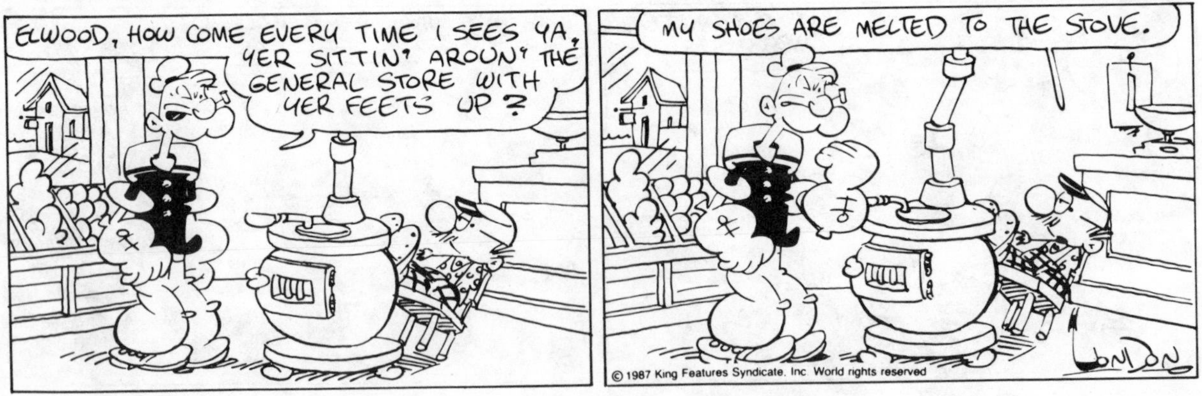
ELWOOD, HOW COME EVERY TIME I SEES YA, YER SITTIN' AROUN' THE GENERAL STORE WITH YER FEETS UP?
MY SHOES ARE MELTED TO THE STOVE.
LONDON
© 1987 King Features Syndicate, Inc. World rights reserved

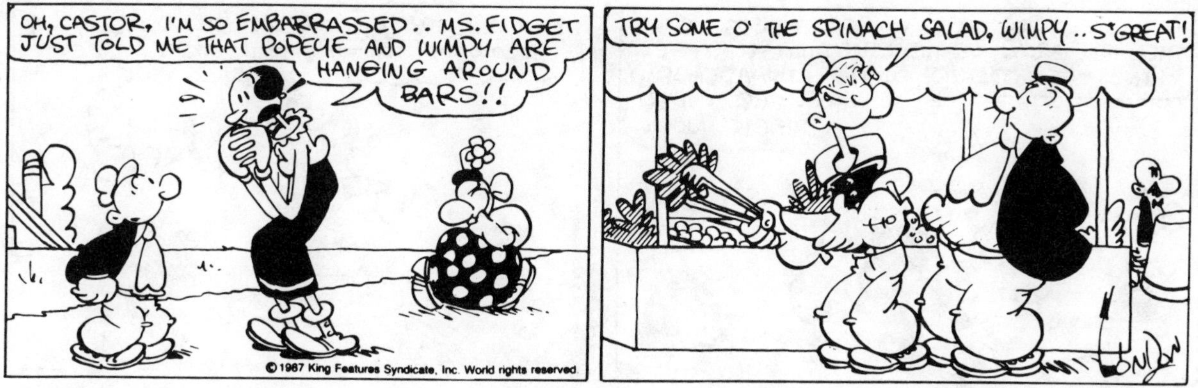
OH, CASTOR, I'M SO EMBARRASSED.. MS. FIDGET JUST TOLD ME THAT POPEYE AND WIMPY ARE HANGING AROUND BARS!!
© 1987 King Features Syndicate, Inc. World rights reserved.
TRY SOME O' THE SPINACH SALAD, WIMPY.. S'GREAT!

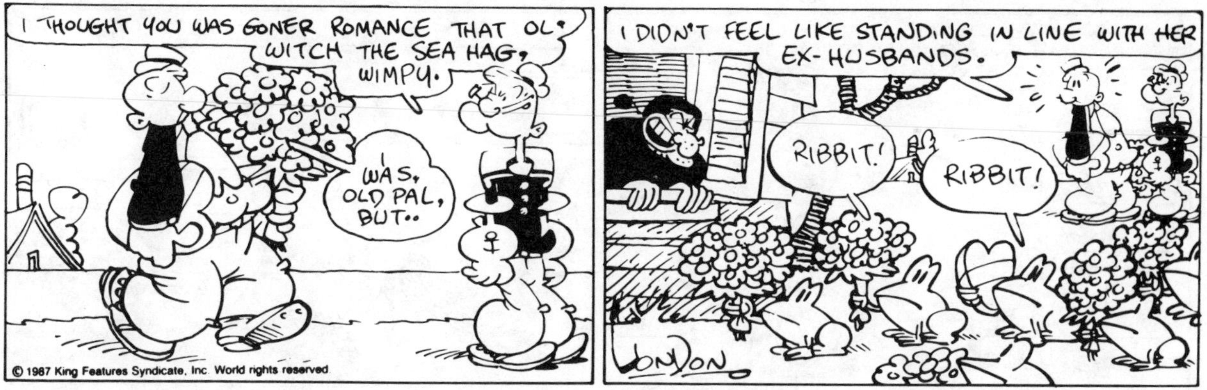
I THOUGHT YOU WAS GONER ROMANCE THAT OL' WITCH THE SEA HAG, WIMPY.
I WAS, OLD PAL, BUT..
© 1987 King Features Syndicate, Inc. World rights reserved.
I DIDN'T FEEL LIKE STANDING IN LINE WITH HER EX-HUSBANDS.
RIBBIT!
RIBBIT!

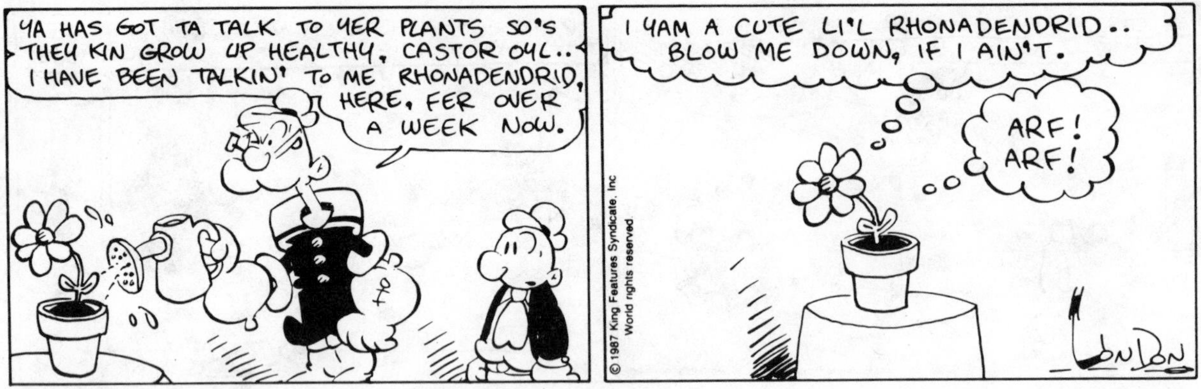
YA HAS GOT TA TALK TO YER PLANTS SO'S THEY KIN GROW UP HEALTHY, CASTOR OYL.. I HAVE BEEN TALKIN' TO ME RHONADENDRID, HERE, FER OVER A WEEK NOW.
I YAM A CUTE LI'L RHONADENDRID.. BLOW ME DOWN, IF I AIN'T.
ARF! ARF!
© 1987 King Features Syndicate, Inc. World rights reserved.
LONDON

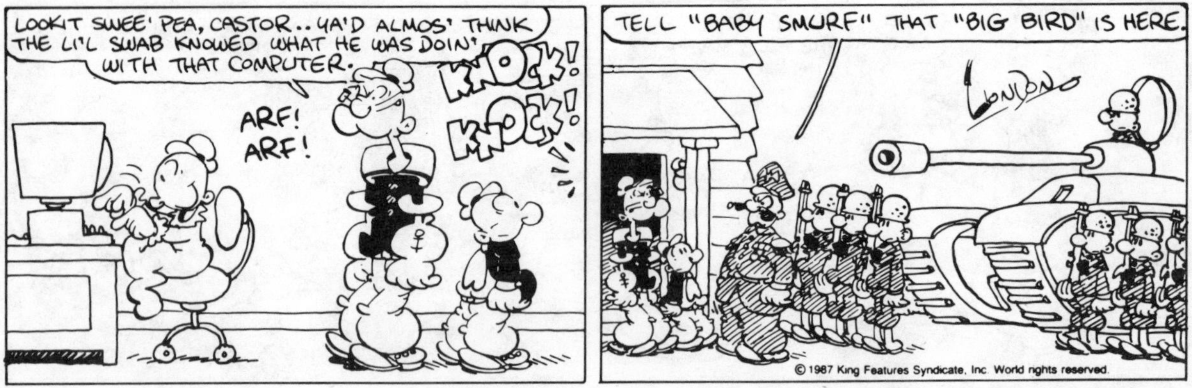
LOOKIT SWEE' PEA, CASTOR.. YA'D ALMOS' THINK THE LI'L SWAB KNOWED WHAT HE WAS DOIN' WITH THAT COMPUTER.
ARF! ARF!
KNOCK! KNOCK!
TELL "BABY SMURF" THAT "BIG BIRD" IS HERE.
LONDON
© 1987 King Features Syndicate, Inc. World rights reserved.

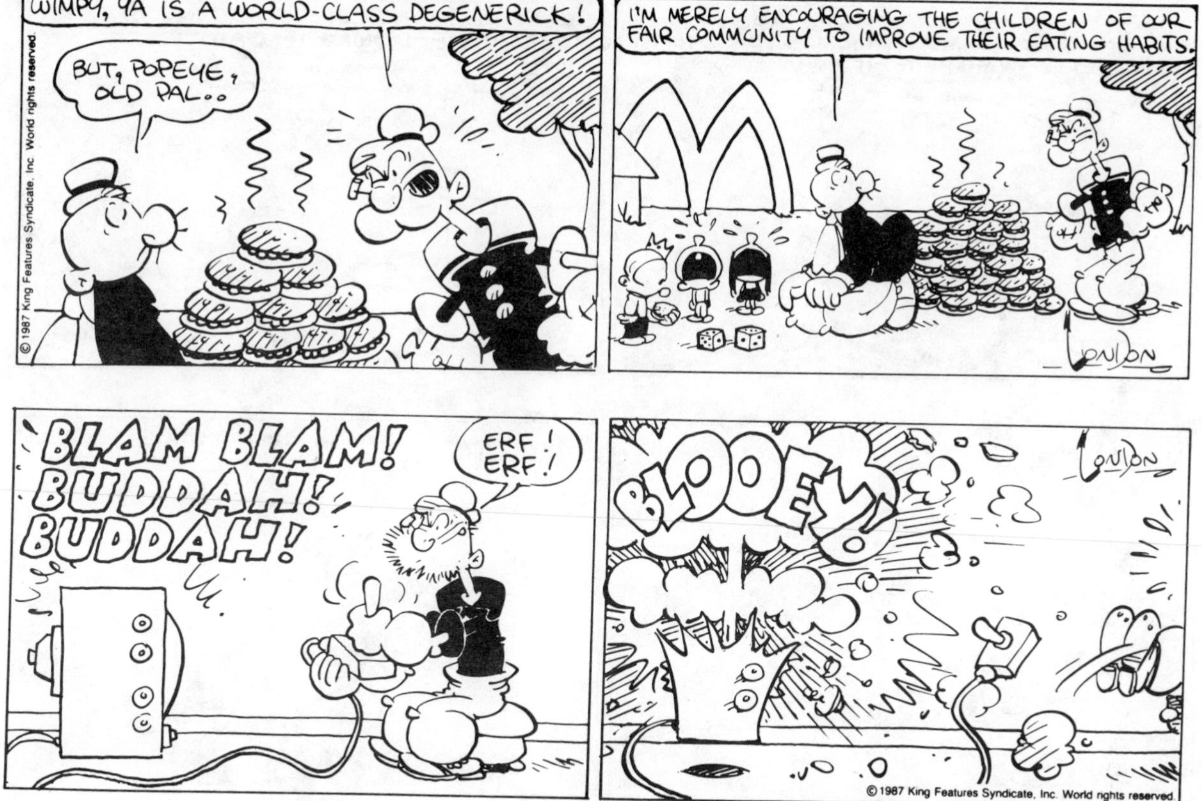
WIMPY, YA IS A WORLD-CLASS DEGENERICK!
BUT, POPEYE, OLD PAL..
I'M MERELY ENCOURAGING THE CHILDREN OF OUR FAIR COMMUNITY TO IMPROVE THEIR EATING HABITS.
LONDON
BLAM BLAM! BUDDAH! BUDDAH!
ERF! ERF!
BLOOEY!
LONDON

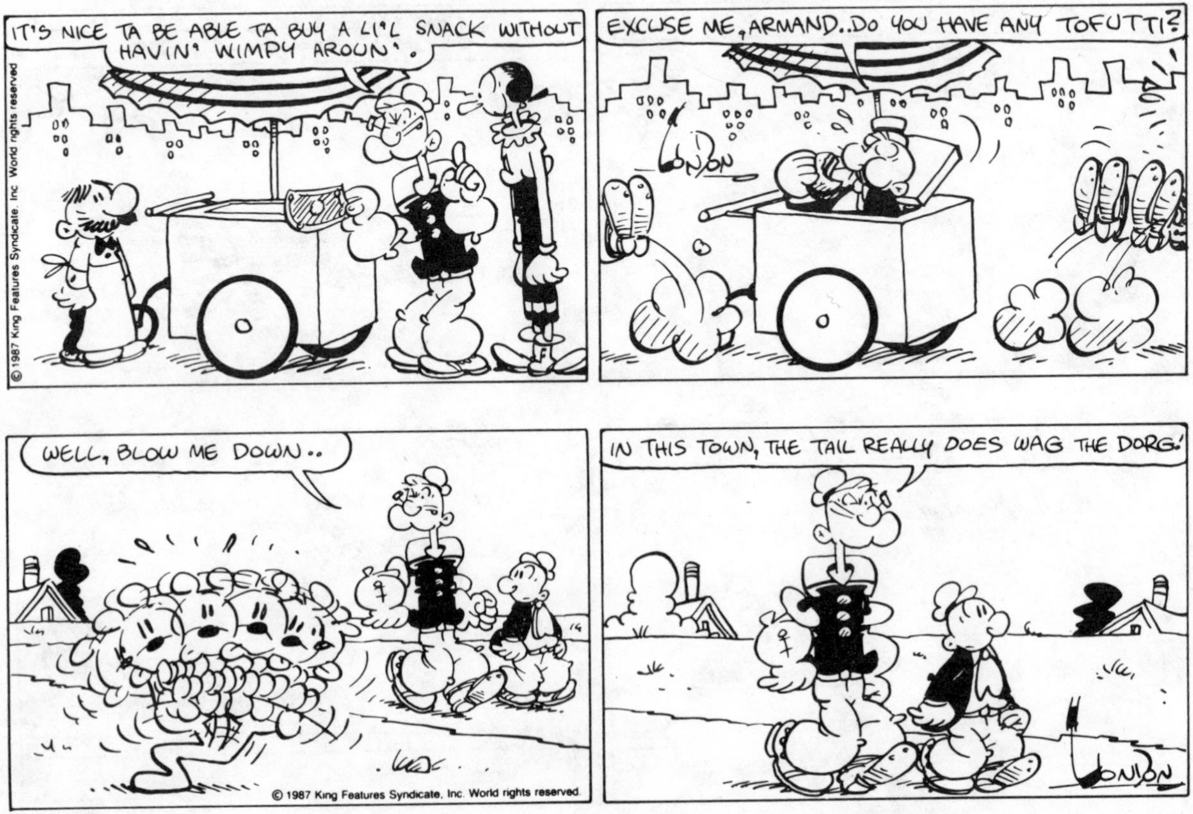
IT'S NICE TA BE ABLE TA BUY A LI'L SNACK WITHOUT HAVIN' WIMPY AROUN'.
© 1987 King Features Syndicate, Inc. World rights reserved
EXCUSE ME, ARMAND..DO YOU HAVE ANY TOFUTTI?
WELL, BLOW ME DOWN..
© 1987 King Features Syndicate, Inc. World rights reserved.
IN THIS TOWN, THE TAIL REALLY DOES WAG THE DORG!
LONDON

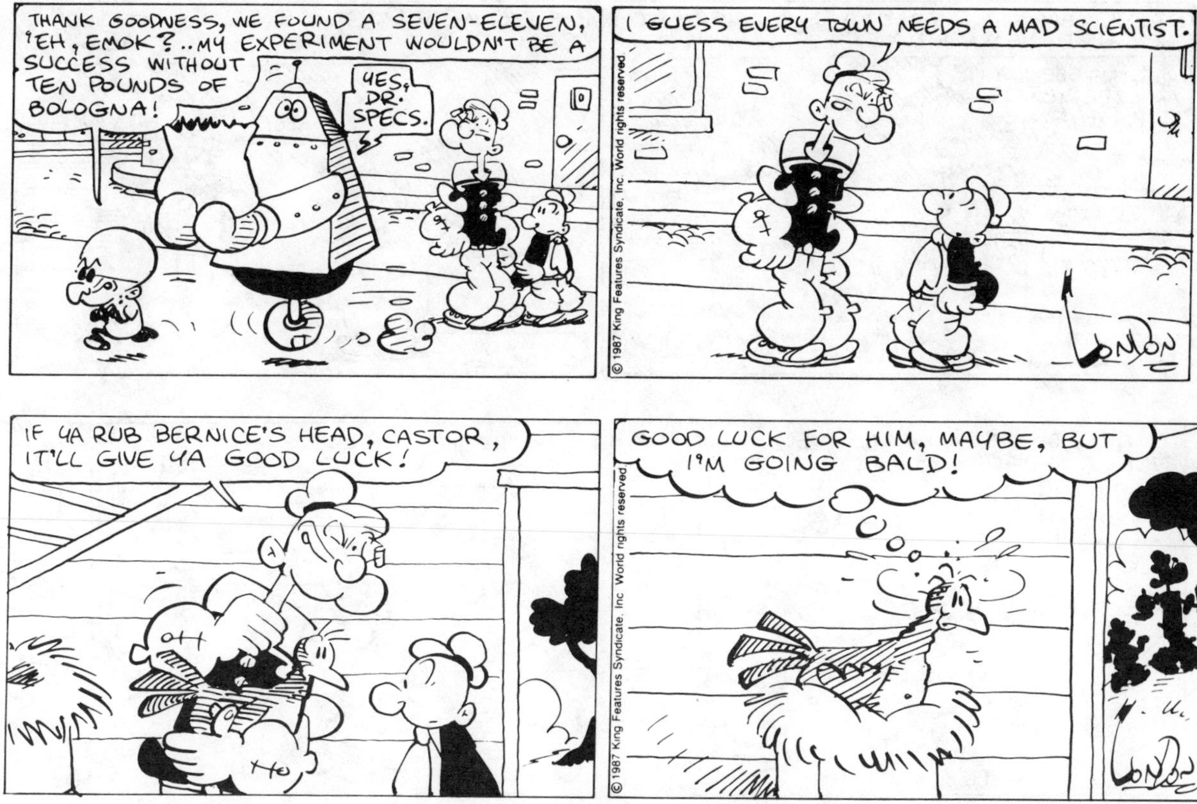
THANK GOODNESS, WE FOUND A SEVEN-ELEVEN, 'EH, EMOK? .. MY EXPERIMENT WOULDN'T BE A SUCCESS WITHOUT TEN POUNDS OF BOLOGNA!
YES, DR. SPECS.
I GUESS EVERY TOWN NEEDS A MAD SCIENTIST.
© 1987 King Features Syndicate, Inc. World rights reserved.
LONDON
IF YA RUB BERNICE'S HEAD, CASTOR, IT'LL GIVE YA GOOD LUCK!
GOOD LUCK FOR HIM, MAYBE, BUT I'M GOING BALD!
© 1987 King Features Syndicate, Inc. World rights reserved.
LONDON

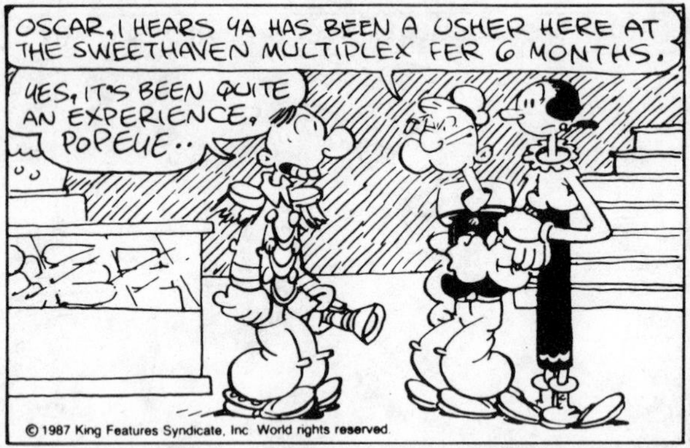
OSCAR, I HEARS YA HAS BEEN A USHER HERE AT THE SWEETHAVEN MULTIPLEX FER 6 MONTHS.
YES, IT'S BEEN QUITE AN EXPERIENCE, POPEYE..
I'VE BECOME HYPOGLYCEMIC AND I'VE SEEN "BACK TO THE FUTURE" 517 TIMES.
LONDON
© 1987 King Features Syndicate, Inc. World rights reserved.

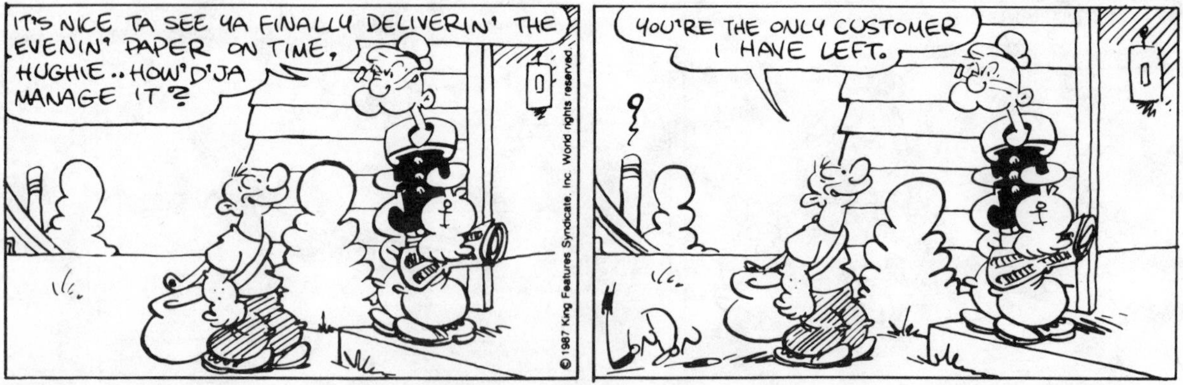
IT'S NICE TA SEE YA FINALLY DELIVERIN' THE EVENIN' PAPER ON TIME, HUGHIE.. HOW'D'JA MANAGE IT?
YOU'RE THE ONLY CUSTOMER I HAVE LEFT.
LONDON
© 1987 King Features Syndicate, Inc. World rights reserved.

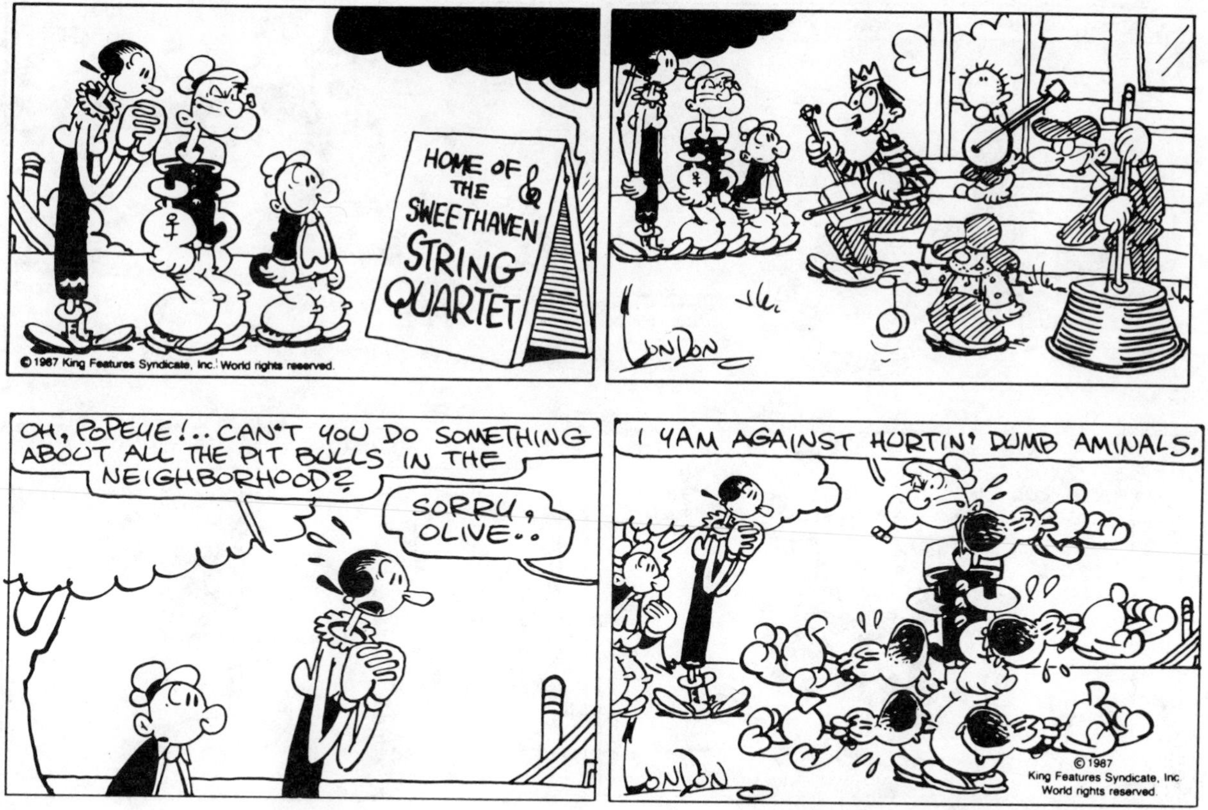
HOME OF THE SWEETHAVEN STRING QUARTET
© 1987 King Features Syndicate, Inc. World rights reserved.
LONDON
OH, POPEYE!.. CAN'T YOU DO SOMETHING ABOUT ALL THE PIT BULLS IN THE NEIGHBORHOOD?
SORRY, OLIVE..
I YAM AGAINST HURTIN' DUMB AMINALS.
LONDON
© 1987 King Features Syndicate, Inc. World rights reserved.

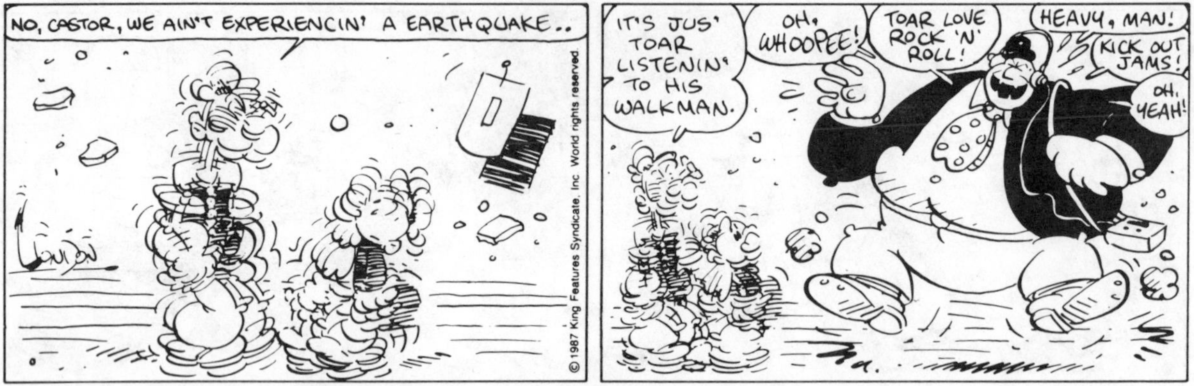
NO, CASTOR, WE AIN'T EXPERIENCIN' A EARTHQUAKE..
© 1987 King Features Syndicate, Inc. World rights reserved.
IT'S JUS' TOAR LISTENIN' TO HIS WALKMAN.
OH, WHOOPEE!
TOAR LOVE ROCK 'N' ROLL!
HEAVY, MAN!
KICK OUT JAMS!
OH, YEAH!

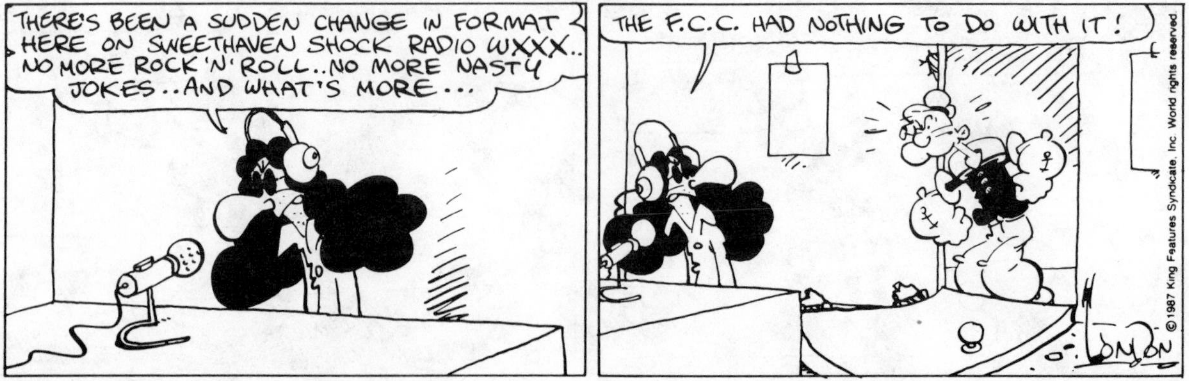
THERE'S BEEN A SUDDEN CHANGE IN FORMAT HERE ON SWEETHAVEN SHOCK RADIO WXXX.. NO MORE ROCK 'N' ROLL.. NO MORE NASTY JOKES.. AND WHAT'S MORE...
THE F.C.C. HAD NOTHING TO DO WITH IT!
© 1987 King Features Syndicate, Inc. World rights reserved.
LONDON

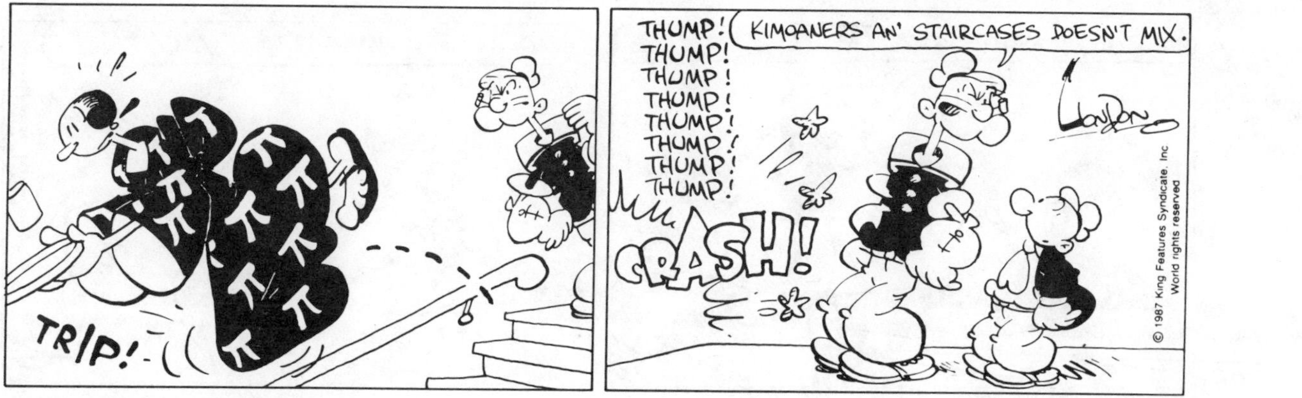
TRIP!
THUMP! THUMP! THUMP! THUMP! THUMP! THUMP! THUMP! THUMP!
CRASH!
KIMOANERS AN' STAIRCASES DOESN'T MIX.
© 1987 King Features Syndicate, Inc. World rights reserved

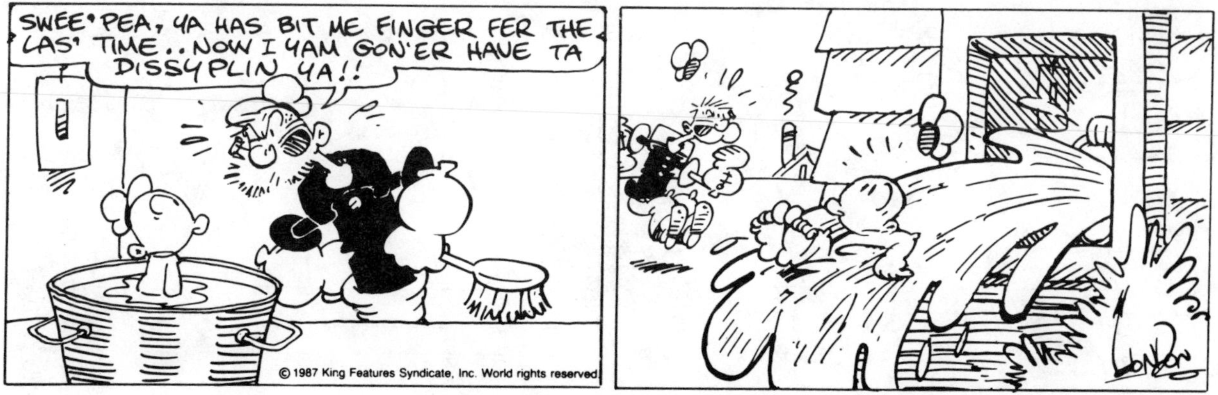
SWEE'PEA, YA HAS BIT ME FINGER FER THE LAS' TIME.. NOW I YAM GON'ER HAVE TA DISSYPLIN YA!!
© 1987 King Features Syndicate, Inc. World rights reserved

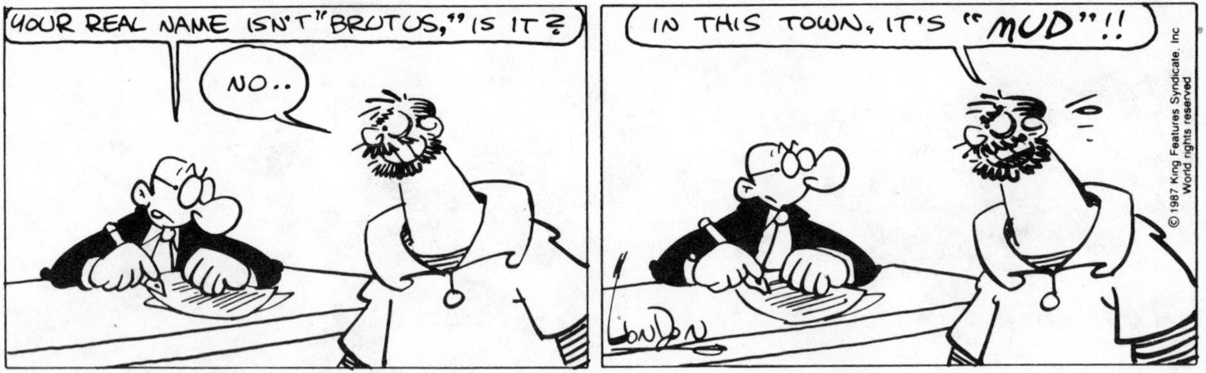
YOUR REAL NAME ISN'T "BRUTUS," IS IT?
NO..
IN THIS TOWN, IT'S "MUD"!!
LONDON
© 1987 King Features Syndicate, Inc
World rights reserved

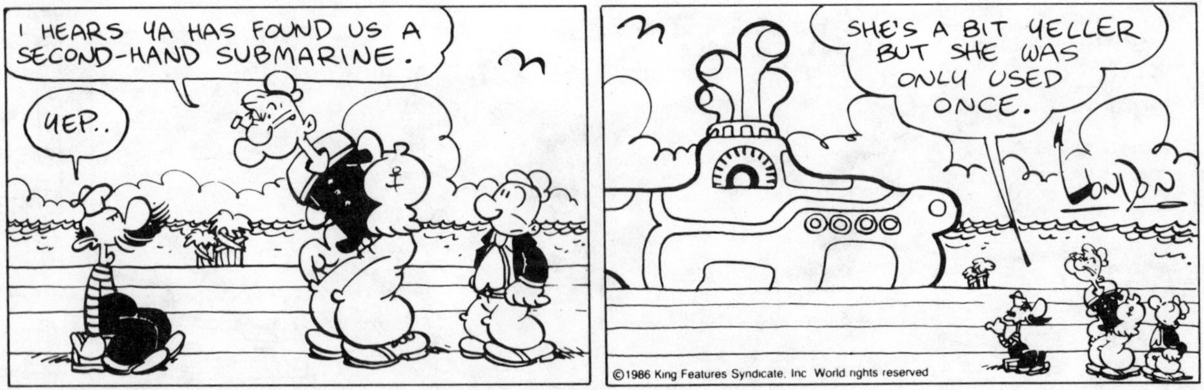
I HEARS YA HAS FOUND US A SECOND-HAND SUBMARINE.
YEP..
SHE'S A BIT YELLER BUT SHE WAS ONLY USED ONCE.
LONDON
©1986 King Features Syndicate, Inc World rights reserved

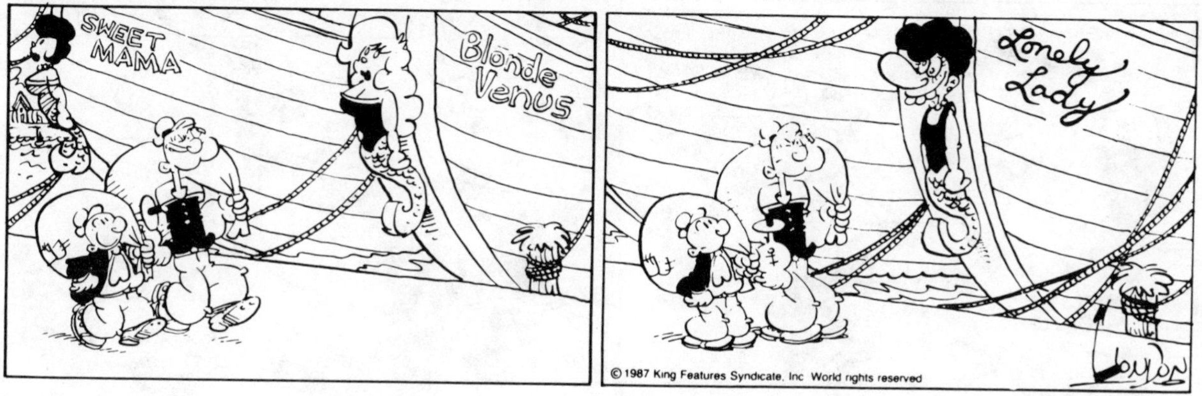
SWEET MAMA
Blonde Venus
Lonely Lady
© 1987 King Features Syndicate, Inc World rights reserved

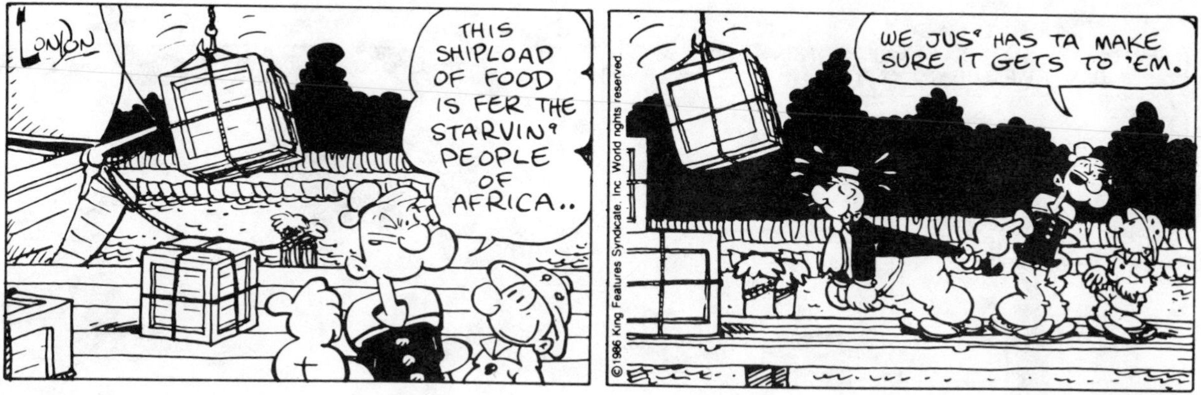
THIS SHIPLOAD OF FOOD IS FER THE STARVIN' PEOPLE OF AFRICA..
WE JUS' HAS TA MAKE SURE IT GETS TO 'EM.
© 1986 King Features Syndicate, Inc World rights reserved

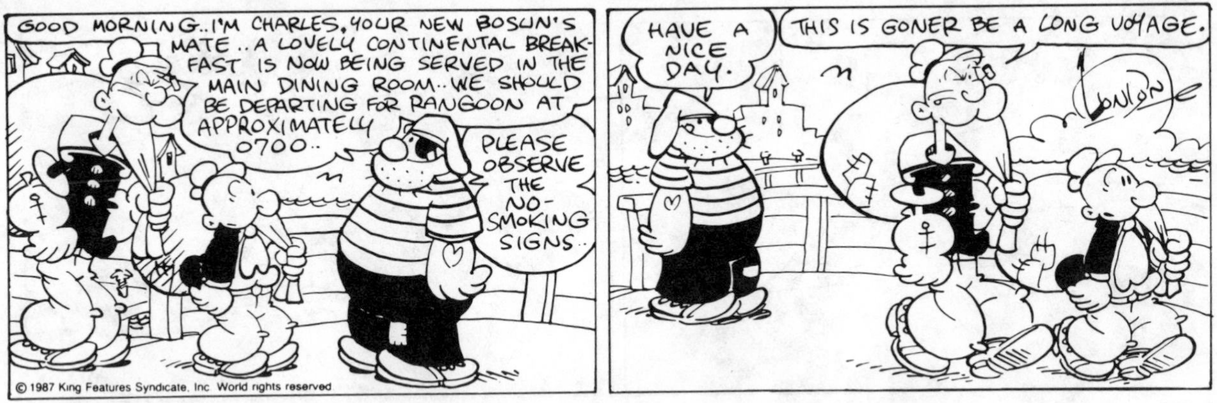
GOOD MORNING..I'M CHARLES, YOUR NEW BOSUN'S MATE..A LOVELY CONTINENTAL BREAK-FAST IS NOW BEING SERVED IN THE MAIN DINING ROOM..WE SHOULD BE DEPARTING FOR RANGOON AT APPROXIMATELY 0700..
PLEASE OBSERVE THE NO-SMOKING SIGNS..
HAVE A NICE DAY.
THIS IS GONER BE A LONG VOYAGE.
LONDON



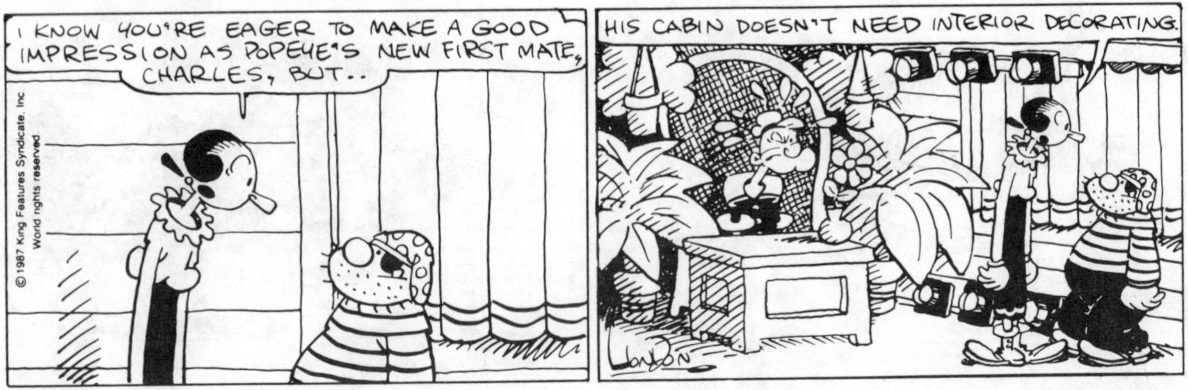
I KNOW YOU'RE EAGER TO MAKE A GOOD IMPRESSION AS POPEYE'S NEW FIRST MATE, CHARLES, BUT..
HIS CABIN DOESN'T NEED INTERIOR DECORATING.
LONDON

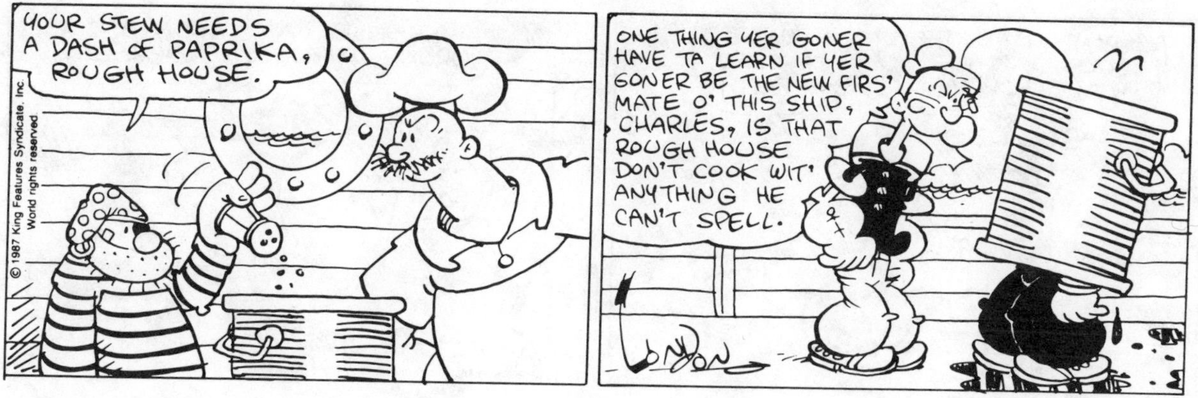
YOUR STEW NEEDS A DASH OF PAPRIKA, ROUGH HOUSE.
© 1987 King Features Syndicate, Inc. World rights reserved
ONE THING YER GONER HAVE TA LEARN IF YER GONER BE THE NEW FIRS' MATE O' THIS SHIP, CHARLES, IS THAT ROUGH HOUSE DON'T COOK WIT' ANYTHING HE CAN'T SPELL.
LONDON

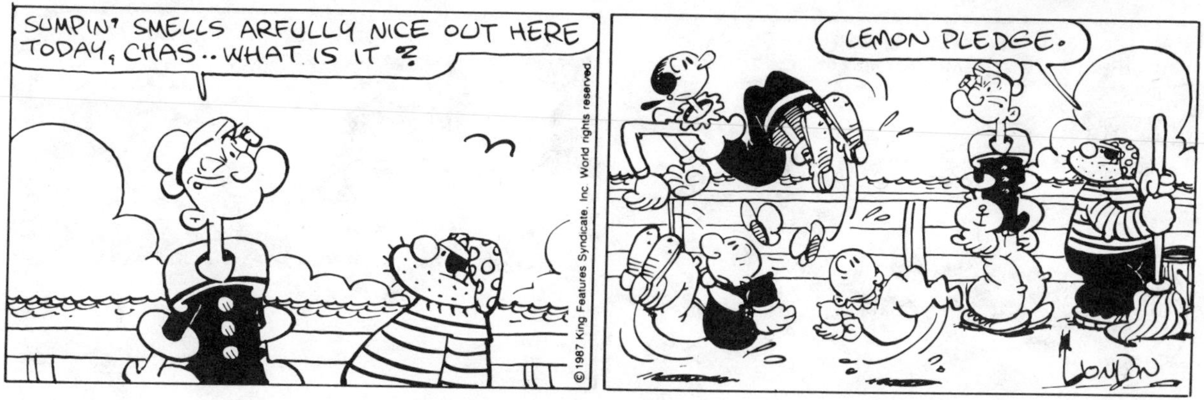
SUMPIN' SMELLS ARFULLY NICE OUT HERE TODAY, CHAS.. WHAT IS IT ?
© 1987 King Features Syndicate, Inc. World rights reserved
LEMON PLEDGE.
LONDON

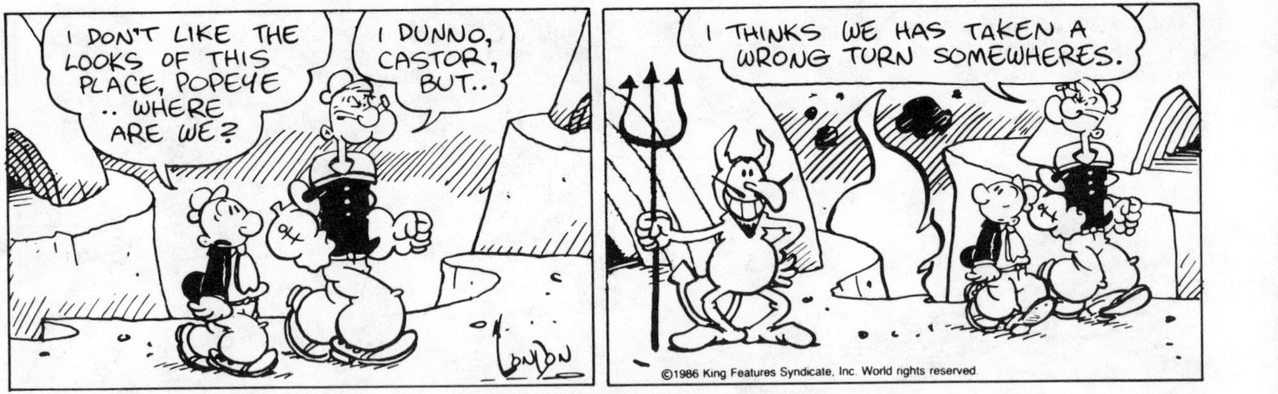
I DON'T LIKE THE LOOKS OF THIS PLACE, POPEYE .. WHERE ARE WE?
I DUNNO, CASTOR, BUT..
I THINKS WE HAS TAKEN A WRONG TURN SOMEWHERES.
©1986 King Features Syndicate, Inc. World rights reserved.

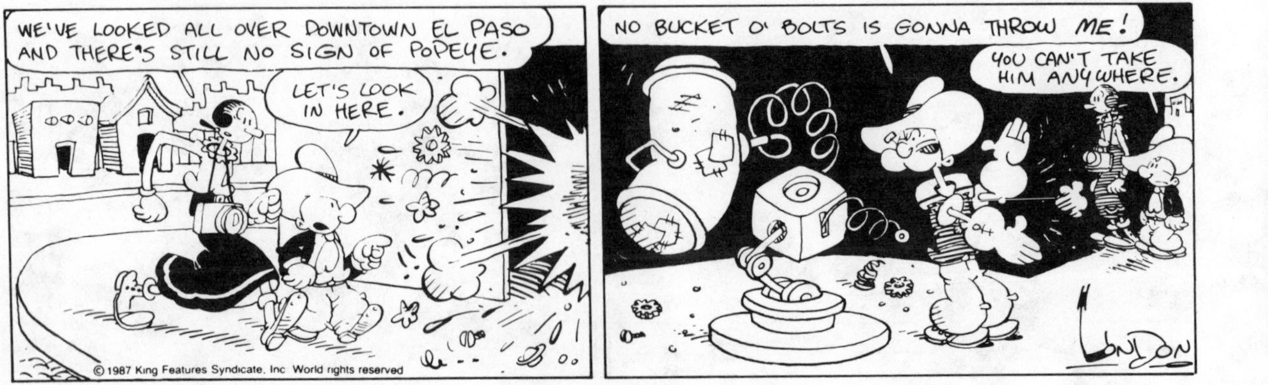
WE'VE LOOKED ALL OVER DOWNTOWN EL PASO AND THERE'S STILL NO SIGN OF POPEYE.
LET'S LOOK IN HERE.
© 1987 King Features Syndicate, Inc World rights reserved
NO BUCKET O' BOLTS IS GONNA THROW *ME*!
YOU CAN'T TAKE HIM ANYWHERE.

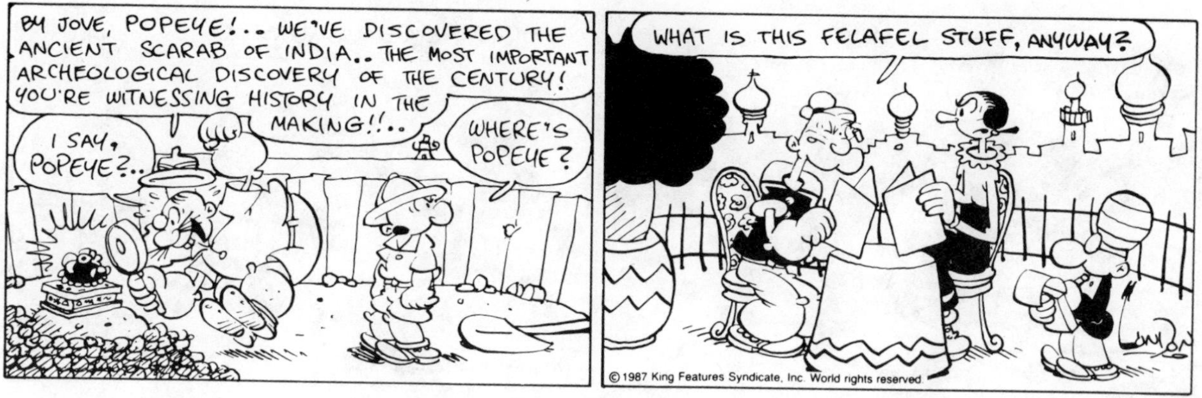
BY JOVE, POPEYE!.. WE'VE DISCOVERED THE ANCIENT SCARAB OF INDIA.. THE MOST IMPORTANT ARCHEOLOGICAL DISCOVERY OF THE CENTURY! YOU'RE WITNESSING HISTORY IN THE MAKING!!..
I SAY, POPEYE?..
WHERE'S POPEYE?
WHAT IS THIS FELAFEL STUFF, ANYWAY?


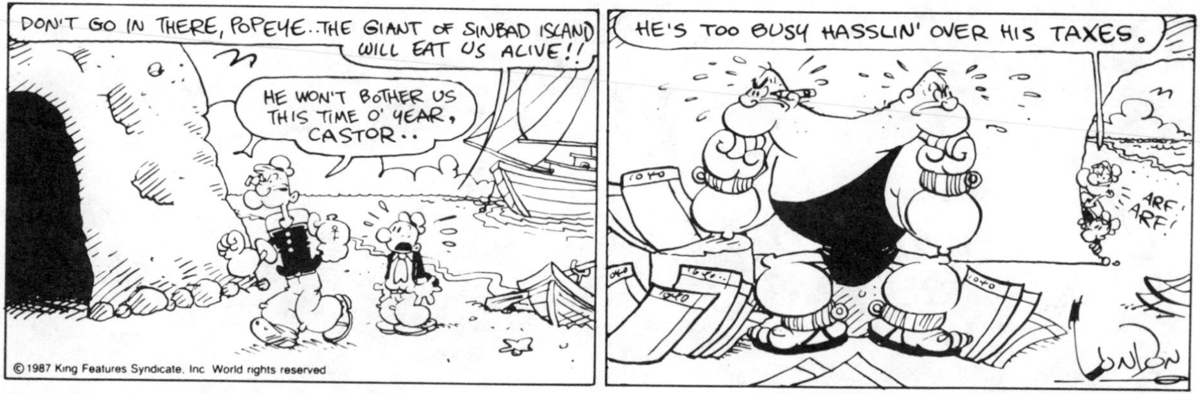
DON'T GO IN THERE, POPEYE..THE GIANT OF SINBAD ISLAND WILL EAT US ALIVE!!
HE WON'T BOTHER US THIS TIME O' YEAR, CASTOR..
HE'S TOO BUSY HASSLIN' OVER HIS TAXES.
ARF! ARF!

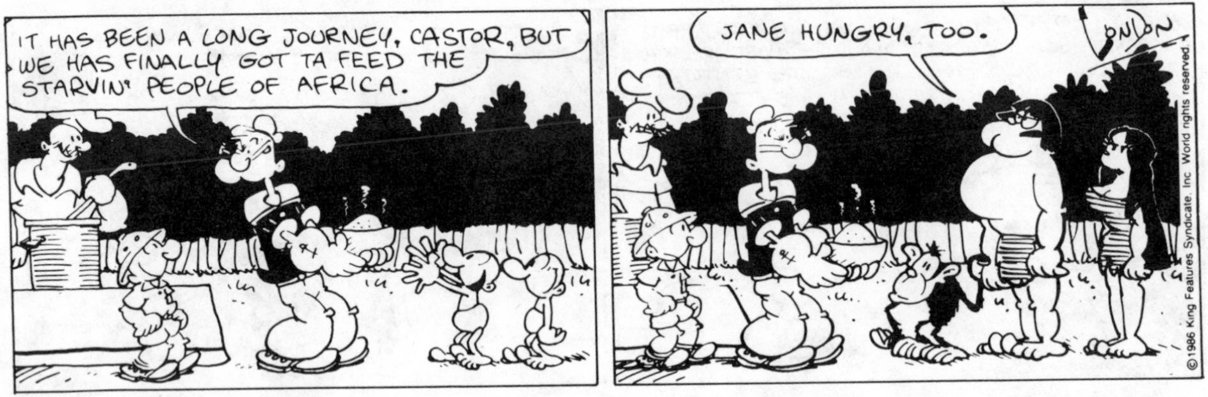

IT HAS BEEN A LONG JOURNEY, CASTOR, BUT WE HAS FINALLY GOT TA FEED THE STARVIN' PEOPLE OF AFRICA.
JANE HUNGRY, TOO.
LONDON
©1986 King Features Syndicate, Inc World rights reserved.


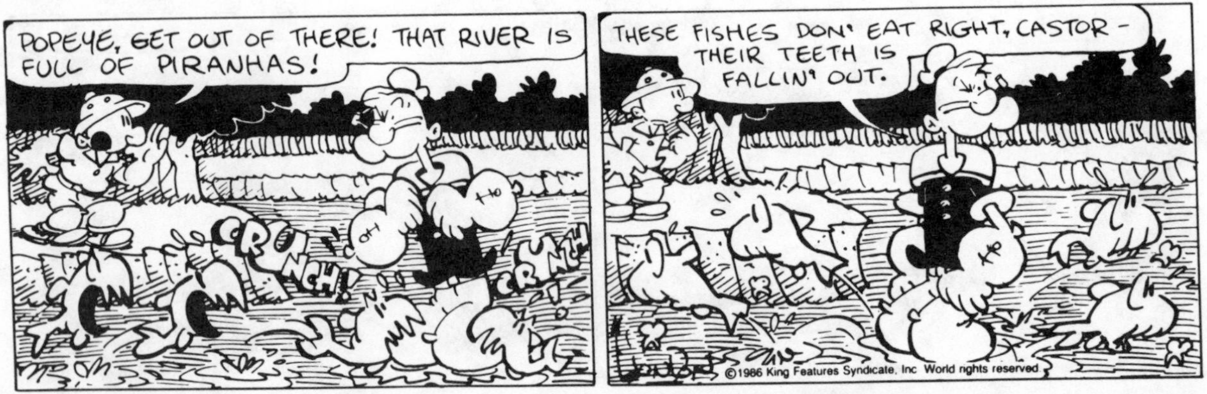

POPEYE, GET OUT OF THERE! THAT RIVER IS FULL OF PIRANHAS!
CRUNCH!
CRUNCH
THESE FISHES DON' EAT RIGHT, CASTOR – THEIR TEETH IS FALLIN' OUT.
©1986 King Features Syndicate, Inc World rights reserved.

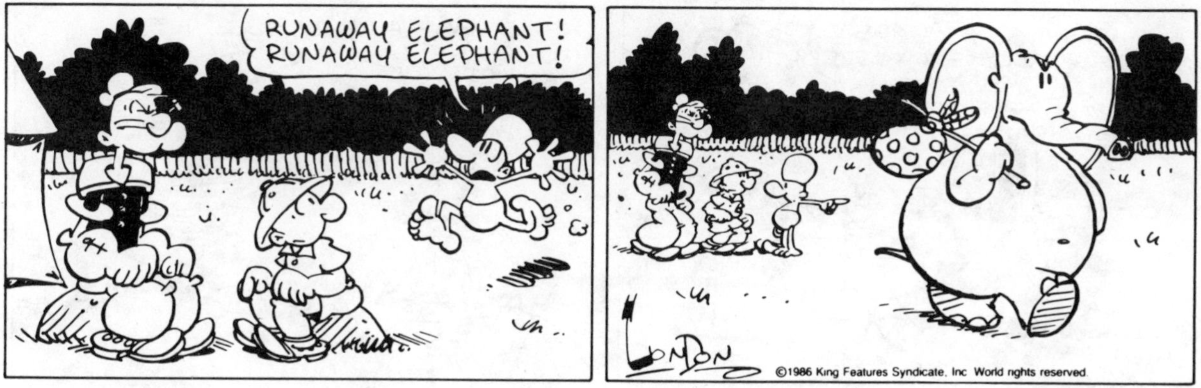
RUNAWAY ELEPHANT! RUNAWAY ELEPHANT!
LONDON
©1986 King Features Syndicate, Inc World rights reserved.

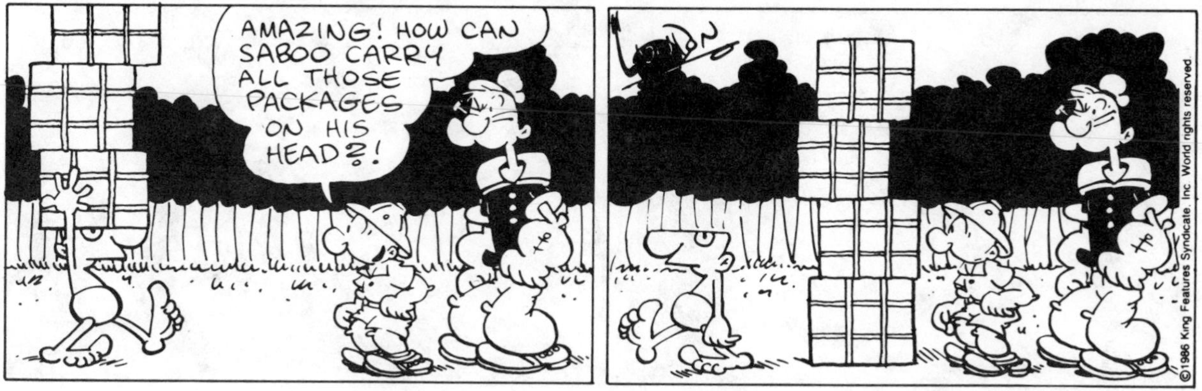
AMAZING! HOW CAN SABOO CARRY ALL THOSE PACKAGES ON HIS HEAD?!
LONDON
©1986 King Features Syndicate, Inc. World rights reserved

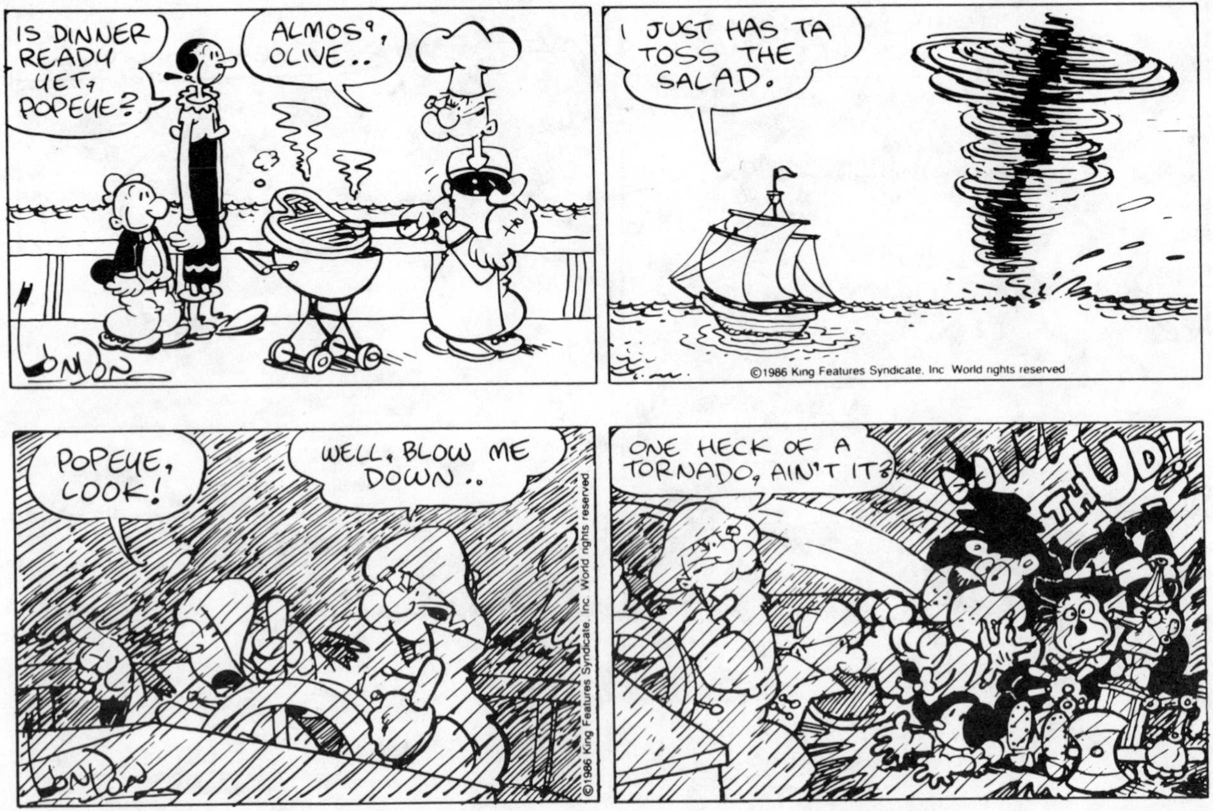
IS DINNER READY YET, POPEYE?
ALMOST, OLIVE..
I JUST HAS TA TOSS THE SALAD.
©1986 King Features Syndicate, Inc World rights reserved
POPEYE, LOOK!
WELL, BLOW ME DOWN..
©1986 King Features Syndicate, Inc. World rights reserved
ONE HECK OF A TORNADO, AIN'T IT?
THUD!!

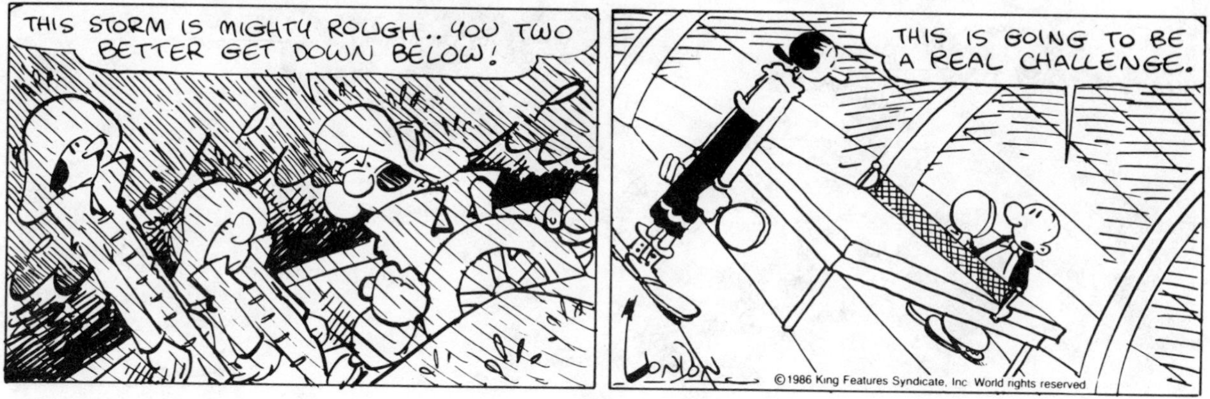
THIS STORM IS MIGHTY ROUGH.. YOU TWO BETTER GET DOWN BELOW!
THIS IS GOING TO BE A REAL CHALLENGE.
LONDON
©1986 King Features Syndicate, Inc World rights reserved

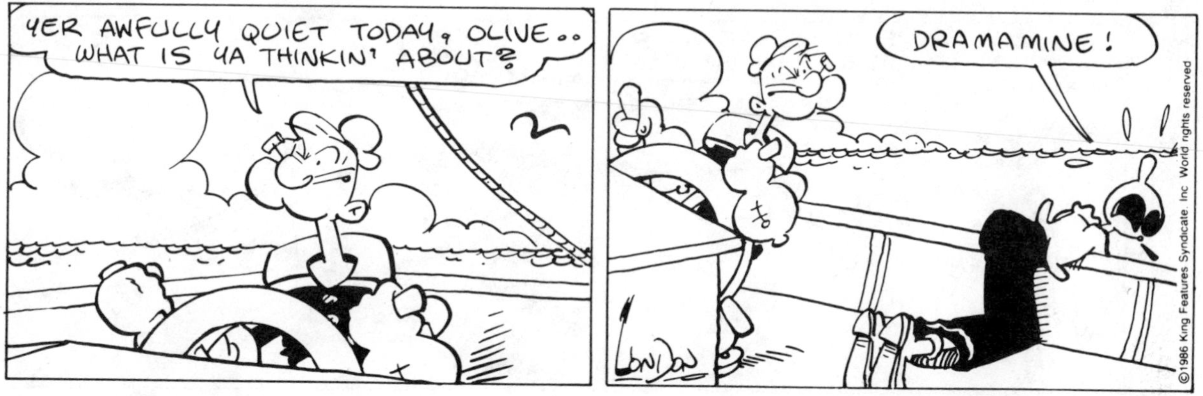
YER AWFULLY QUIET TODAY, OLIVE.. WHAT IS YA THINKIN' ABOUT?
DRAMAMINE!
LONDON
©1986 King Features Syndicate, Inc World rights reserved

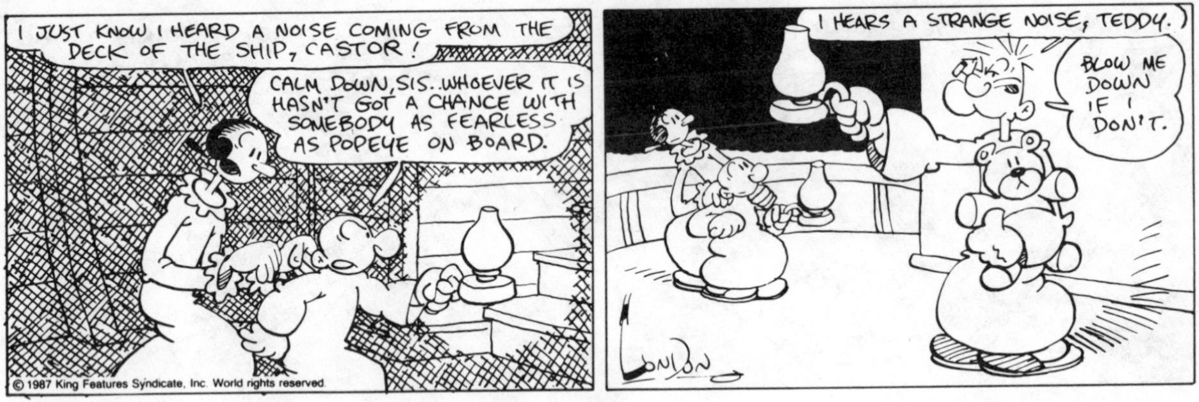
I JUST KNOW I HEARD A NOISE COMING FROM THE DECK OF THE SHIP, CASTOR!
CALM DOWN, SIS.. WHOEVER IT IS HASN'T GOT A CHANCE WITH SOMEBODY AS FEARLESS AS POPEYE ON BOARD.
© 1987 King Features Syndicate, Inc. World rights reserved.
I HEARS A STRANGE NOISE, TEDDY.
BLOW ME DOWN IF I DON'T.

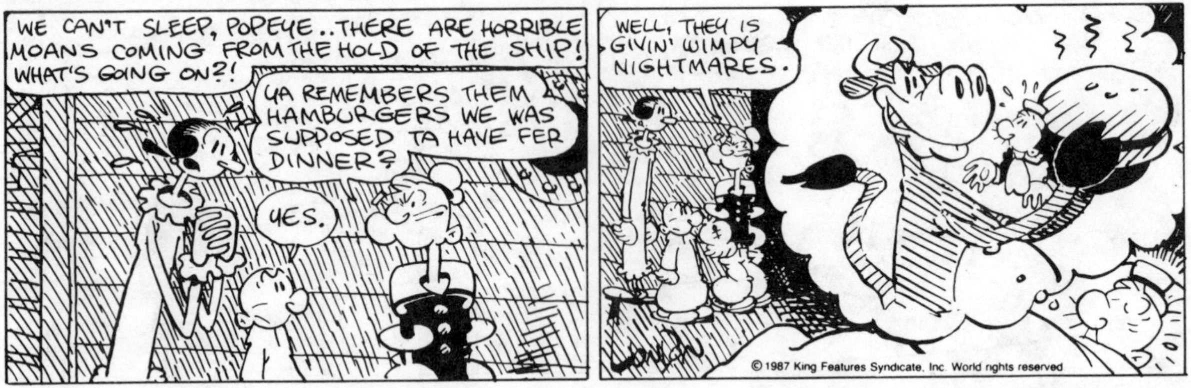
WE CAN'T SLEEP, POPEYE.. THERE ARE HORRIBLE MOANS COMING FROM THE HOLD OF THE SHIP! WHAT'S GOING ON?!
YA REMEMBERS THEM HAMBURGERS WE WAS SUPPOSED TA HAVE FER DINNER?
YES.
WELL, THEY IS GIVIN' WIMPY NIGHTMARES.
© 1987 King Features Syndicate, Inc. World rights reserved

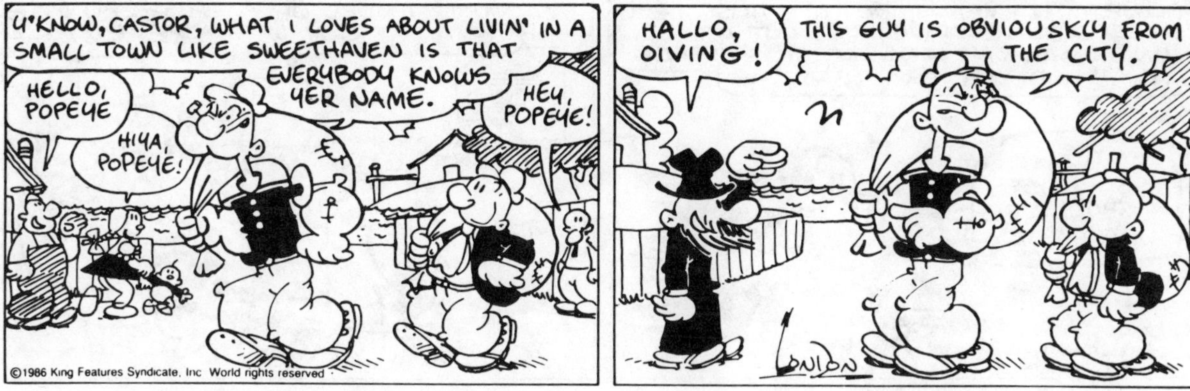
Y'KNOW, CASTOR, WHAT I LOVES ABOUT LIVIN' IN A SMALL TOWN LIKE SWEETHAVEN IS THAT EVERYBODY KNOWS YER NAME.
HELLO, POPEYE
HIYA, POPEYE!
HEY, POPEYE!
HALLO, OIVING!
THIS GUY IS OBVIOUSKLY FROM THE CITY.
LONDON
©1986 King Features Syndicate, Inc World rights reserved

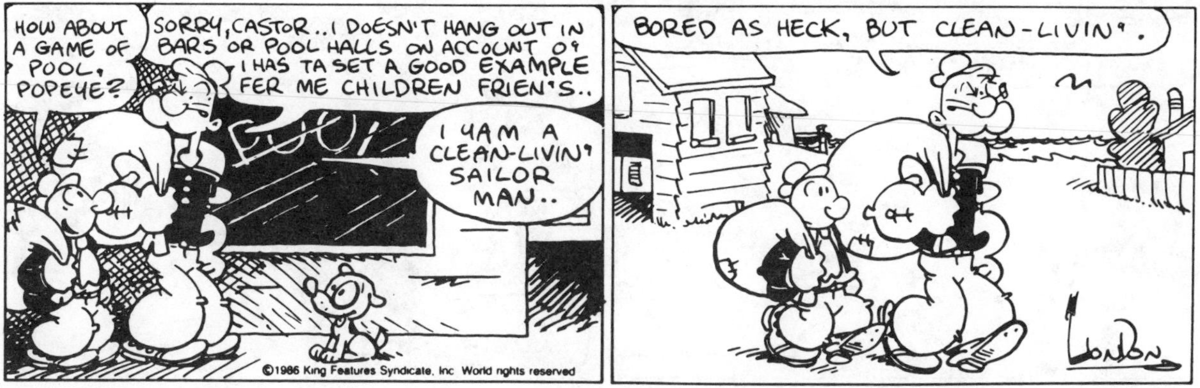
HOW ABOUT A GAME OF POOL, POPEYE?
SORRY, CASTOR.. I DOESN'T HANG OUT IN BARS OR POOL HALLS ON ACCOUNT O' I HAS TA SET A GOOD EXAMPLE FER ME CHILDREN FRIEN'S..
I YAM A CLEAN-LIVIN' SAILOR MAN..
BORED AS HECK, BUT CLEAN-LIVIN'.
LONDON
©1986 King Features Syndicate, Inc World rights reserved

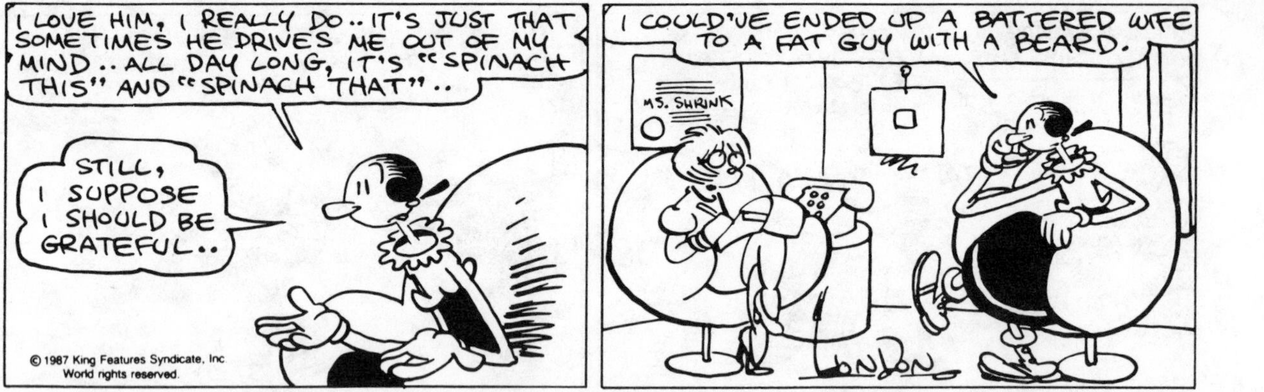

I LOVE HIM, I REALLY DO.. IT'S JUST THAT SOMETIMES HE DRIVES ME OUT OF MY MIND.. ALL DAY LONG, IT'S "SPINACH THIS" AND "SPINACH THAT"..
STILL, I SUPPOSE I SHOULD BE GRATEFUL..
© 1987 King Features Syndicate, Inc. World rights reserved.
I COULD'VE ENDED UP A BATTERED WIFE TO A FAT GUY WITH A BEARD.
MS. SHRINK
LONDON


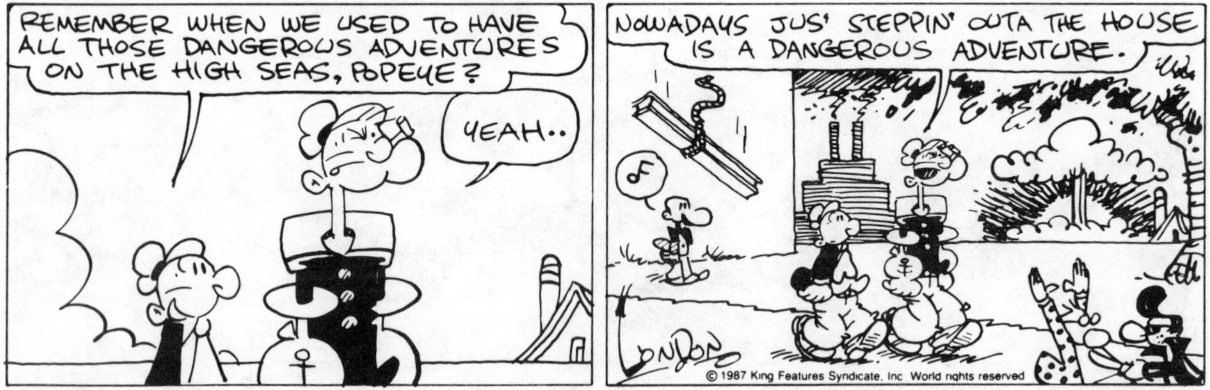

REMEMBER WHEN WE USED TO HAVE ALL THOSE DANGEROUS ADVENTURES ON THE HIGH SEAS, POPEYE?
YEAH..
NOWADAYS JUS' STEPPIN' OUTA THE HOUSE IS A DANGEROUS ADVENTURE.
LONDON
© 1987 King Features Syndicate, Inc World rights reserved

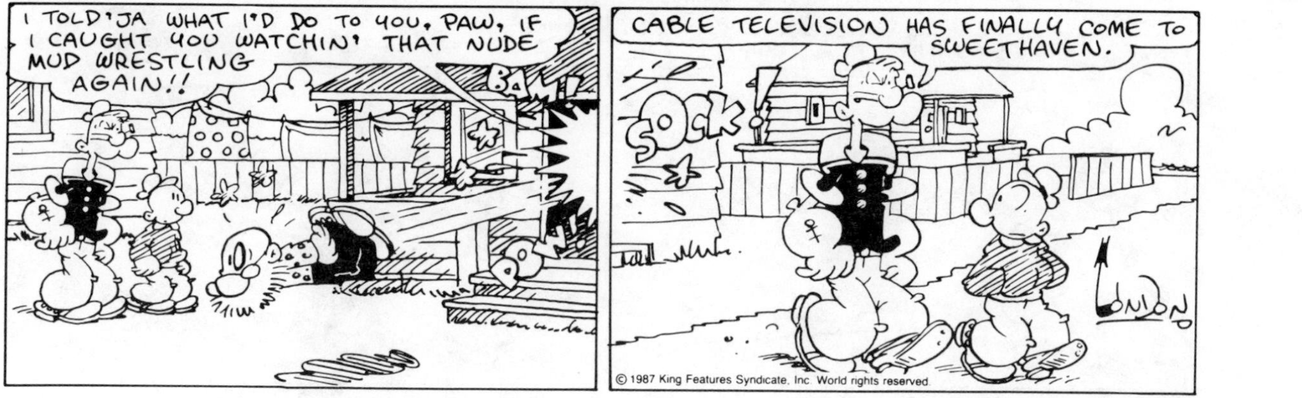

I TOLD'JA WHAT I'D DO TO YOU, PAW, IF I CAUGHT YOU WATCHIN' THAT NUDE MUD WRESTLING AGAIN!!
BAM!
POW!
SOCK!
CABLE TELEVISION HAS FINALLY COME TO SWEETHAVEN.
LONDON



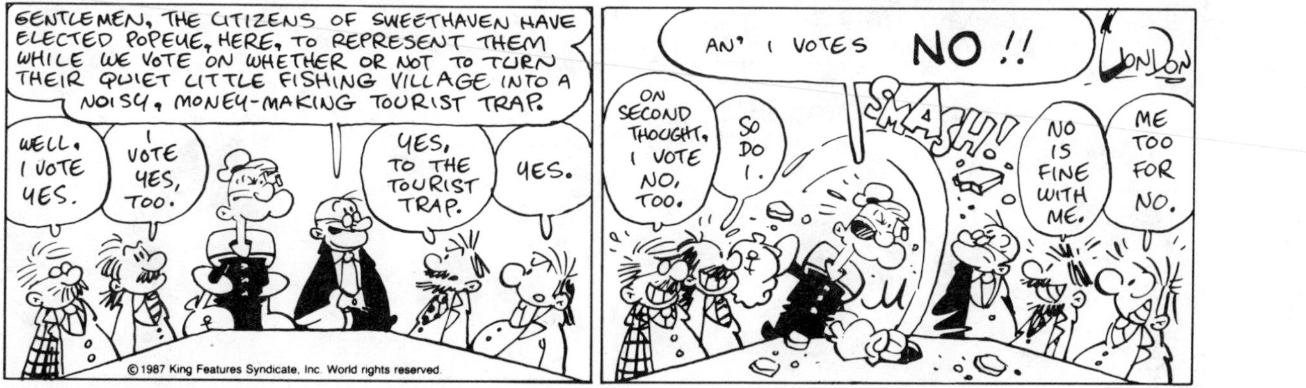

GENTLEMEN, THE CITIZENS OF SWEETHAVEN HAVE ELECTED POPEYE, HERE, TO REPRESENT THEM WHILE WE VOTE ON WHETHER OR NOT TO TURN THEIR QUIET LITTLE FISHING VILLAGE INTO A NOISY, MONEY-MAKING TOURIST TRAP.
WELL, I VOTE YES.
I VOTE YES, TOO.
YES, TO THE TOURIST TRAP.
YES.
AN' I VOTES NO !!
SMASH!
ON SECOND THOUGHT, I VOTE NO, TOO.
SO DO I.
NO IS FINE WITH ME.
ME TOO FOR NO.
LONDON

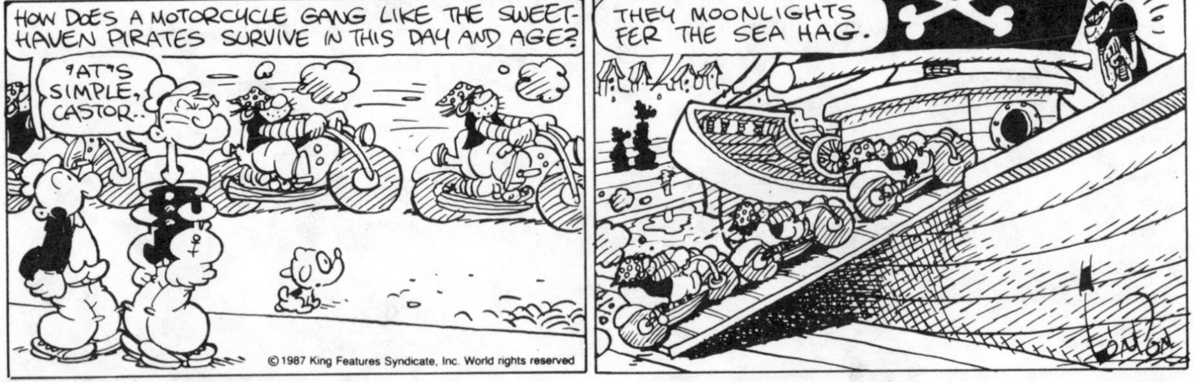
HOW DOES A MOTORCYCLE GANG LIKE THE SWEET-HAVEN PIRATES SURVIVE IN THIS DAY AND AGE?
'AT'S SIMPLE, CASTOR..
THEY MOONLIGHTS FER THE SEA HAG.
© 1987 King Features Syndicate, Inc. World rights reserved

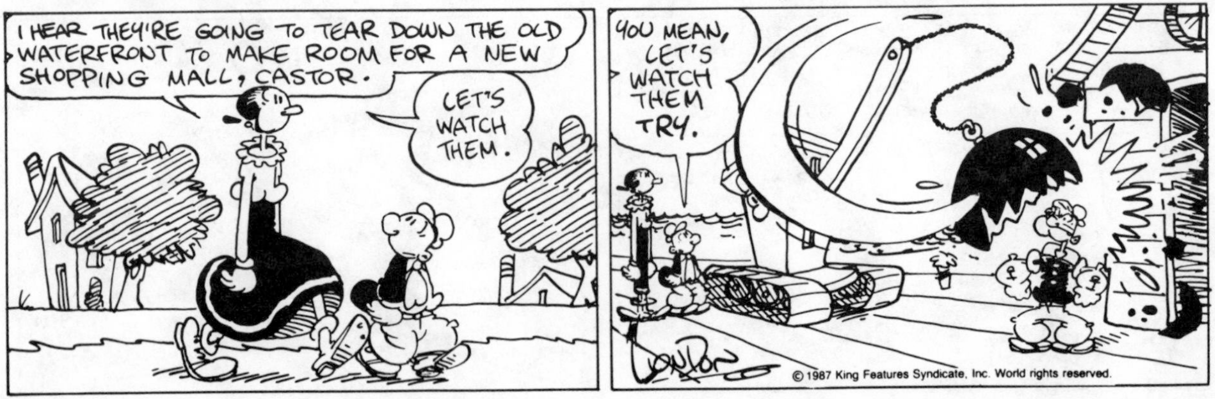
I HEAR THEY'RE GOING TO TEAR DOWN THE OLD WATERFRONT TO MAKE ROOM FOR A NEW SHOPPING MALL, CASTOR.
LET'S WATCH THEM.
YOU MEAN, LET'S WATCH THEM TRY.
© 1987 King Features Syndicate, Inc. World rights reserved.

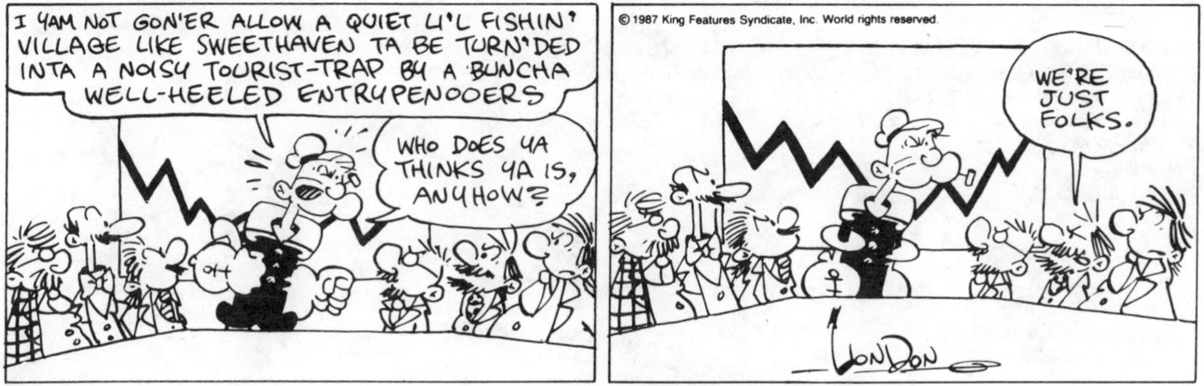
I YAM NOT GON'ER ALLOW A QUIET LI'L FISHIN' VILLAGE LIKE SWEETHAVEN TA BE TURN'DED INTA A NOISY TOURIST-TRAP BY A BUNCHA WELL-HEELED ENTRUPENOOERS
WHO DOES YA THINKS YA IS, ANYHOW?
© 1987 King Features Syndicate, Inc. World rights reserved.
WE'RE JUST FOLKS.
LONDON

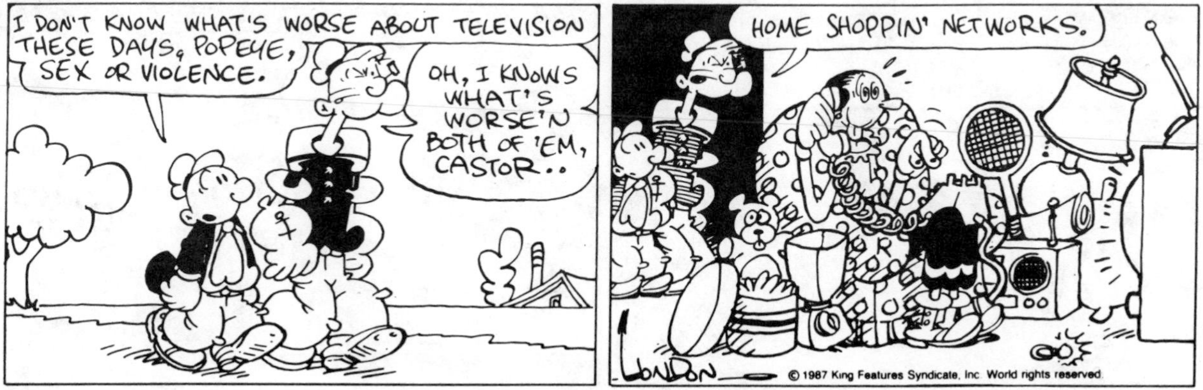
I DON'T KNOW WHAT'S WORSE ABOUT TELEVISION THESE DAYS, POPEYE, SEX OR VIOLENCE.
OH, I KNOWS WHAT'S WORSE'N BOTH OF 'EM, CASTOR..
HOME SHOPPIN' NETWORKS.
LONDON
© 1987 King Features Syndicate, Inc. World rights reserved.

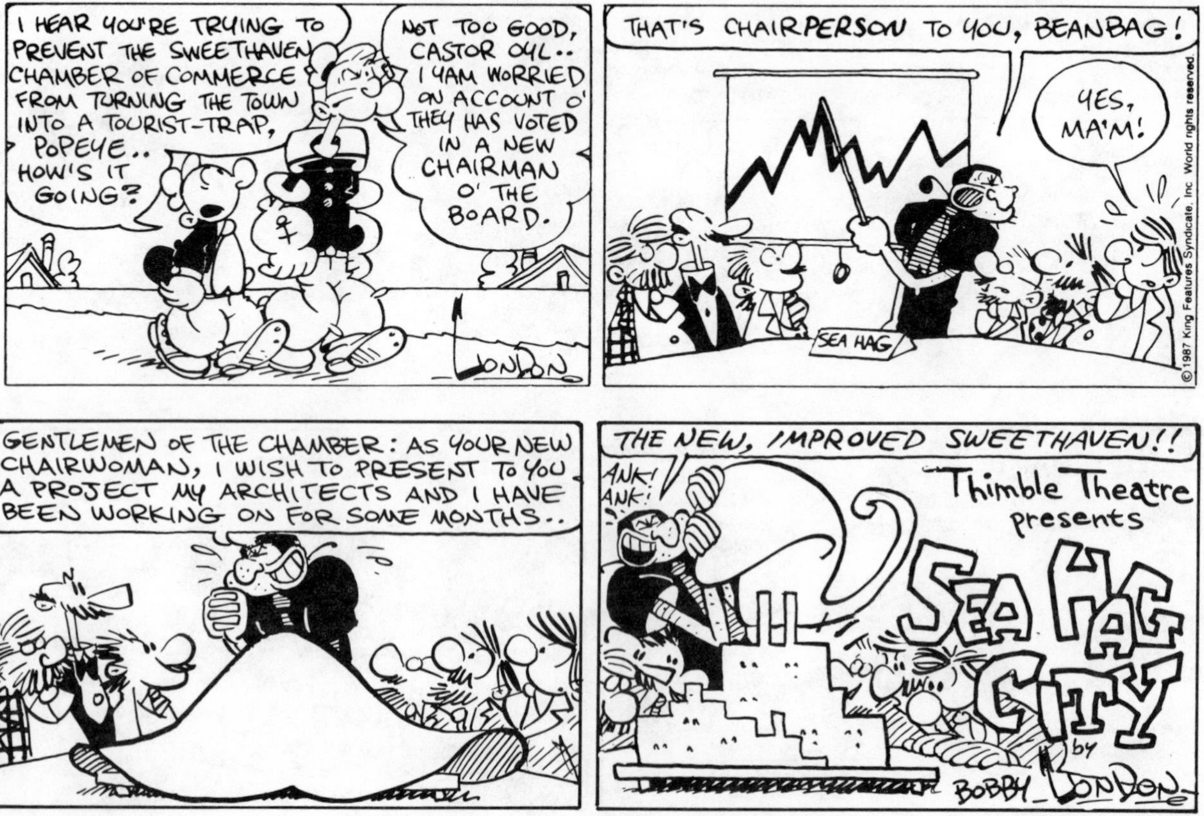
I HEAR YOU'RE TRYING TO PREVENT THE SWEETHAVEN CHAMBER OF COMMERCE FROM TURNING THE TOWN INTO A TOURIST-TRAP, POPEYE.. HOW'S IT GOING?
NOT TOO GOOD, CASTOR OYL.. I YAM WORRIED ON ACCOUNT O' THEY HAS VOTED IN A NEW CHAIRMAN O' THE BOARD.
LONDON
THAT'S CHAIRPERSON TO YOU, BEANBAG!
YES, MA'M!
SEA HAG
© 1987 King Features Syndicate, Inc. World rights reserved.
GENTLEMEN OF THE CHAMBER: AS YOUR NEW CHAIRWOMAN, I WISH TO PRESENT TO YOU A PROJECT MY ARCHITECTS AND I HAVE BEEN WORKING ON FOR SOME MONTHS..
THE NEW, IMPROVED SWEETHAVEN!!
ANK! ANK!
Thimble Theatre presents
SEA HAG CITY
by BOBBY LONDON

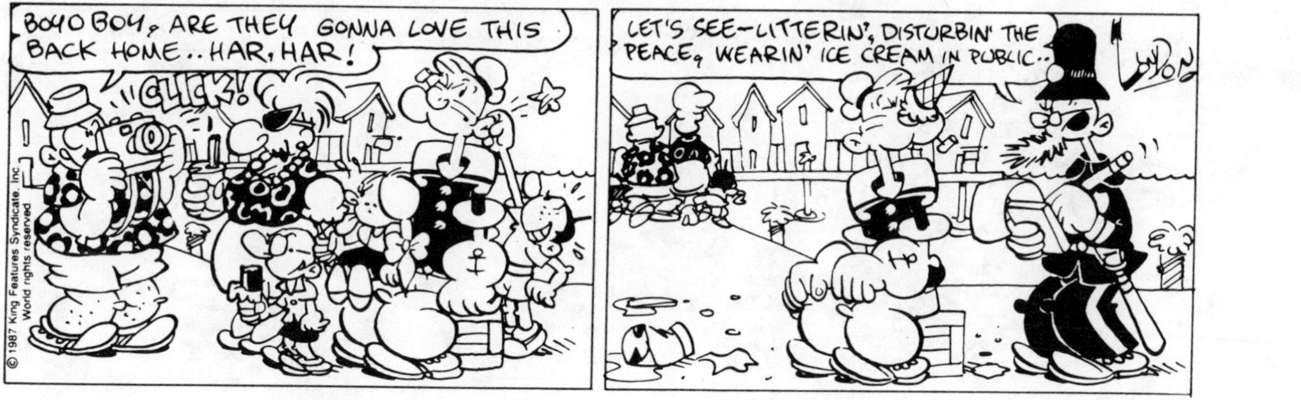
BOY O BOY, ARE THEY GONNA LOVE THIS BACK HOME.. HAR, HAR!
CLICK!
LET'S SEE—LITTERIN', DISTURBIN' THE PEACE, WEARIN' ICE CREAM IN PUBLIC..
LONDON
© 1987 King Features Syndicate, Inc. World rights reserved

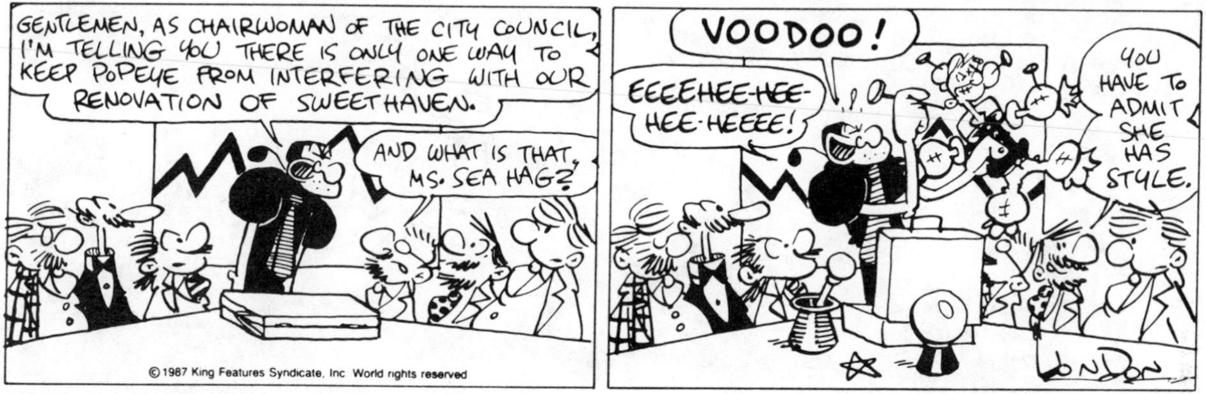
GENTLEMEN, AS CHAIRWOMAN OF THE CITY COUNCIL, I'M TELLING YOU THERE IS ONLY ONE WAY TO KEEP POPEYE FROM INTERFERING WITH OUR RENOVATION OF SWEETHAVEN.
AND WHAT IS THAT, MS. SEA HAG?
© 1987 King Features Syndicate, Inc. World rights reserved
VOODOO!
EEEEHEE-HEE-HEE-HEEEE!
YOU HAVE TO ADMIT SHE HAS STYLE.
LONDON

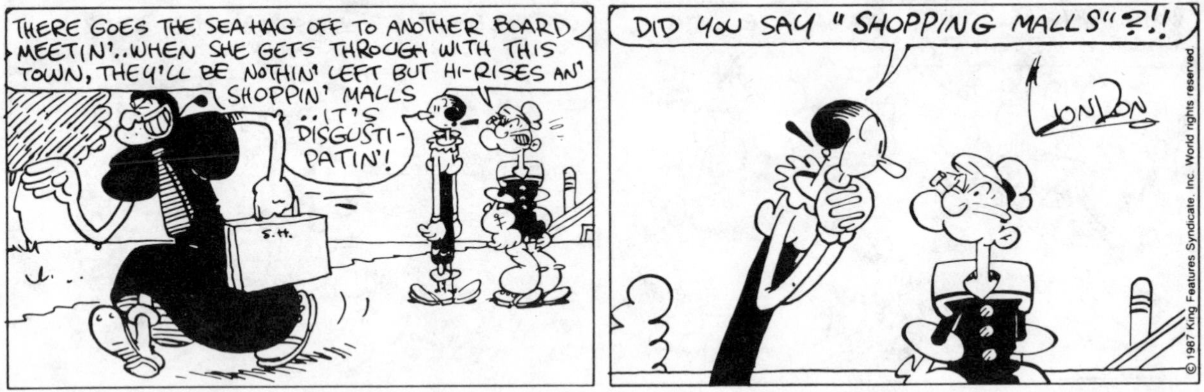
THERE GOES THE SEA HAG OFF TO ANOTHER BOARD MEETIN'..WHEN SHE GETS THROUGH WITH THIS TOWN, THEY'LL BE NOTHIN' LEFT BUT HI-RISES AN' SHOPPIN' MALLS
..IT'S DISGUSTI-PATIN'!
S.H.
DID YOU SAY "SHOPPING MALLS"?!!
LONDON
© 1987 King Features Syndicate, Inc. World rights reserved.

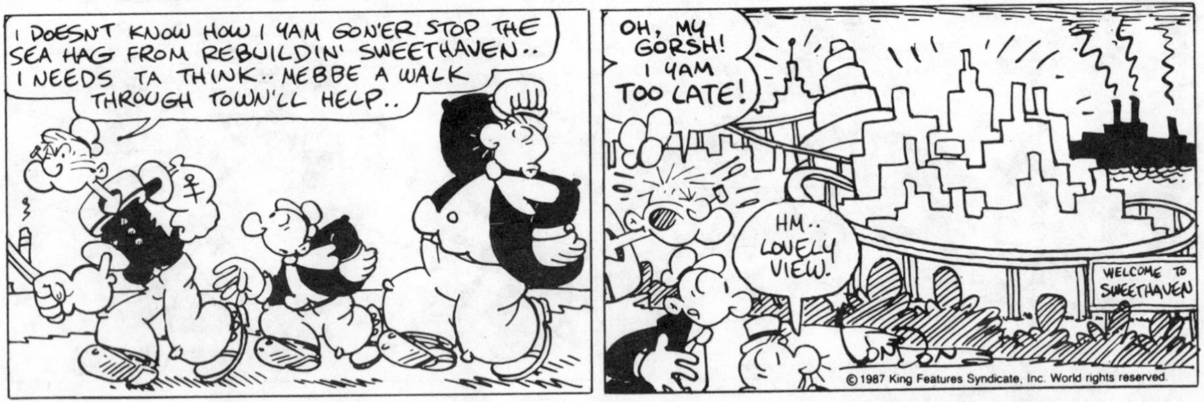
I DOESN'T KNOW HOW I YAM GON'ER STOP THE SEA HAG FROM REBUILDIN' SWEETHAVEN.. I NEEDS TA THINK.. MEBBE A WALK THROUGH TOWN'LL HELP..
OH, MY GORSH! I YAM TOO LATE!
HM.. LOVELY VIEW.
WELCOME TO SWEETHAVEN
LONDON
© 1987 King Features Syndicate, Inc. World rights reserved.

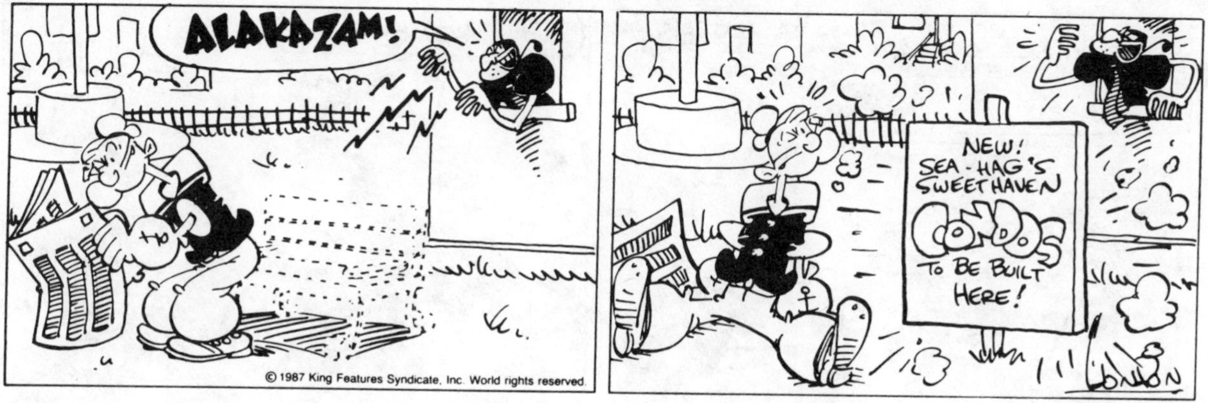
ALAKAZAM!
NEW! SEA-HAG'S SWEETHAVEN CONDOS TO BE BUILT HERE!
LONDON
© 1987 King Features Syndicate, Inc. World rights reserved.

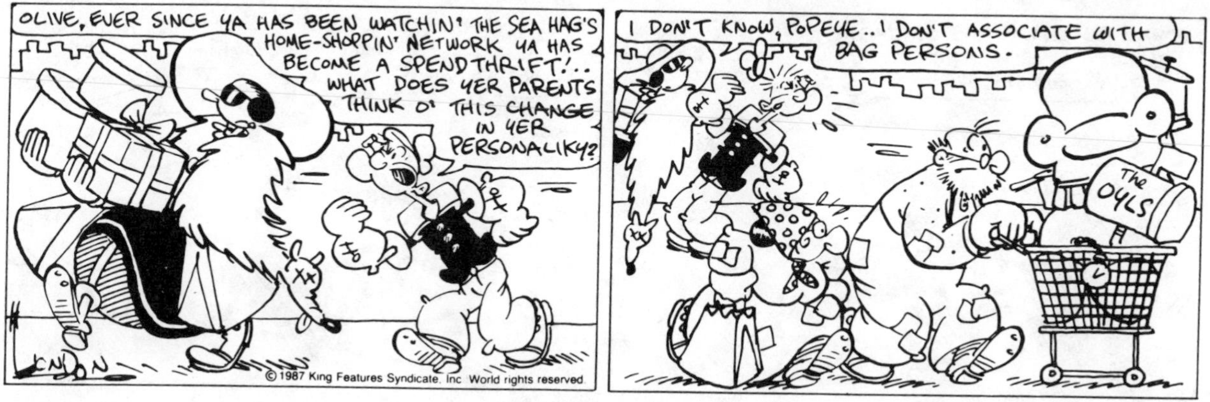
OLIVE, EVER SINCE YA HAS BEEN WATCHIN' THE SEA HAG'S HOME-SHOPPIN' NETWORK YA HAS BECOME A SPENDTHRIFT!.. WHAT DOES YER PARENTS THINK O' THIS CHANGE IN YER PERSONALIKY?
I DON'T KNOW, POPEYE.. I DON'T ASSOCIATE WITH BAG PERSONS.
THE OYLS
LONDON
© 1987 King Features Syndicate, Inc. World rights reserved.

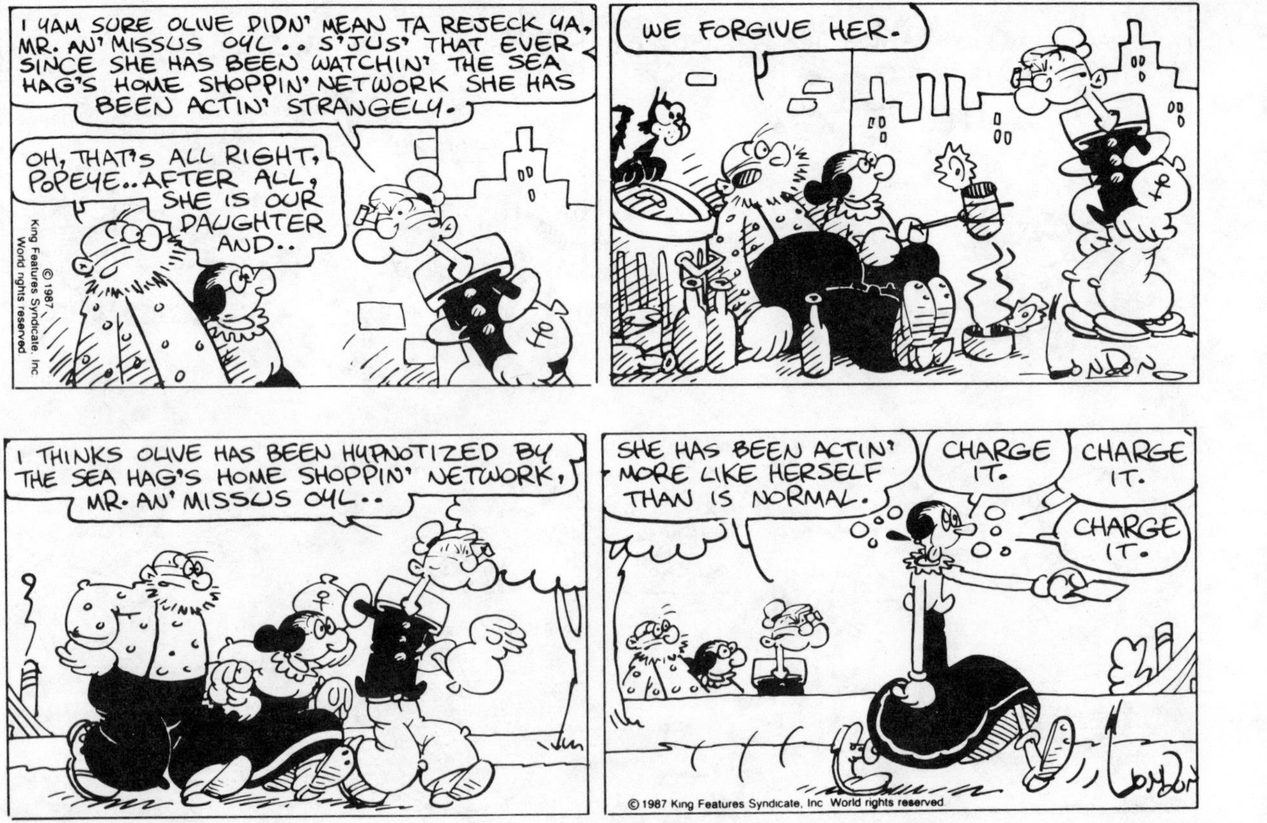
I YAM SURE OLIVE DIDN' MEAN TA REJECK YA, MR. AN' MISSUS OYL.. S'JUS' THAT EVER SINCE SHE HAS BEEN WATCHIN' THE SEA HAG'S HOME SHOPPIN' NETWORK SHE HAS BEEN ACTIN' STRANGELY.
OH, THAT'S ALL RIGHT, POPEYE.. AFTER ALL, SHE IS OUR DAUGHTER AND..
© 1987 King Features Syndicate, Inc. World rights reserved.
WE FORGIVE HER.
LONDON
I THINKS OLIVE HAS BEEN HYPNOTIZED BY THE SEA HAG'S HOME SHOPPIN' NETWORK, MR. AN' MISSUS OYL..
SHE HAS BEEN ACTIN' MORE LIKE HERSELF THAN IS NORMAL.
CHARGE IT.
CHARGE IT.
CHARGE IT.
LONDON
© 1987 King Features Syndicate, Inc World rights reserved.

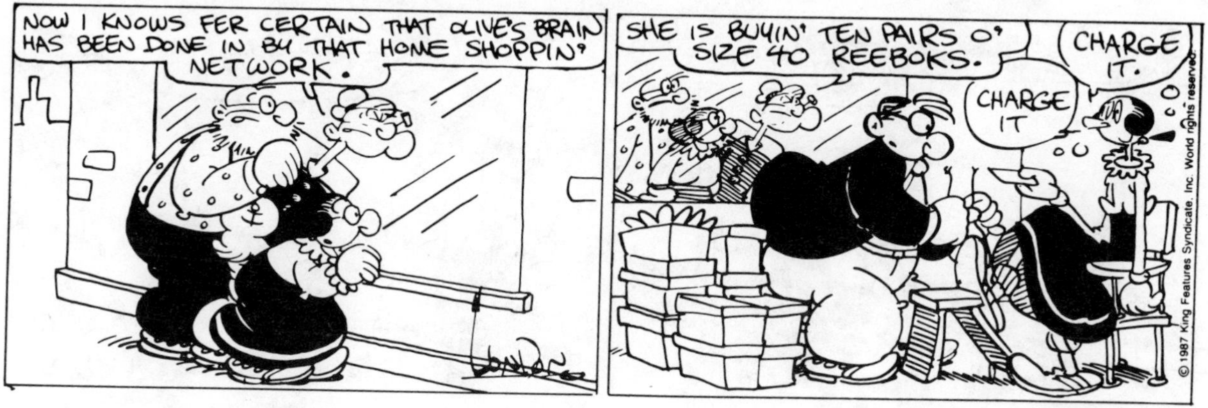
NOW I KNOWS FER CERTAIN THAT OLIVE'S BRAIN HAS BEEN DONE IN BY THAT HOME SHOPPIN' NETWORK.
SHE IS BUYIN' TEN PAIRS O' SIZE 40 REEBOKS.
CHARGE IT.
CHARGE IT
© 1987 King Features Syndicate, Inc. World rights reserved

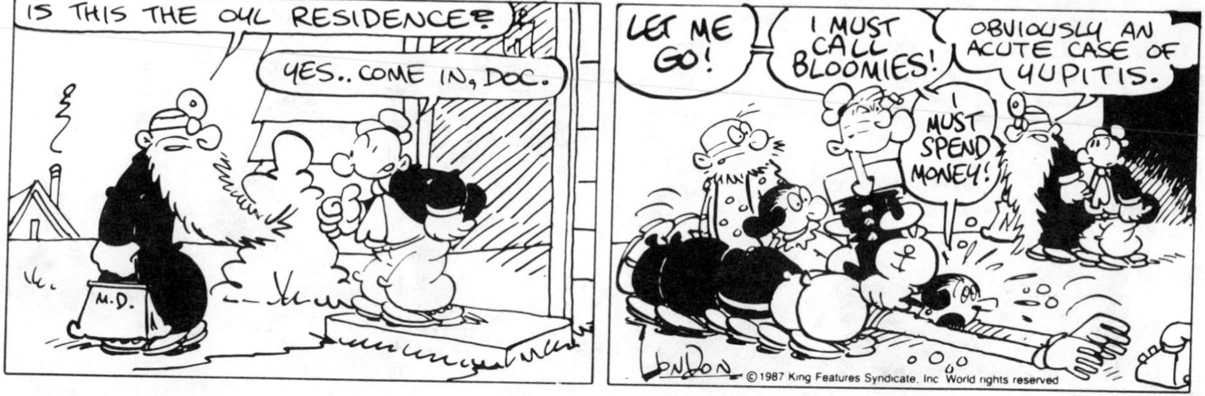
IS THIS THE OYL RESIDENCE?
YES.. COME IN, DOC.
M.D.
LET ME GO!
I MUST CALL BLOOMIES!
OBVIOUSLY AN ACUTE CASE OF YUPITIS.
I MUST SPEND MONEY!
© 1987 King Features Syndicate, Inc. World rights reserved

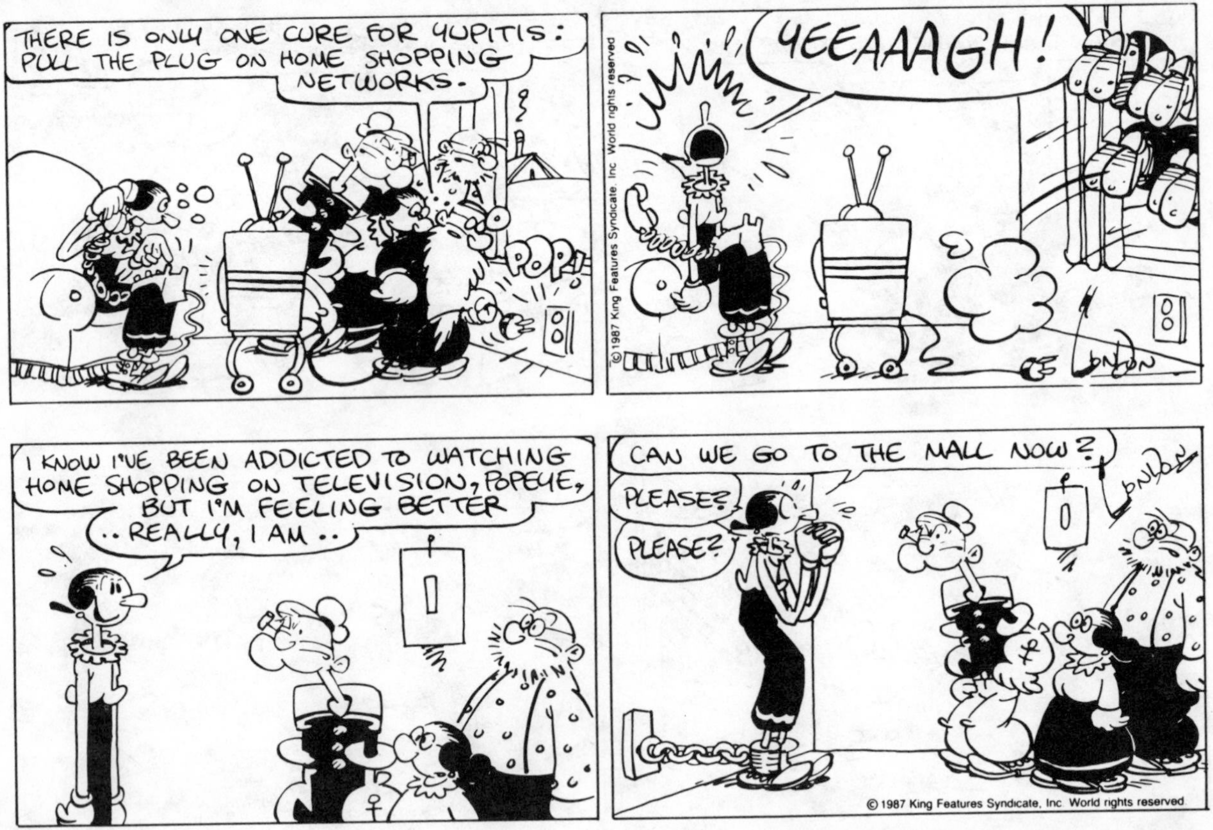
THERE IS ONLY ONE CURE FOR YUPITIS: PULL THE PLUG ON HOME SHOPPING NETWORKS.
POP!
YEEAAAAGH!
© 1987 King Features Syndicate, Inc. World rights reserved
I KNOW I'VE BEEN ADDICTED TO WATCHING HOME SHOPPING ON TELEVISION, POPEYE, BUT I'M FEELING BETTER .. REALLY, I AM ..
CAN WE GO TO THE MALL NOW?
PLEASE?
PLEASE?
© 1987 King Features Syndicate, Inc. World rights reserved

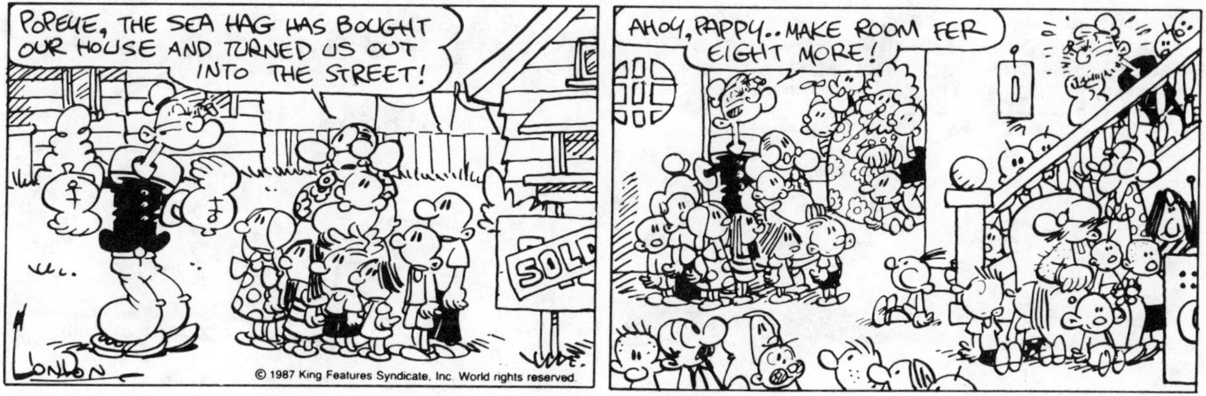
POPEYE, THE SEA HAG HAS BOUGHT OUR HOUSE AND TURNED US OUT INTO THE STREET!
SOLD
© 1987 King Features Syndicate, Inc. World rights reserved.
AHOY, PAPPY.. MAKE ROOM FER EIGHT MORE!

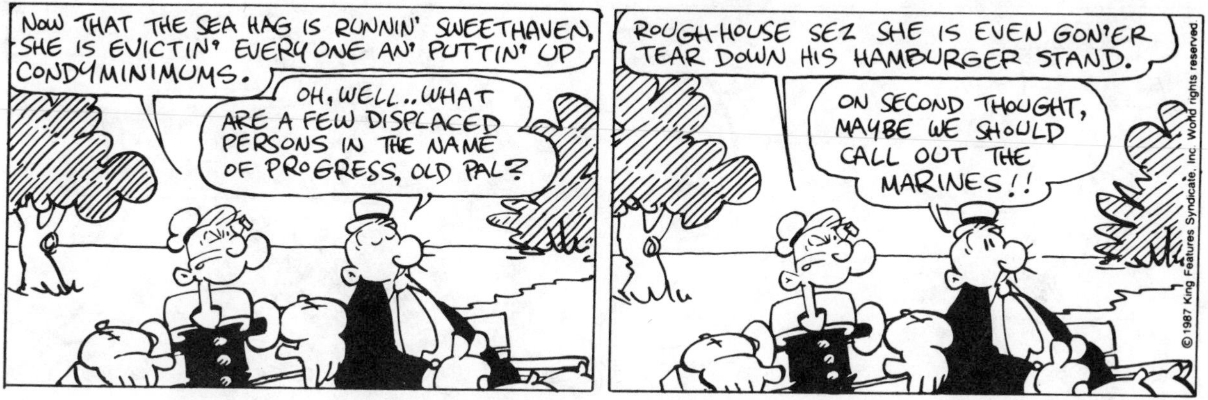
NOW THAT THE SEA HAG IS RUNNIN' SWEETHAVEN, SHE IS EVICTIN' EVERYONE AN' PUTTIN' UP CONDYMINIMUMS.
OH, WELL.. WHAT ARE A FEW DISPLACED PERSONS IN THE NAME OF PROGRESS, OLD PAL?
ROUGH-HOUSE SEZ SHE IS EVEN GON'ER TEAR DOWN HIS HAMBURGER STAND.
ON SECOND THOUGHT, MAYBE WE SHOULD CALL OUT THE MARINES!!
© 1987 King Features Syndicate, Inc. World rights reserved.

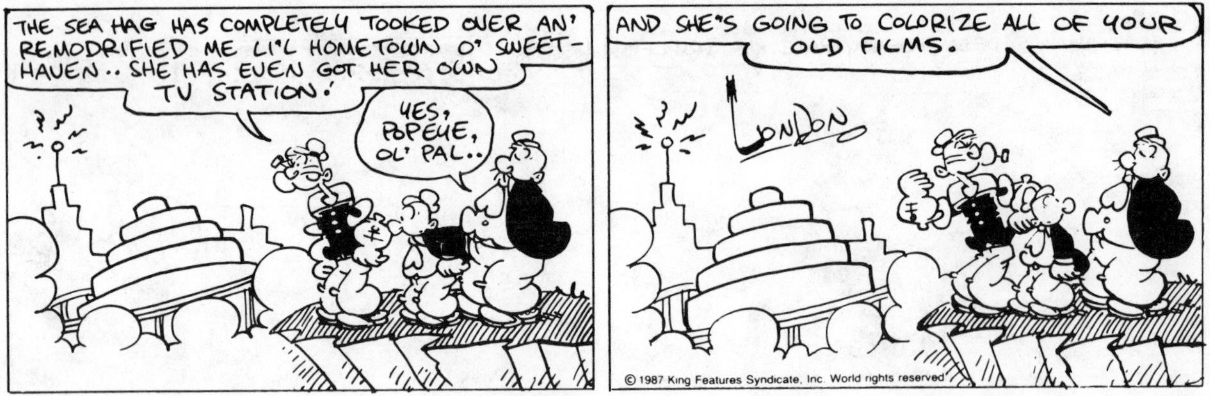
THE SEA HAG HAS COMPLETELY TOOKED OVER AN' REMODRIFIED ME LI'L HOMETOWN O' SWEET-HAVEN.. SHE HAS EVEN GOT HER OWN TV STATION!
YES, POPEYE, OL' PAL..
AND SHE'S GOING TO COLORIZE ALL OF YOUR OLD FILMS.
LONDON
© 1987 King Features Syndicate, Inc. World rights reserved

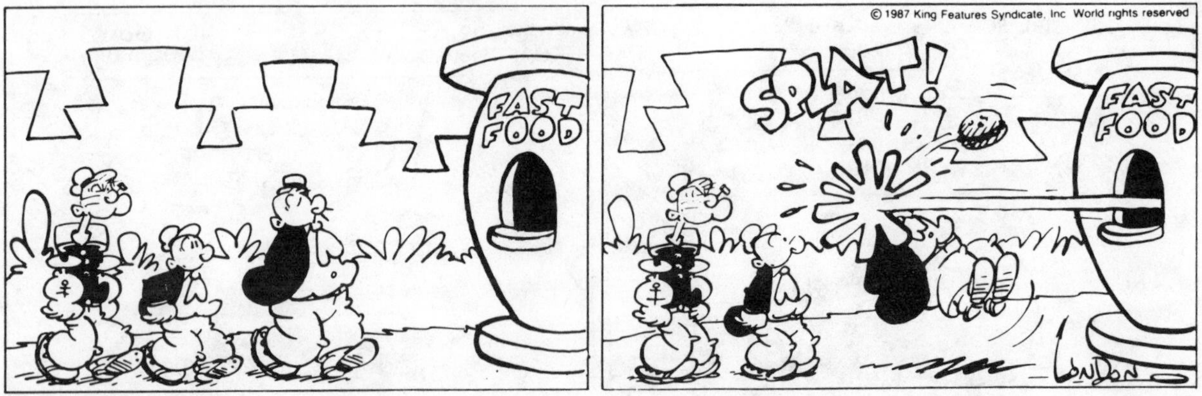
© 1987 King Features Syndicate, Inc World rights reserved
FAST FOOD
SPLAT!
FAST FOOD
LONDON

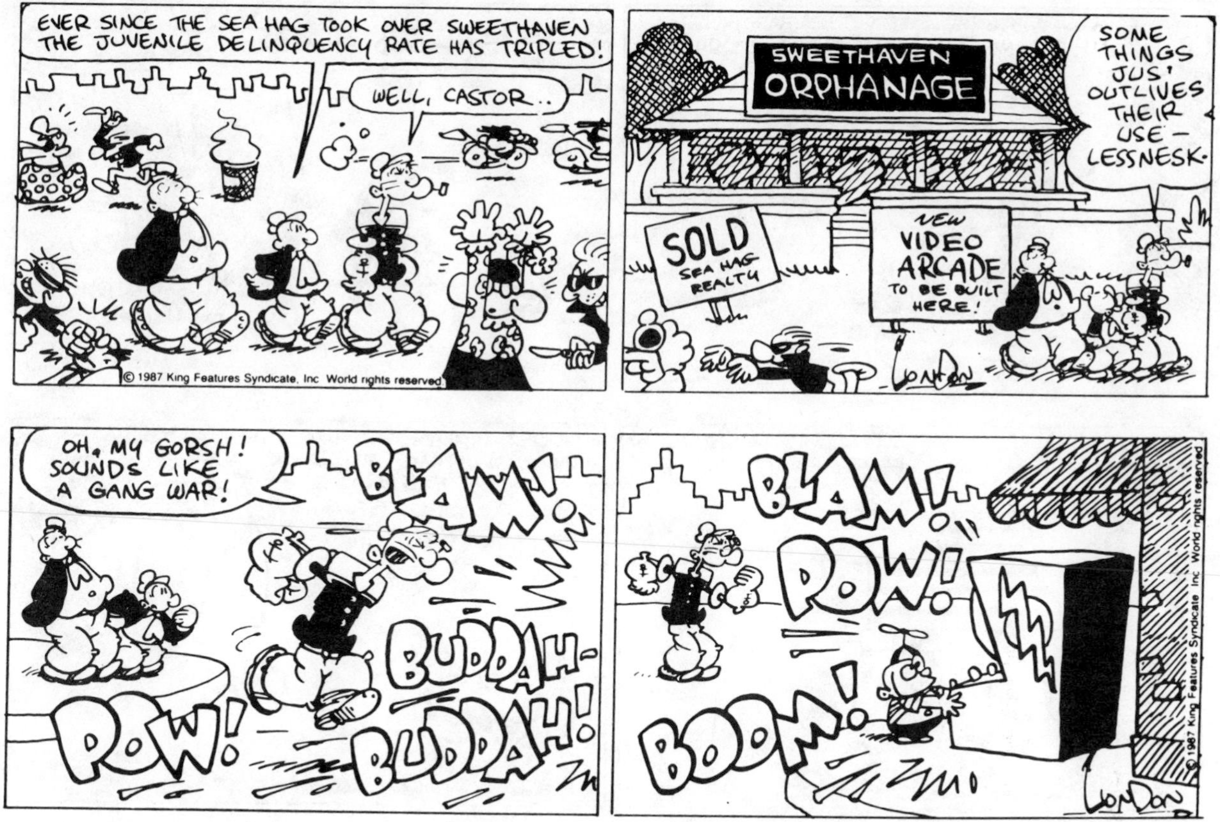
EVER SINCE THE SEA HAG TOOK OVER SWEETHAVEN THE JUVENILE DELINQUENCY RATE HAS TRIPLED!
WELL, CASTOR..
© 1987 King Features Syndicate, Inc World rights reserved
SWEETHAVEN ORPHANAGE
SOME THINGS JUS' OUTLIVES THEIR USE-LESSNESK.
SOLD SEA HAG REALTY
NEW VIDEO ARCADE TO BE BUILT HERE!
LONDON
OH, MY GORSH! SOUNDS LIKE A GANG WAR!
BLAM!
BUDDAH-BUDDAH!
POW!
BLAM!
POW!
BOOM!
© 1987 King Features Syndicate Inc World rights reserved
LONDON

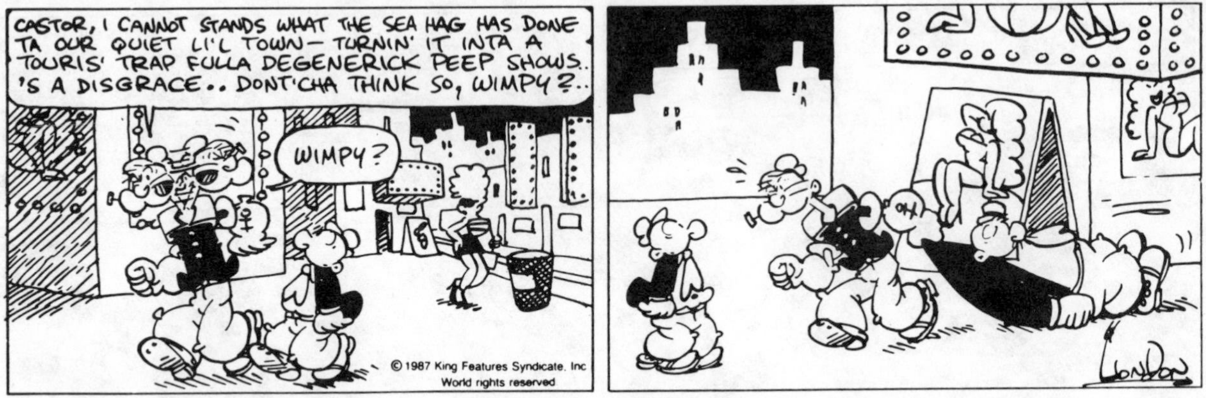
CASTOR, I CANNOT STANDS WHAT THE SEA HAG HAS DONE TA OUR QUIET LI'L TOWN— TURNIN' IT INTA A TOURIS' TRAP FULLA DEGENERICK PEEP SHOWS.. 'S A DISGRACE.. DONT'CHA THINK SO, WIMPY ?..
WIMPY?
© 1987 King Features Syndicate, Inc
World rights reserved
LONDON

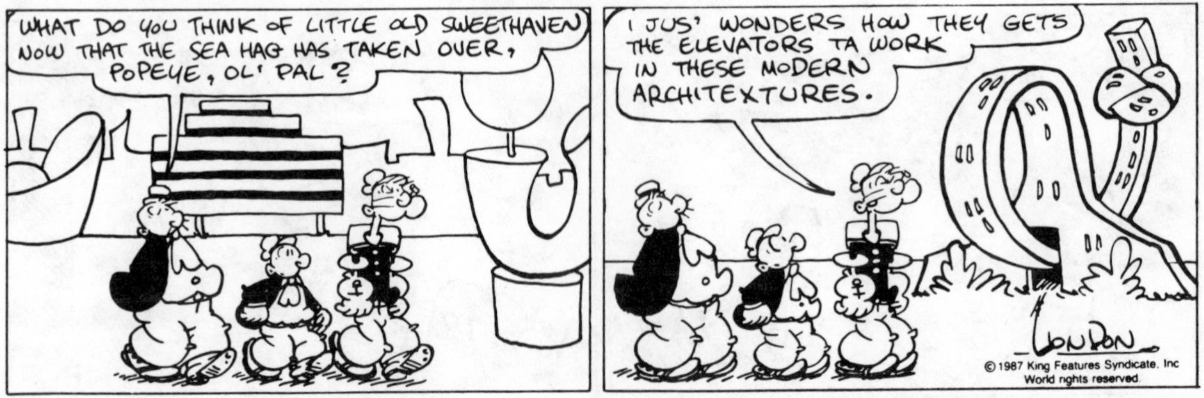
WHAT DO YOU THINK OF LITTLE OLD SWEETHAVEN NOW THAT THE SEA HAG HAS TAKEN OVER, POPEYE, OL' PAL ?
I JUS' WONDERS HOW THEY GETS THE ELEVATORS TA WORK IN THESE MODERN ARCHITEXTURES.
LONDON
© 1987 King Features Syndicate, Inc
World rights reserved.

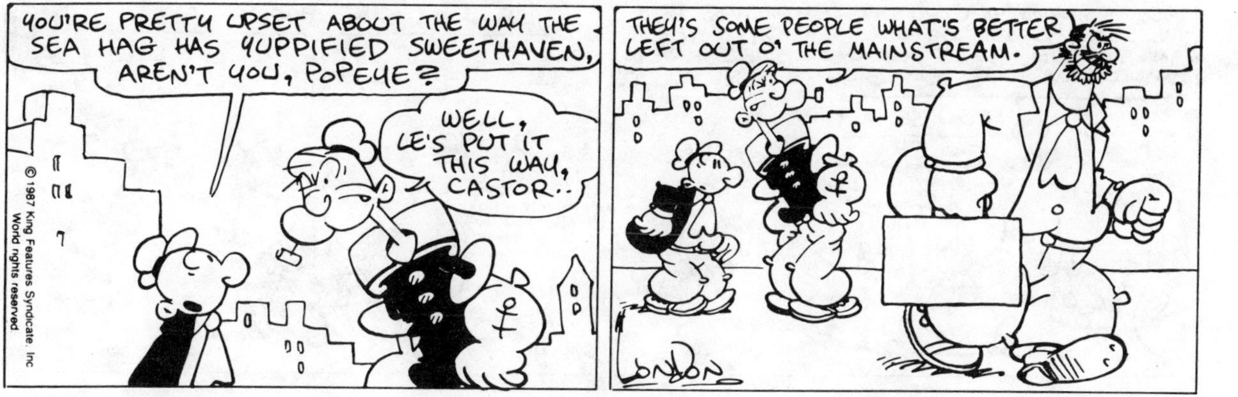
YOU'RE PRETTY UPSET ABOUT THE WAY THE SEA HAG HAS YUPPIFIED SWEETHAVEN, AREN'T YOU, POPEYE?
WELL, LE'S PUT IT THIS WAY, CASTOR..
THEY'S SOME PEOPLE WHAT'S BETTER LEFT OUT O' THE MAINSTREAM.
LONDON
© 1987 King Features Syndicate, Inc
World rights reserved

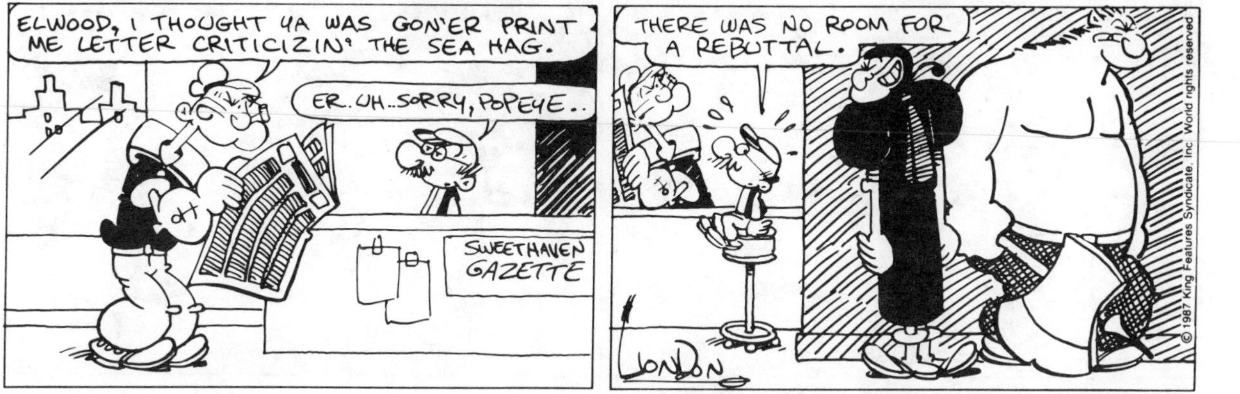
ELWOOD, I THOUGHT YA WAS GON'ER PRINT ME LETTER CRITICIZIN' THE SEA HAG.
ER..UH..SORRY, POPEYE..
SWEETHAVEN GAZETTE
THERE WAS NO ROOM FOR A REBUTTAL.
LONDON
© 1987 King Features Syndicate, Inc. World rights reserved

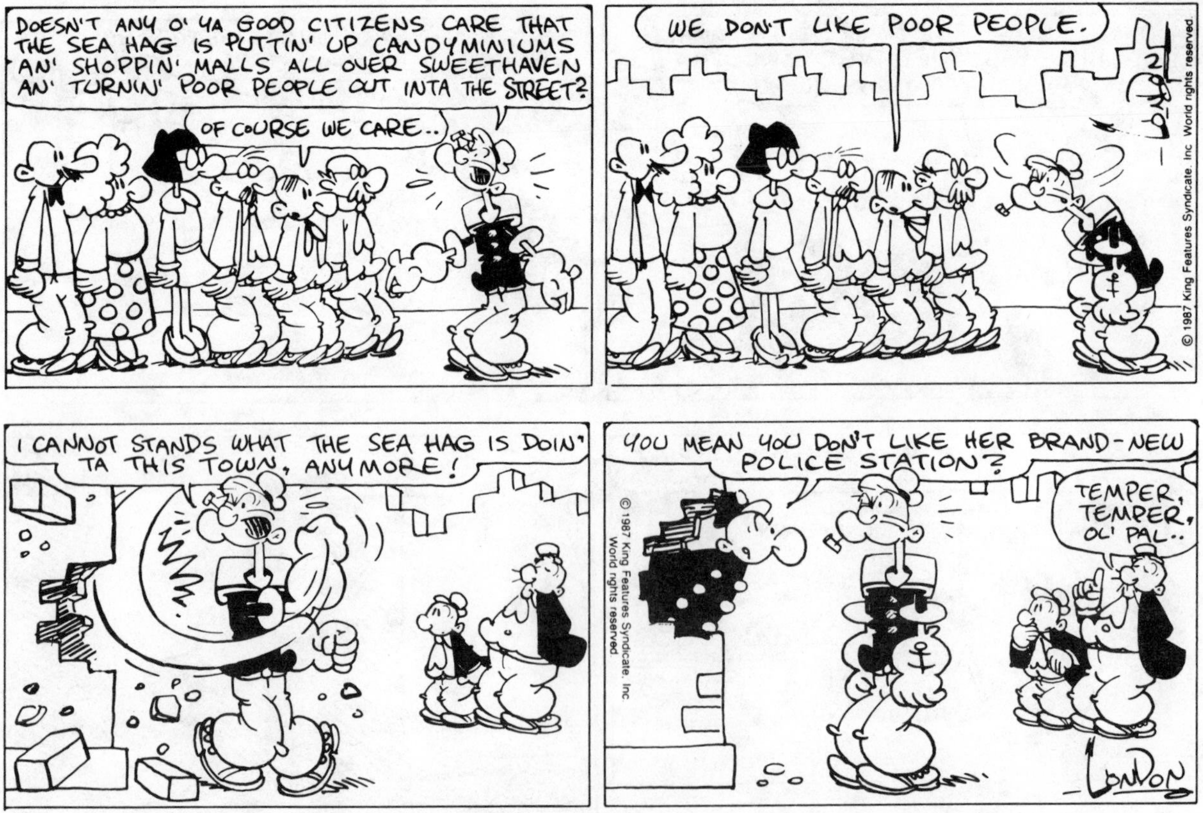

DOESN'T ANY O' YA GOOD CITIZENS CARE THAT THE SEA HAG IS PUTTIN' UP CANDYMINIUMS AN' SHOPPIN' MALLS ALL OVER SWEETHAVEN AN' TURNIN' POOR PEOPLE OUT INTA THE STREET?
OF COURSE WE CARE..
WE DON'T LIKE POOR PEOPLE.
© 1987 King Features Syndicate, Inc. World rights reserved
I CANNOT STANDS WHAT THE SEA HAG IS DOIN' TA THIS TOWN, ANYMORE!
YOU MEAN YOU DON'T LIKE HER BRAND-NEW POLICE STATION?
TEMPER, TEMPER, OL' PAL..
© 1987 King Features Syndicate, Inc. World rights reserved.
LONDON

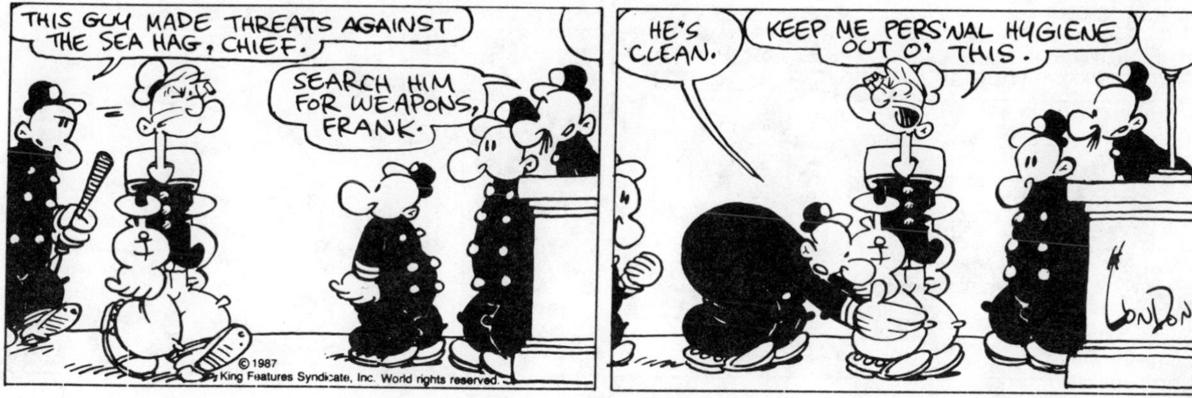
THIS GUY MADE THREATS AGAINST THE SEA HAG, CHIEF.
SEARCH HIM FOR WEAPONS, FRANK.
© 1987 King Features Syndicate, Inc. World rights reserved.
HE'S CLEAN.
KEEP ME PERS'NAL HYGIENE OUT O' THIS.

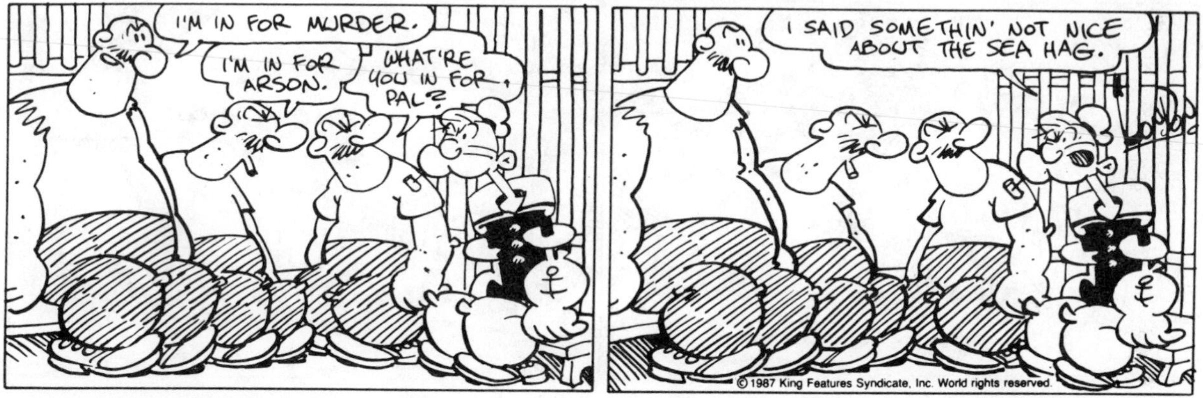
I'M IN FOR MURDER.
I'M IN FOR ARSON.
WHAT'RE YOU IN FOR, PAL?
I SAID SOMETHIN' NOT NICE ABOUT THE SEA HAG.
© 1987 King Features Syndicate, Inc. World rights reserved.

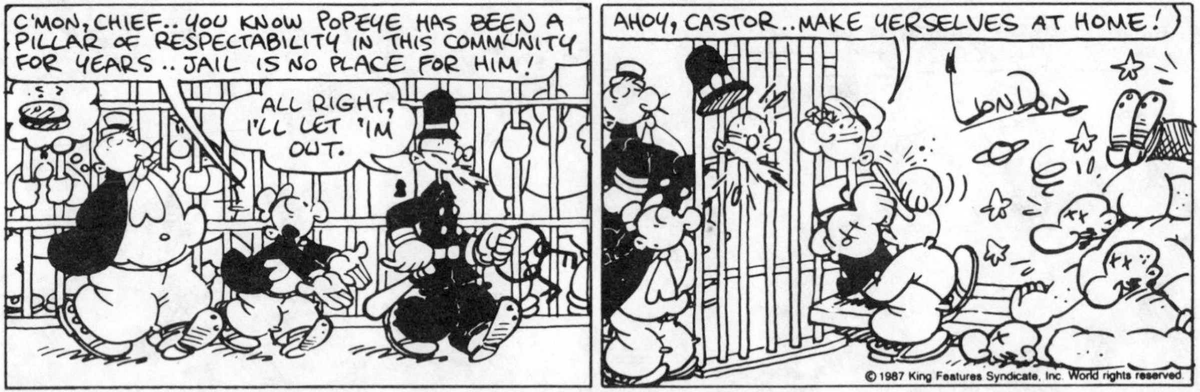
C'MON, CHIEF.. YOU KNOW POPEYE HAS BEEN A PILLAR OF RESPECTABILITY IN THIS COMMUNITY FOR YEARS.. JAIL IS NO PLACE FOR HIM!
ALL RIGHT, I'LL LET 'IM OUT.
AHOY, CASTOR.. MAKE YERSELVES AT HOME!
LONDON
© 1987 King Features Syndicate, Inc. World rights reserved.

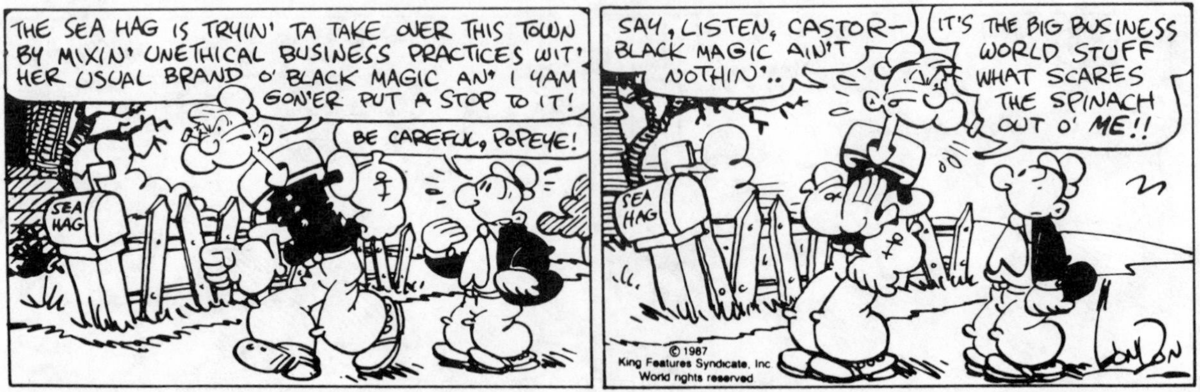
THE SEA HAG IS TRYIN' TA TAKE OVER THIS TOWN BY MIXIN' UNETHICAL BUSINESS PRACTICES WIT' HER USUAL BRAND O' BLACK MAGIC AN' I YAM GON'ER PUT A STOP TO IT!
BE CAREFUL, POPEYE!
SEA HAG
SAY, LISTEN, CASTOR– BLACK MAGIC AIN'T NOTHIN'..
IT'S THE BIG BUSINESS WORLD STUFF WHAT SCARES THE SPINACH OUT O' ME!!
SEA HAG
© 1987 King Features Syndicate, Inc World rights reserved
LONDON

I SAID BUY BEEZLEBUB INCORPORATED AND SELL LEGS-O'-TOAD!..DO I HAVE TO SAY EVERYTHING IN LATIN?!!..
WELL, BLOW ME DOWN..
YOUR DRINK, MADAME.
WADDYA MEAN, "LET'S DO LUNCH"?!!
THE SEA HAG IS A YUPPIE!
© 1987 King Features Syndicate, Inc. World rights reserved.

VISITORS, MS. SEA HAG.
WELL, IF IT ISN'T POPEYE AND CASTOR OYL.. WHAT CAN I DO FOR YOU, BOYS?
© 1987 King Features Syndicate, Inc. World rights reserved.
WELL, FER ONE THING, YA KIN TELL YER HOUSE-BOY TA PUT THE REST O' HIS SHIRT ON!

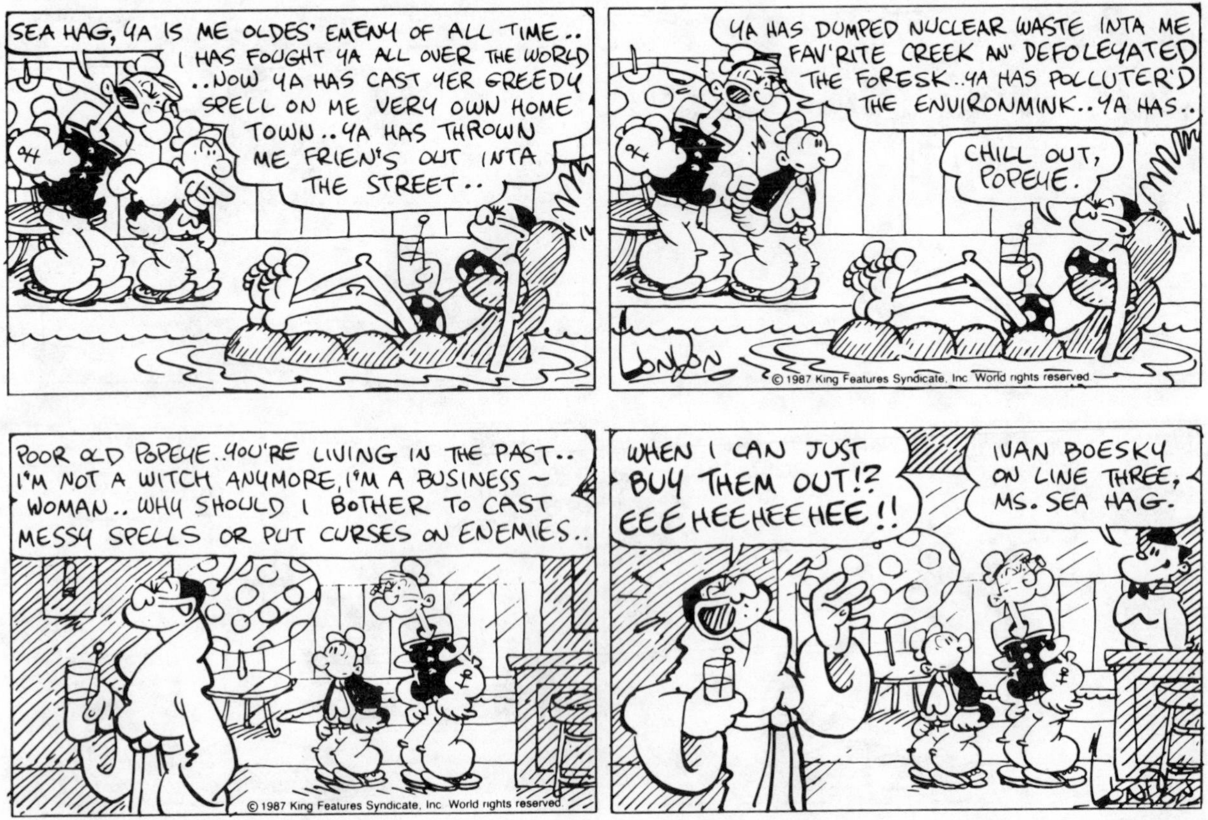
SEA HAG, YA IS ME OLDES' EMENY OF ALL TIME.. I HAS FOUGHT YA ALL OVER THE WORLD ..NOW YA HAS CAST YER GREEDY SPELL ON ME VERY OWN HOME TOWN..YA HAS THROWN ME FRIEN'S OUT INTA THE STREET..
YA HAS DUMPED NUCLEAR WASTE INTA ME FAV'RITE CREEK AN' DEFOLEYATED THE FORESK..YA HAS POLLUTER'D THE ENVIRONMINK..YA HAS..
CHILL OUT, POPEYE.
LONDON
© 1987 King Features Syndicate, Inc World rights reserved
POOR OLD POPEYE..YOU'RE LIVING IN THE PAST.. I'M NOT A WITCH ANYMORE, I'M A BUSINESS~WOMAN..WHY SHOULD I BOTHER TO CAST MESSY SPELLS OR PUT CURSES ON ENEMIES..
© 1987 King Features Syndicate, Inc World rights reserved
WHEN I CAN JUST BUY THEM OUT!? EEEHEEHEEHEE!!
IVAN BOESKY ON LINE THREE, MS. SEA HAG.

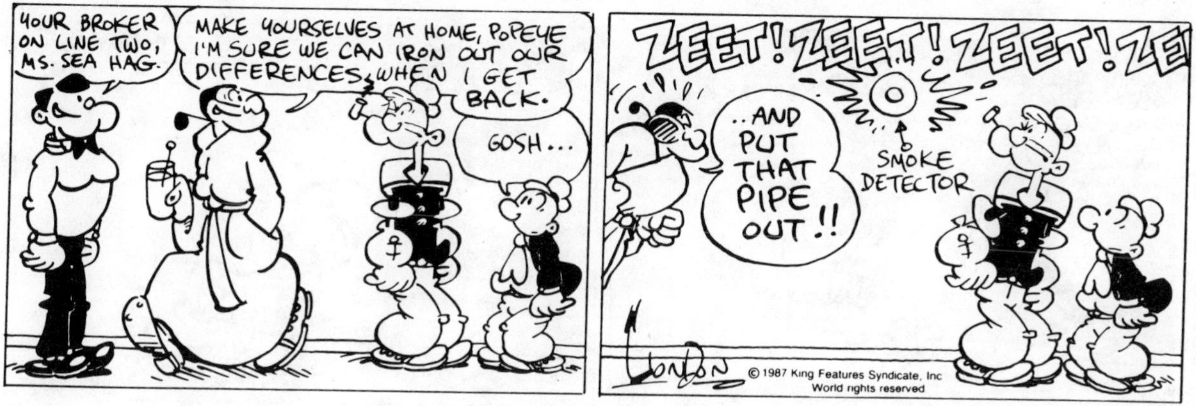
YOUR BROKER ON LINE TWO, MS. SEA HAG.
MAKE YOURSELVES AT HOME, POPEYE I'M SURE WE CAN IRON OUT OUR DIFFERENCES, WHEN I GET BACK.
GOSH...
ZEET! ZEET! ZEET! ZE
..AND PUT THAT PIPE OUT!!
SMOKE DETECTOR
LONDON
© 1987 King Features Syndicate, Inc
World rights reserved

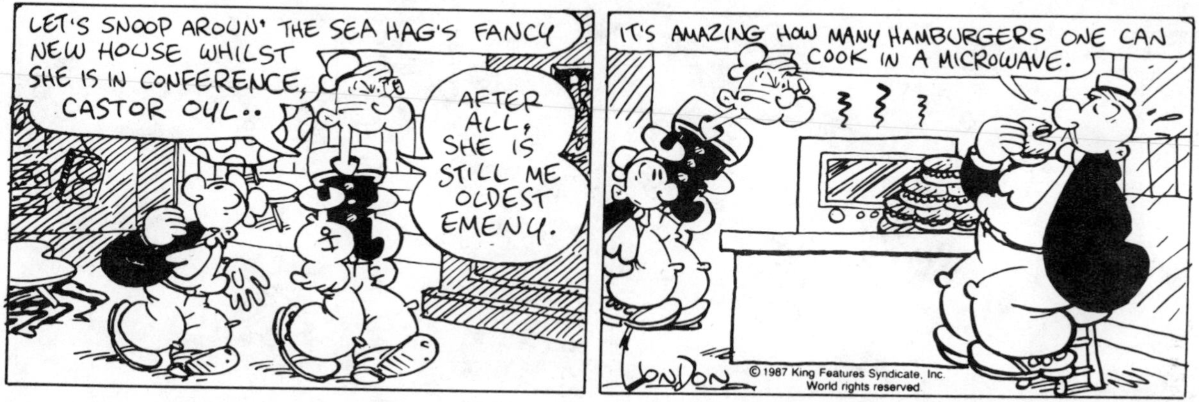
LET'S SNOOP AROUN' THE SEA HAG'S FANCY NEW HOUSE WHILST SHE IS IN CONFERENCE, CASTOR OYL..
AFTER ALL, SHE IS STILL ME OLDEST EMENY.
IT'S AMAZING HOW MANY HAMBURGERS ONE CAN COOK IN A MICROWAVE.
LONDON
© 1987 King Features Syndicate, Inc.
World rights reserved

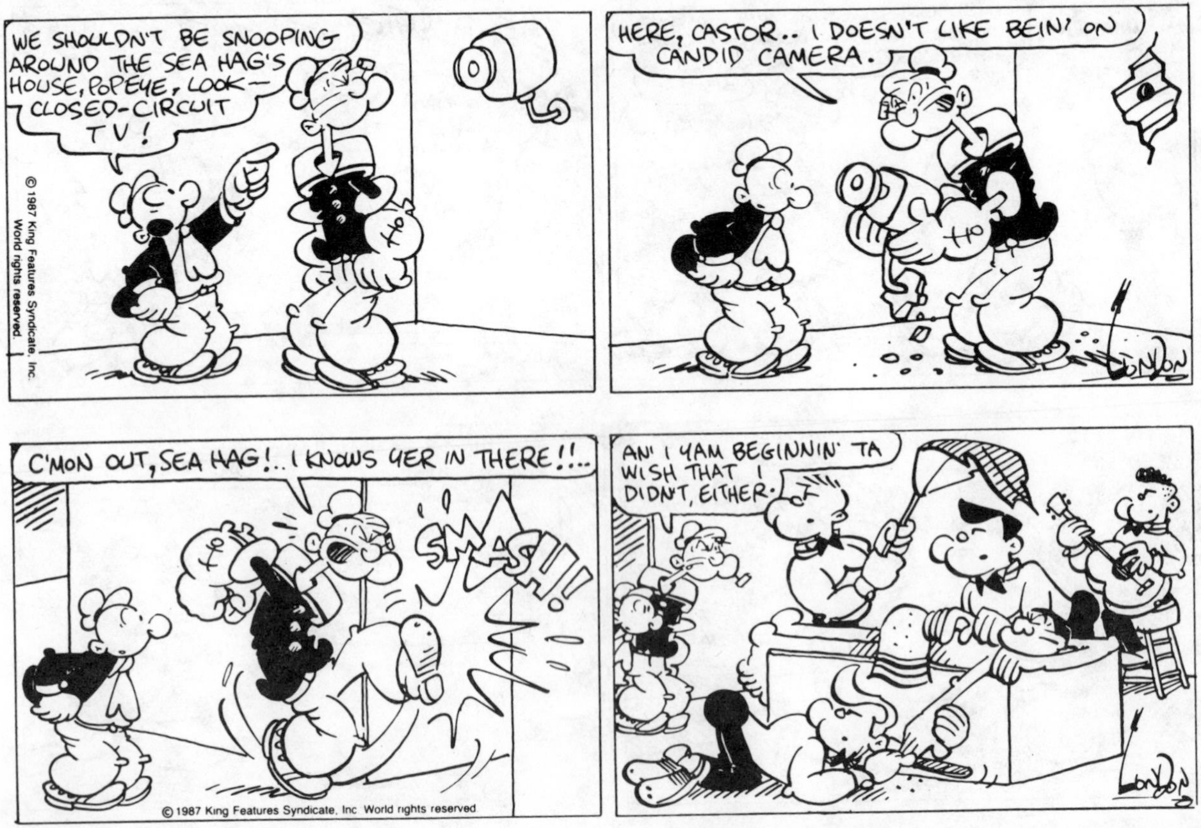
WE SHOULDN'T BE SNOOPING AROUND THE SEA HAG'S HOUSE, POPEYE, LOOK— CLOSED-CIRCUIT TV!
© 1987 King Features Syndicate, Inc. World rights reserved.
HERE, CASTOR.. I DOESN'T LIKE BEIN' ON CANDID CAMERA.
C'MON OUT, SEA HAG!.. I KNOWS YER IN THERE!!..
SMASH!!
© 1987 King Features Syndicate, Inc World rights reserved
AN' I YAM BEGINNIN' TA WISH THAT I DIDN'T, EITHER.

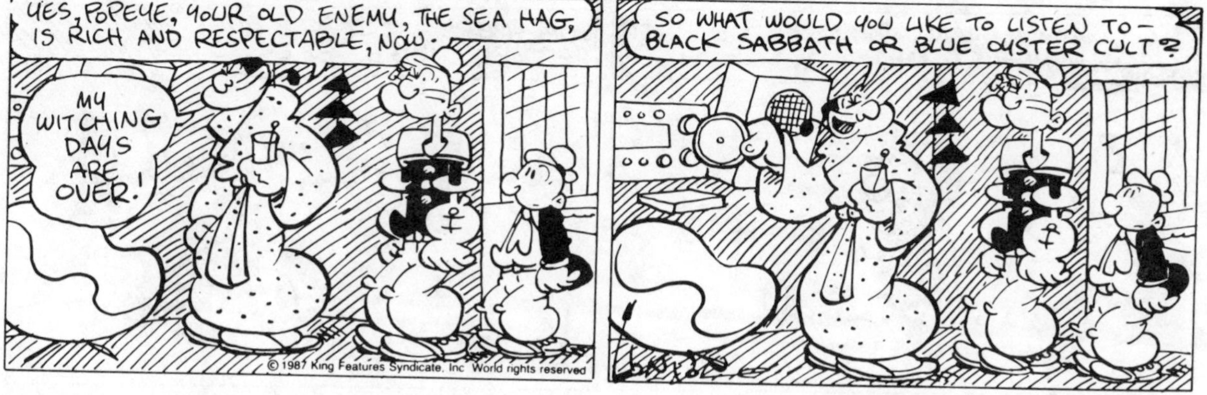
YES, POPEYE, YOUR OLD ENEMY, THE SEA HAG, IS RICH AND RESPECTABLE, NOW.
MY WITCHING DAYS ARE OVER!
© 1987 King Features Syndicate, Inc World rights reserved
SO WHAT WOULD YOU LIKE TO LISTEN TO— BLACK SABBATH OR BLUE OYSTER CULT?

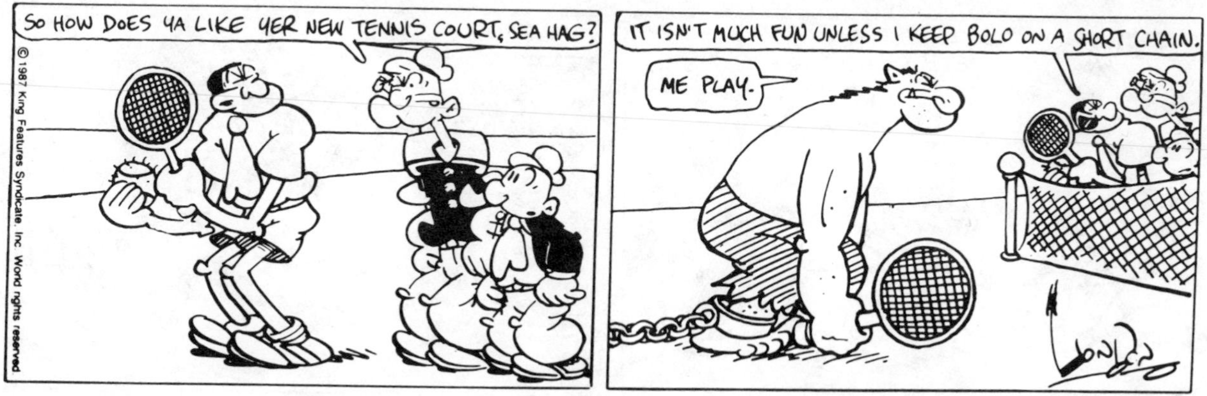
SO HOW DOES YA LIKE YER NEW TENNIS COURT, SEA HAG?
© 1987 King Features Syndicate, Inc World rights reserved
IT ISN'T MUCH FUN UNLESS I KEEP BOLO ON A SHORT CHAIN.
ME PLAY.

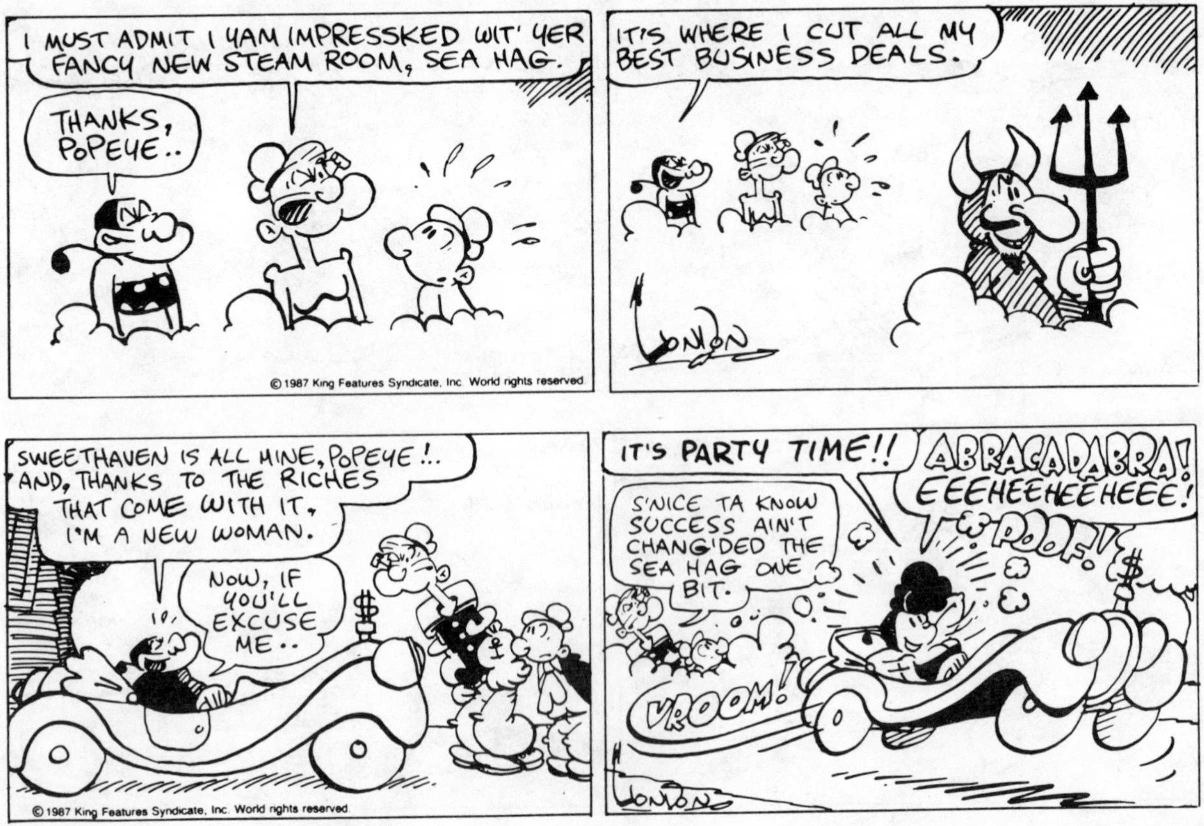
I MUST ADMIT I YAM IMPRESSKED WIT' YER FANCY NEW STEAM ROOM, SEA HAG.
THANKS, POPEYE..
IT'S WHERE I CUT ALL MY BEST BUSINESS DEALS.
LONDON
© 1987 King Features Syndicate, Inc. World rights reserved.
SWEETHAVEN IS ALL MINE, POPEYE!.. AND, THANKS TO THE RICHES THAT COME WITH IT, I'M A NEW WOMAN.
NOW, IF YOU'LL EXCUSE ME..
© 1987 King Features Syndicate, Inc. World rights reserved.
IT'S PARTY TIME!!
ABRACADABRA! EEEHEEHEEHEEE!
POOF!
S'NICE TA KNOW SUCCESS AIN'T CHANG'DED THE SEA HAG ONE BIT.
VROOM!
LONDON

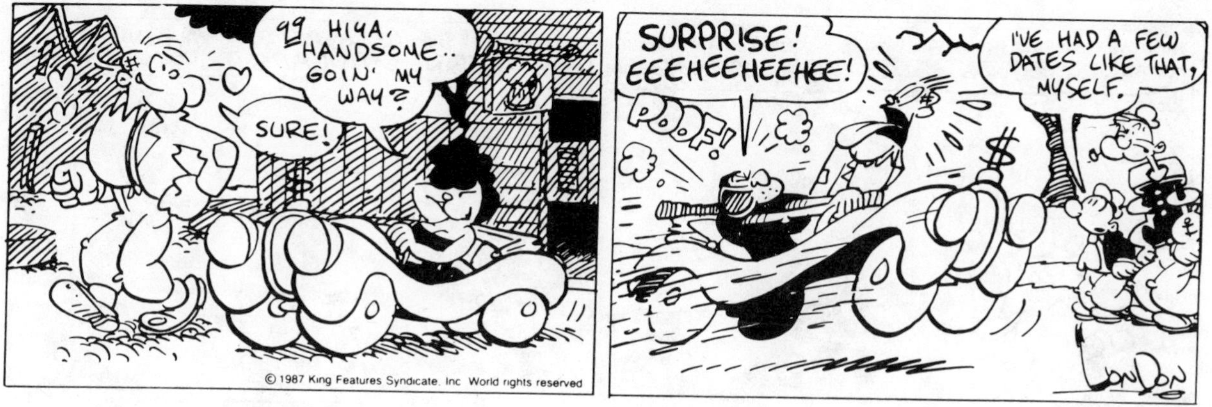
HIYA, HANDSOME.. GOIN' MY WAY?
SURE!
© 1987 King Features Syndicate, Inc. World rights reserved
SURPRISE! EEEHEEHEEHEE!
POOF!
I'VE HAD A FEW DATES LIKE THAT, MYSELF.
LONDON

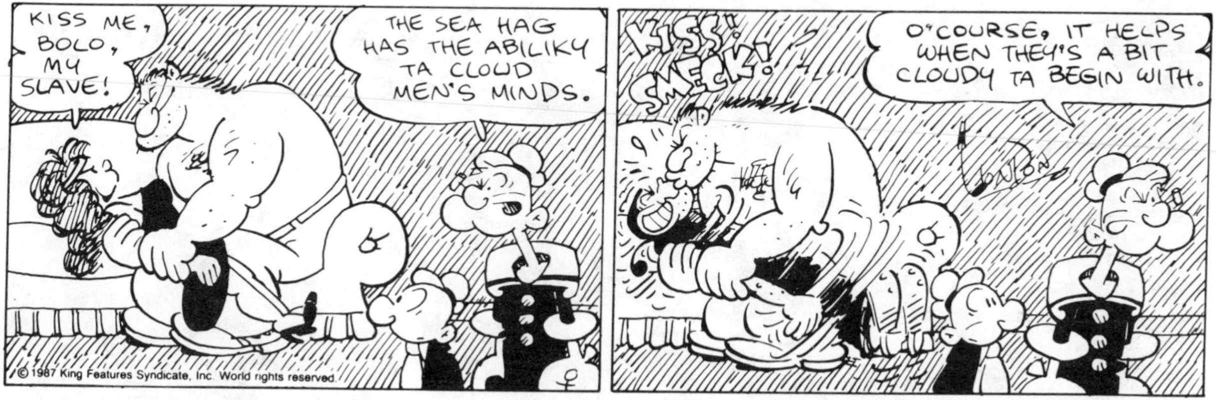
KISS ME, BOLO, MY SLAVE!
THE SEA HAG HAS THE ABILIKY TA CLOUD MEN'S MINDS.
© 1987 King Features Syndicate, Inc. World rights reserved.
KISS! SMECK!
O'COURSE, IT HELPS WHEN THEY'S A BIT CLOUDY TA BEGIN WITH.

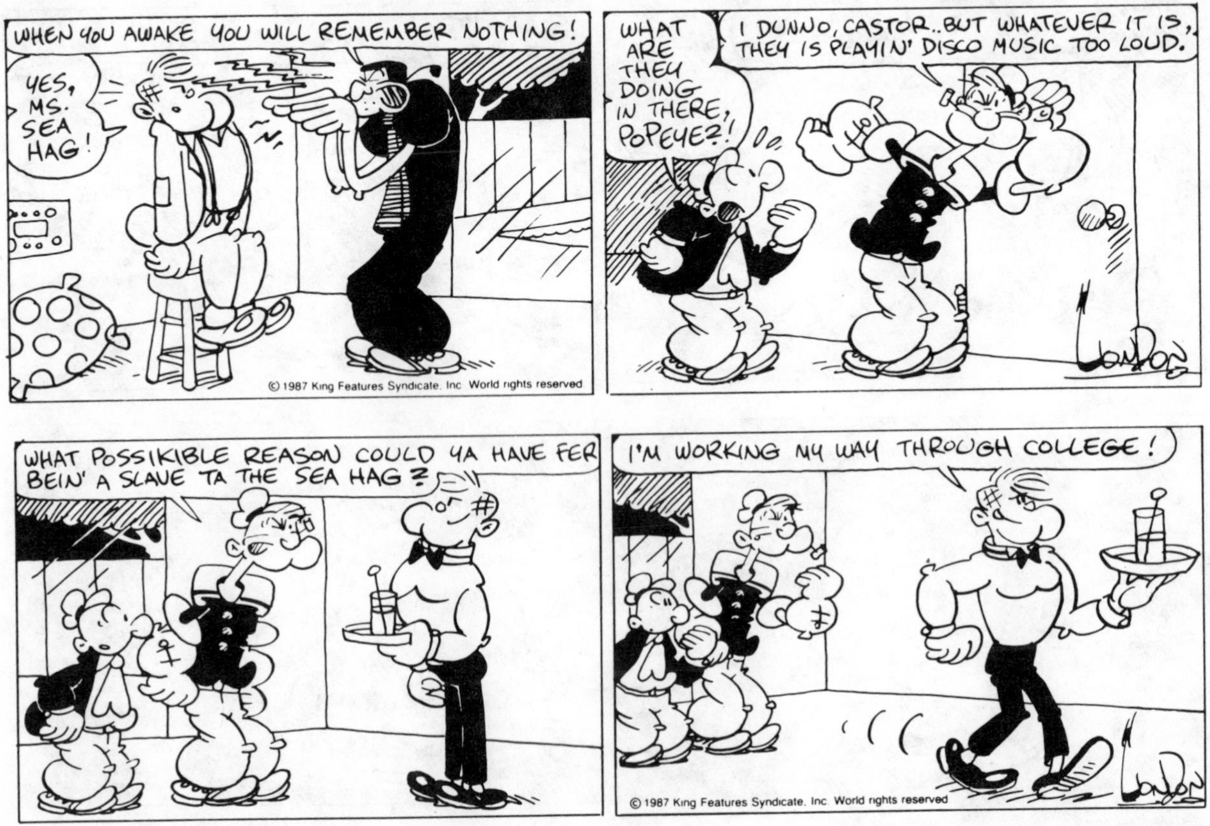
WHEN YOU AWAKE YOU WILL REMEMBER NOTHING!
YES, MS. SEA HAG!
© 1987 King Features Syndicate, Inc. World rights reserved
WHAT ARE THEY DOING IN THERE, POPEYE?!
I DUNNO, CASTOR.. BUT WHATEVER IT IS, THEY IS PLAYIN' DISCO MUSIC TOO LOUD.
LONDON
WHAT POSSIKIBLE REASON COULD YA HAVE FER BEIN' A SLAVE TA THE SEA HAG?
I'M WORKING MY WAY THROUGH COLLEGE!
© 1987 King Features Syndicate, Inc. World rights reserved
LONDON

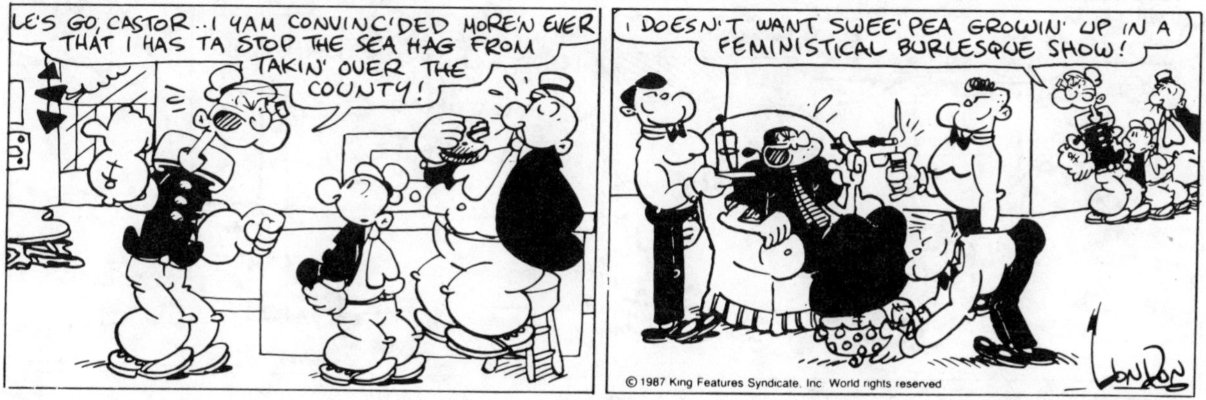
LE'S GO, CASTOR..I YAM CONVINC'DED MORE'N EVER THAT I HAS TA STOP THE SEA HAG FROM TAKIN' OVER THE COUNTY!
I DOESN'T WANT SWEE'PEA GROWIN' UP IN A FEMINISTICAL BURLESQUE SHOW!
© 1987 King Features Syndicate, Inc. World rights reserved
LONDON

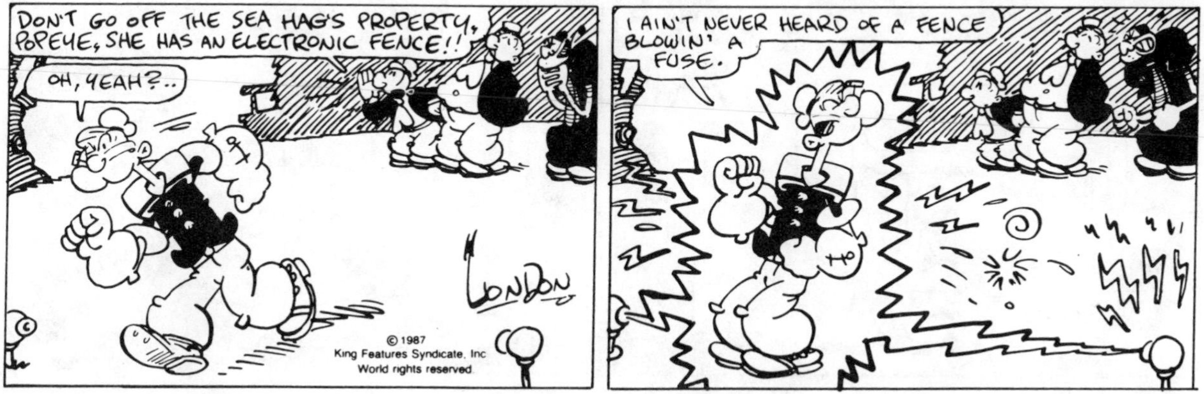
DON'T GO OFF THE SEA HAG'S PROPERTY, POPEYE, SHE HAS AN ELECTRONIC FENCE!!
OH, YEAH?..
LONDON
© 1987 King Features Syndicate, Inc. World rights reserved.
I AIN'T NEVER HEARD OF A FENCE BLOWIN' A FUSE.

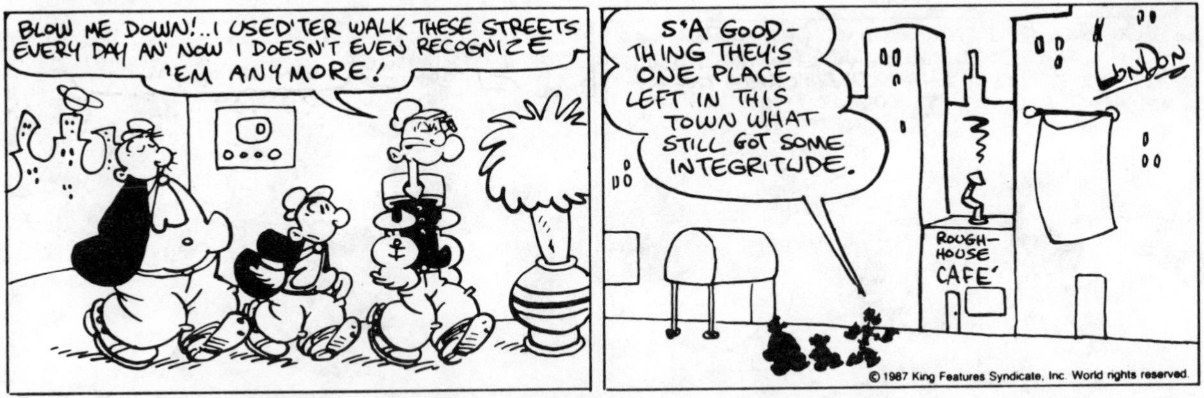
BLOW ME DOWN!..I USED'TER WALK THESE STREETS EVERY DAY AN' NOW I DOESN'T EVEN RECOGNIZE 'EM ANYMORE!
S'A GOOD-THING THEY'S ONE PLACE LEFT IN THIS TOWN WHAT STILL GOT SOME INTEGRITUDE.
ROUGH-HOUSE CAFE'
LONDON
© 1987 King Features Syndicate, Inc. World rights reserved.

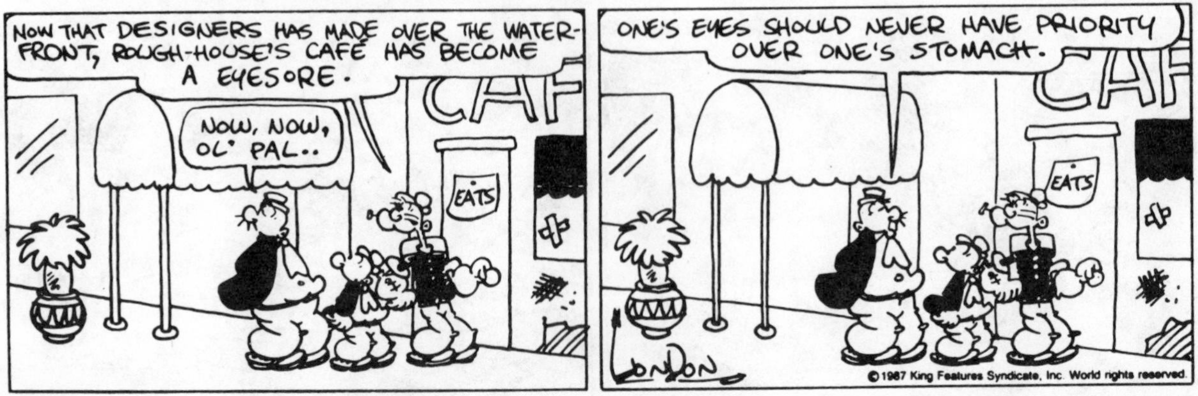
NOW THAT DESIGNERS HAS MADE OVER THE WATER-FRONT, ROUGH-HOUSE'S CAFÉ HAS BECOME A EYESORE.
NOW, NOW, OL' PAL..
CAF
EATS
LONDON
ONE'S EYES SHOULD NEVER HAVE PRIORITY OVER ONE'S STOMACH.
CAF
EATS
© 1987 King Features Syndicate, Inc. World rights reserved.

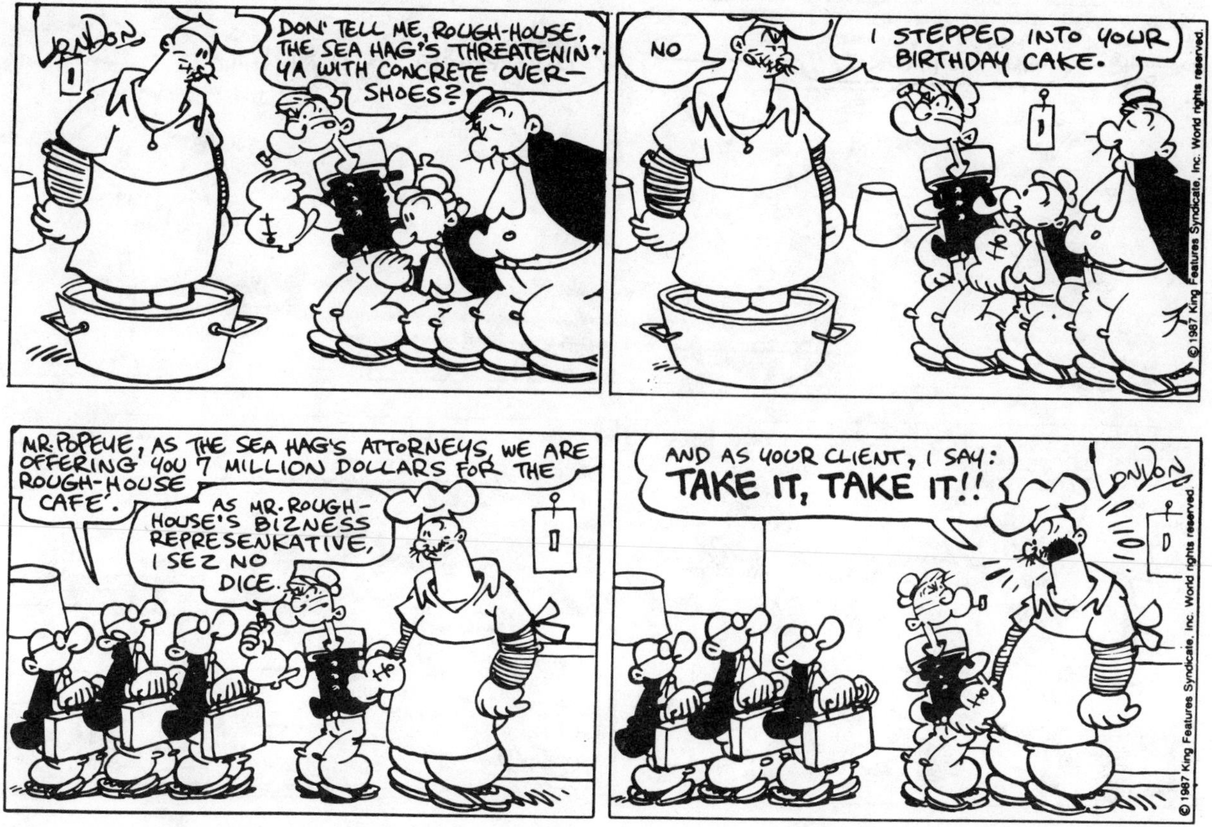
LONDON
DON' TELL ME, ROUGH-HOUSE, THE SEA HAG'S THREATENIN' YA WITH CONCRETE OVER-SHOES?
NO
I STEPPED INTO YOUR BIRTHDAY CAKE.
© 1987 King Features Syndicate, Inc. World rights reserved.
MR. POPEYE, AS THE SEA HAG'S ATTORNEYS, WE ARE OFFERING YOU 7 MILLION DOLLARS FOR THE ROUGH-HOUSE CAFE'.
AS MR. ROUGH-HOUSE'S BIZNESS REPRESENKATIVE, I SEZ NO DICE.
AND AS YOUR CLIENT, I SAY: TAKE IT, TAKE IT!!
LONDON
© 1987 King Features Syndicate, Inc. World rights reserved.

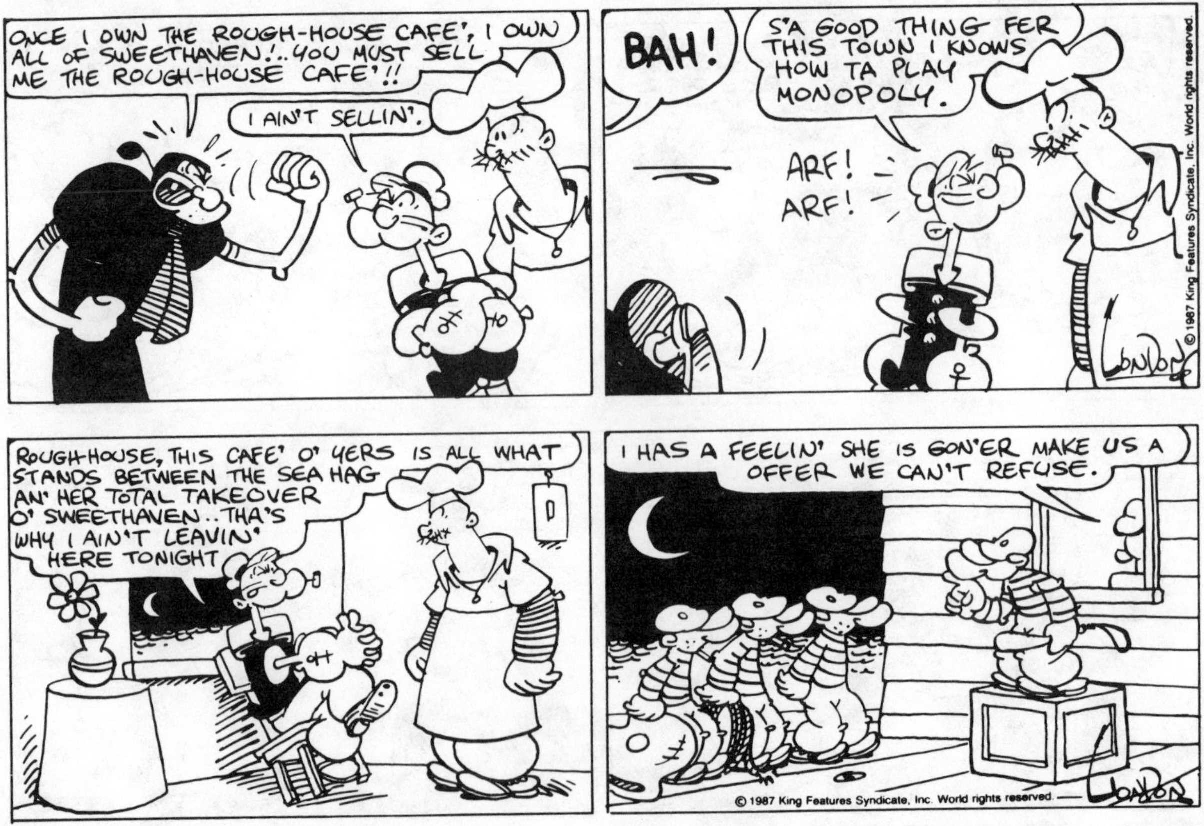
ONCE I OWN THE ROUGH-HOUSE CAFE', I OWN ALL OF SWEETHAVEN!.. YOU MUST SELL ME THE ROUGH-HOUSE CAFE'!!
I AIN'T SELLIN'.
BAH!
S'A GOOD THING FER THIS TOWN I KNOWS HOW TA PLAY MONOPOLY.
ARF! ARF!
© 1987 King Features Syndicate, Inc. World rights reserved.
LONDON
ROUGH-HOUSE, THIS CAFE' O' YERS IS ALL WHAT STANDS BETWEEN THE SEA HAG AN' HER TOTAL TAKEOVER O' SWEETHAVEN.. THA'S WHY I AIN'T LEAVIN' HERE TONIGHT
I HAS A FEELIN' SHE IS GON'ER MAKE US A OFFER WE CAN'T REFUSE.
© 1987 King Features Syndicate, Inc. World rights reserved.
LONDON

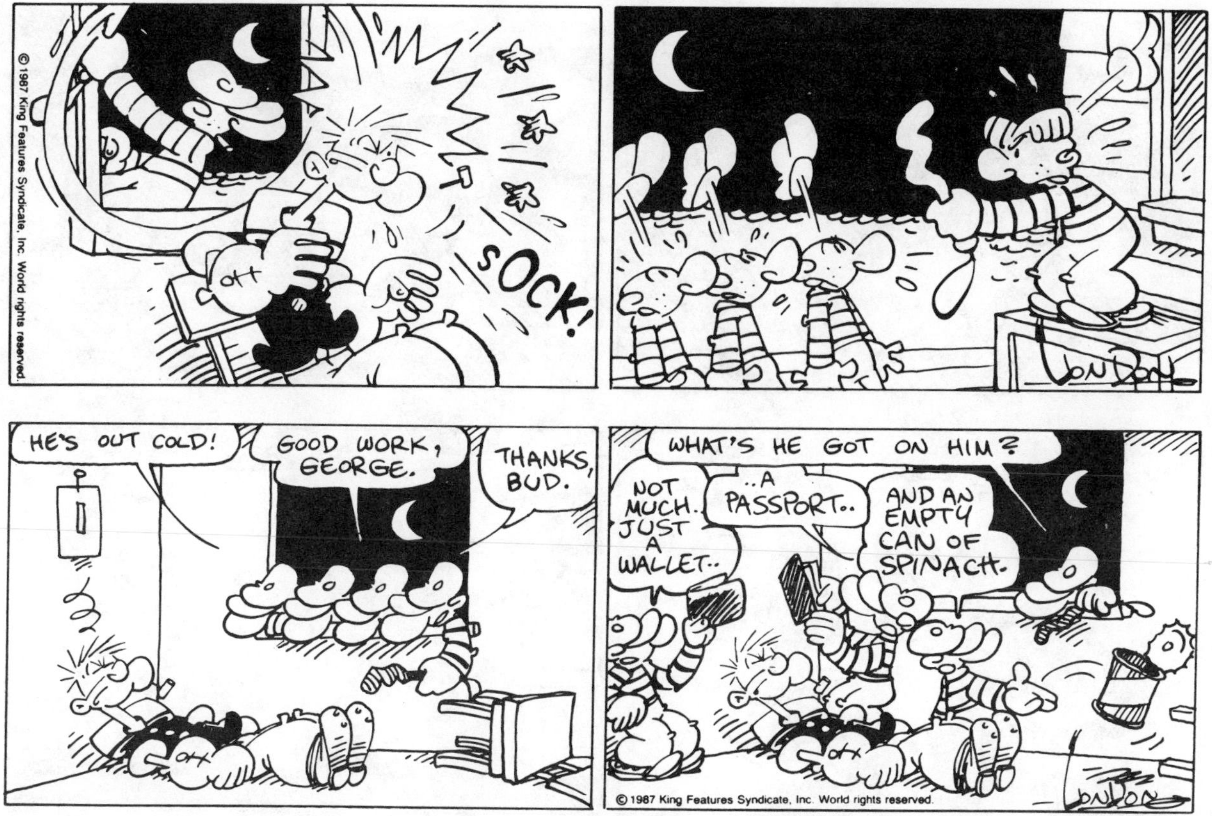
SOCK!
LONDON
HE'S OUT COLD!
GOOD WORK, GEORGE.
THANKS, BUD.
WHAT'S HE GOT ON HIM?
NOT MUCH.. JUST A WALLET..
..A PASSPORT..
AND AN EMPTY CAN OF SPINACH.
LONDON


© 1987 King Features Syndicate, Inc. World rights reserved.

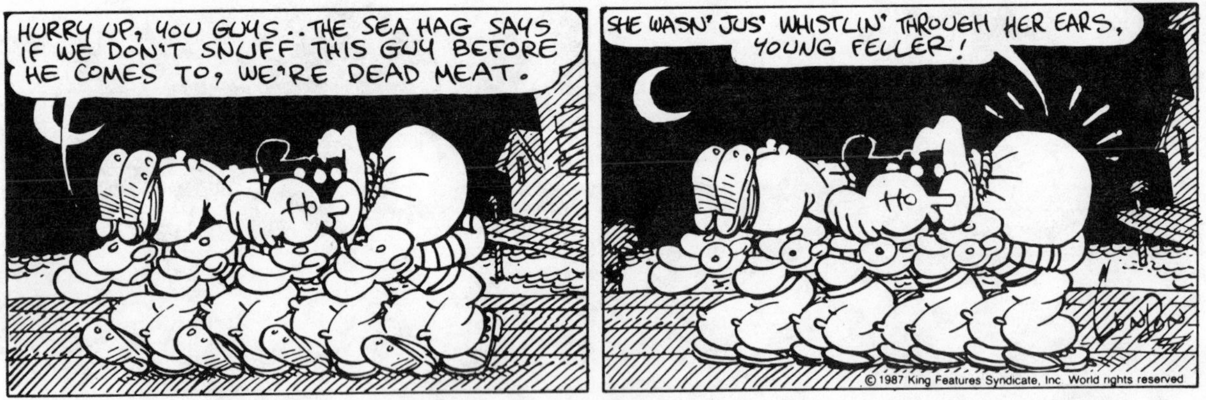
HURRY UP, YOU GUYS..THE SEA HAG SAYS IF WE DON'T SNUFF THIS GUY BEFORE HE COMES TO, WE'RE DEAD MEAT.
SHE WASN' JUS' WHISTLIN' THROUGH HER EARS, YOUNG FELLER!
LONDON


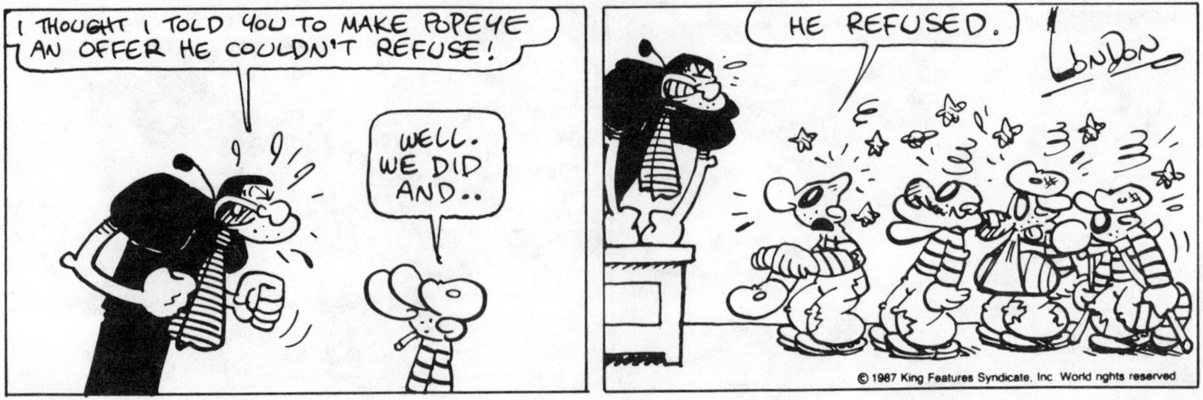
I THOUGHT I TOLD YOU TO MAKE POPEYE AN OFFER HE COULDN'T REFUSE!
WELL. WE DID AND..
HE REFUSED.
LONDON

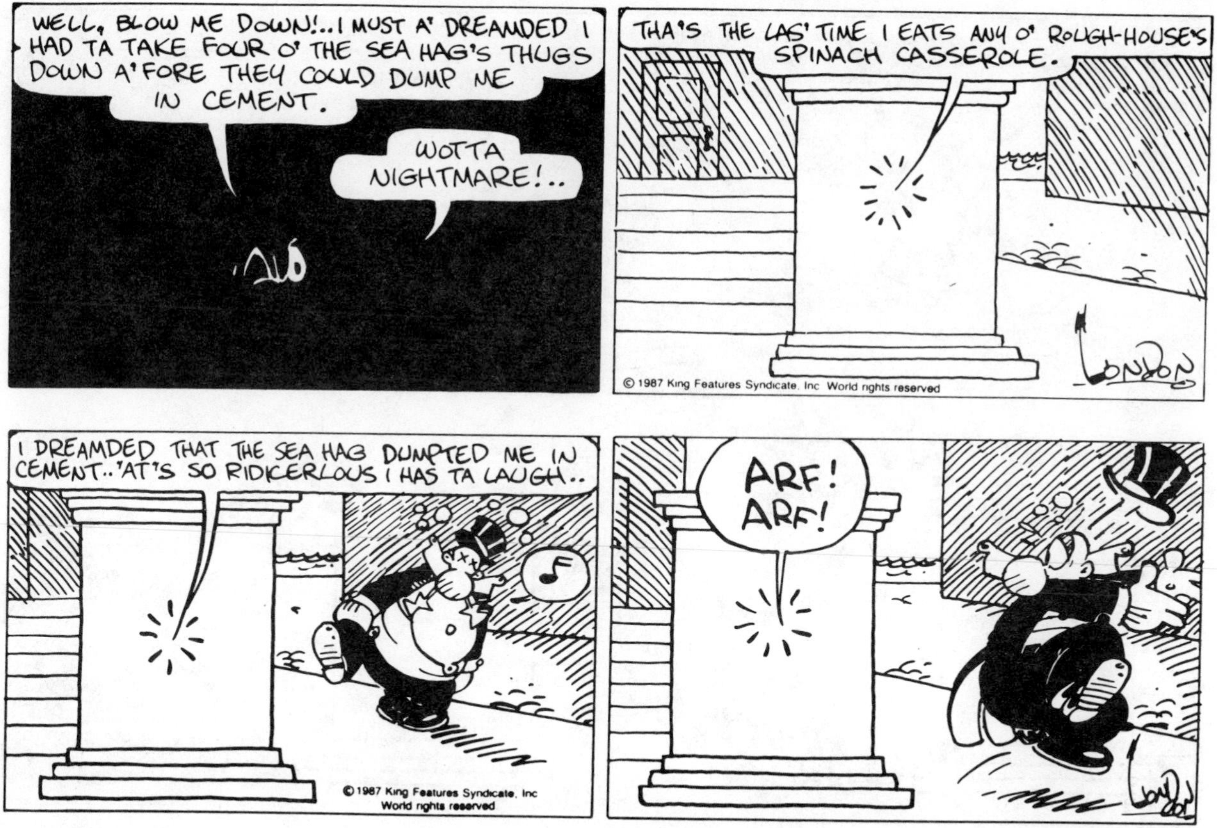

WELL, BLOW ME DOWN!..I MUST A' DREAMDED I HAD TA TAKE FOUR O' THE SEA HAG'S THUGS DOWN A'FORE THEY COULD DUMP ME IN CEMENT.
WOTTA NIGHTMARE!..
THA'S THE LAS' TIME I EATS ANY O' ROUGH-HOUSE'S SPINACH CASSEROLE.
LONDON
© 1987 King Features Syndicate, Inc World rights reserved
I DREAMDED THAT THE SEA HAG DUMPTED ME IN CEMENT..'AT'S SO RIDICERLOUS I HAS TA LAUGH..
© 1987 King Features Syndicate, Inc World rights reserved
ARF! ARF!
LONDON

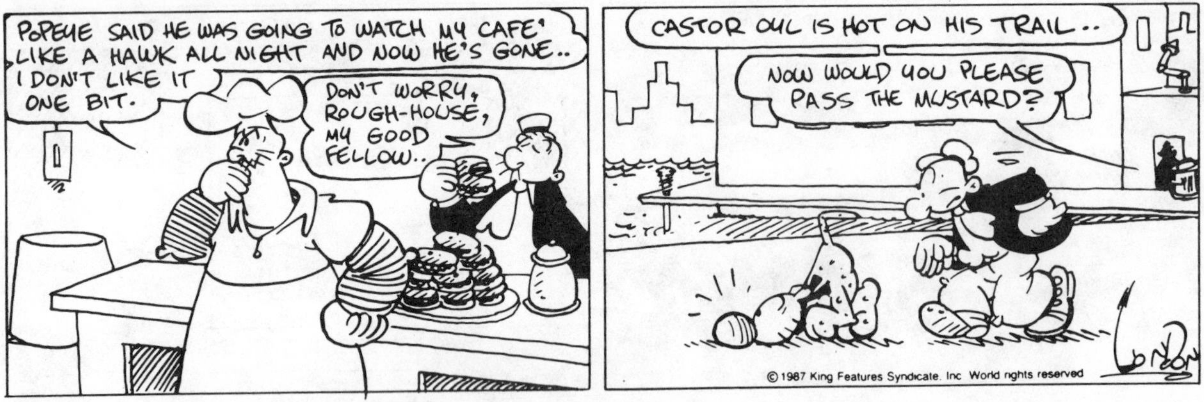
POPEYE SAID HE WAS GOING TO WATCH MY CAFE' LIKE A HAWK ALL NIGHT AND NOW HE'S GONE.. I DON'T LIKE IT ONE BIT.
DON'T WORRY, ROUGH-HOUSE, MY GOOD FELLOW..
CASTOR OYL IS HOT ON HIS TRAIL..
NOW WOULD YOU PLEASE PASS THE MUSTARD?
LONDON
© 1987 King Features Syndicate, Inc World rights reserved

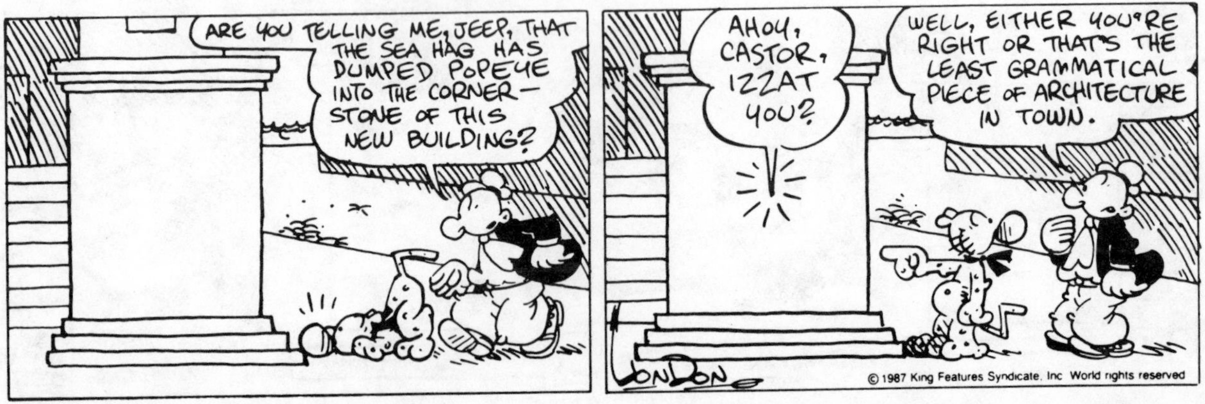
ARE YOU TELLING ME, JEEP, THAT THE SEA HAG HAS DUMPED POPEYE INTO THE CORNER-STONE OF THIS NEW BUILDING?
AHOY, CASTOR, IZZAT YOU?
WELL, EITHER YOU'RE RIGHT OR THAT'S THE LEAST GRAMMATICAL PIECE OF ARCHITECTURE IN TOWN.
LONDON
© 1987 King Features Syndicate, Inc World rights reserved

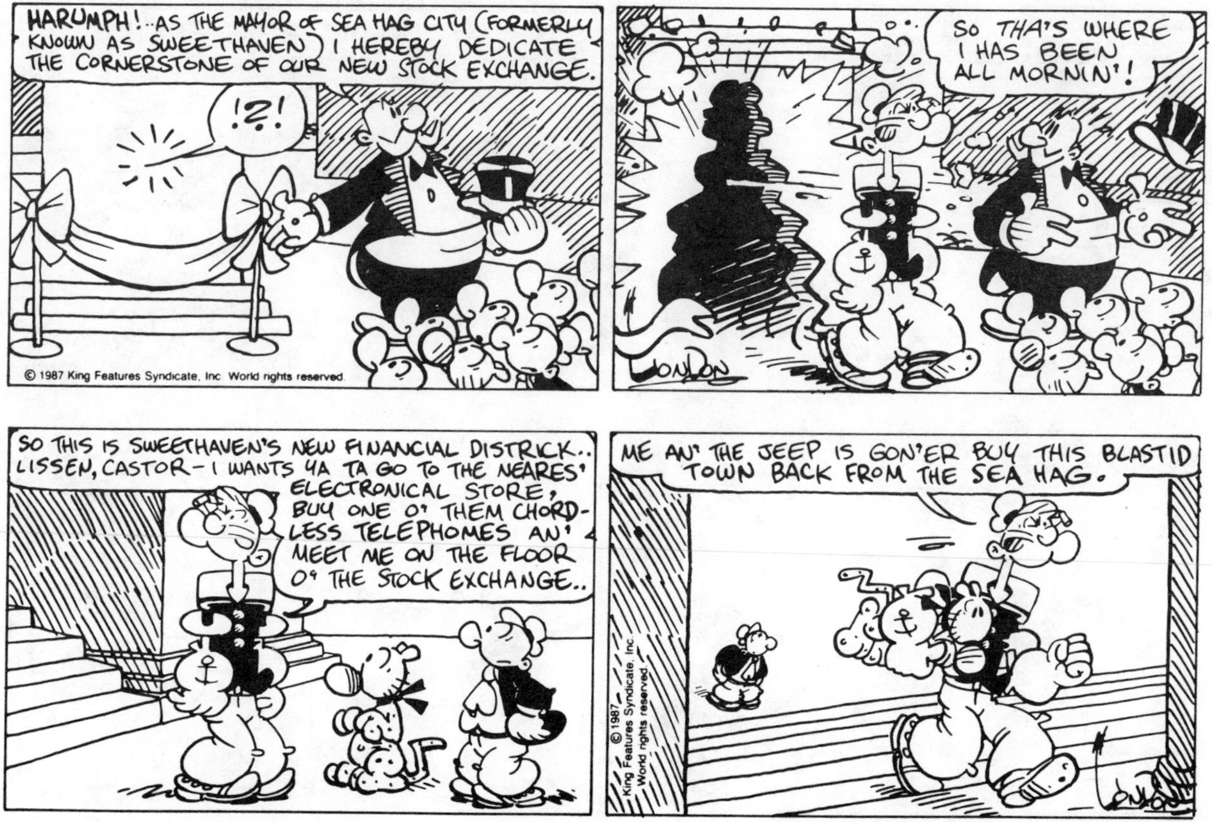
HARUMPH!..AS THE MAYOR OF SEA HAG CITY (FORMERLY KNOWN AS SWEETHAVEN) I HEREBY DEDICATE THE CORNERSTONE OF OUR NEW STOCK EXCHANGE.
!?!
© 1987 King Features Syndicate, Inc. World rights reserved.
SO THA'S WHERE I HAS BEEN ALL MORNIN'!
SO THIS IS SWEETHAVEN'S NEW FINANCIAL DISTRICK.. LISSEN, CASTOR - I WANTS YA TA GO TO THE NEARES' ELECTRONICAL STORE, BUY ONE O' THEM CHORDLESS TELEPHOMES AN' MEET ME ON THE FLOOR O' THE STOCK EXCHANGE..
ME AN' THE JEEP IS GON'ER BUY THIS BLASTID TOWN BACK FROM THE SEA HAG.
© 1987 King Features Syndicate, Inc. World rights reserved.

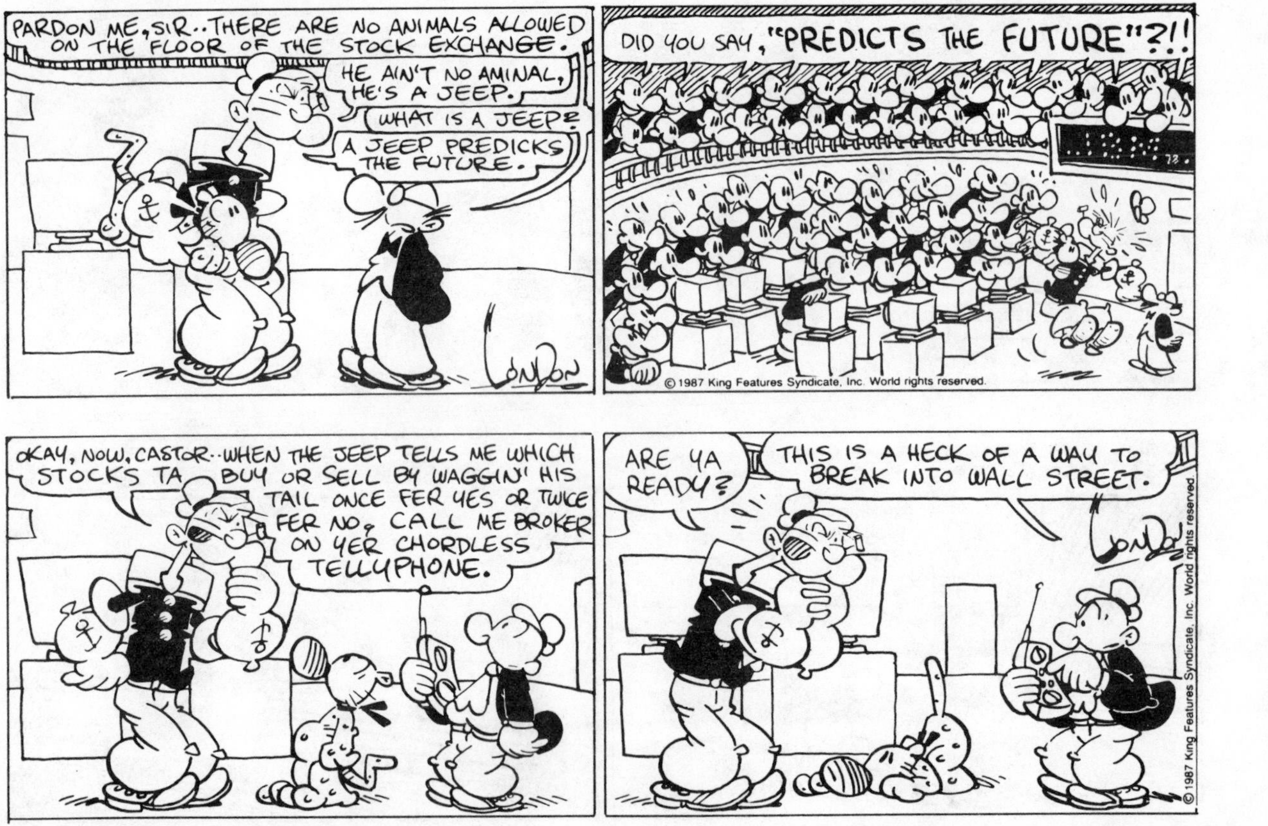
PARDON ME, SIR.. THERE ARE NO ANIMALS ALLOWED ON THE FLOOR OF THE STOCK EXCHANGE.
HE AIN'T NO AMINAL, HE'S A JEEP.
WHAT IS A JEEP?
A JEEP PREDICKS THE FUTURE.
DID YOU SAY, "PREDICTS THE FUTURE"?!!
© 1987 King Features Syndicate, Inc. World rights reserved.
OKAY, NOW, CASTOR.. WHEN THE JEEP TELLS ME WHICH STOCKS TA BUY OR SELL BY WAGGIN' HIS TAIL ONCE FER YES OR TWICE FER NO, CALL ME BROKER ON YER CHORDLESS TELLYPHONE.
ARE YA READY?
THIS IS A HECK OF A WAY TO BREAK INTO WALL STREET.
© 1987 King Features Syndicate, Inc. World rights reserved.

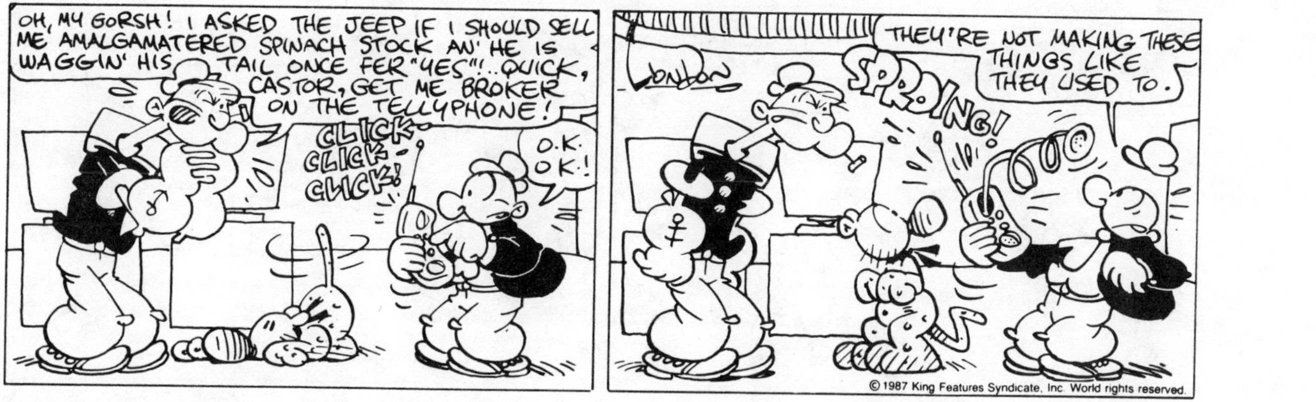
OH, MY GORSH! I ASKED THE JEEP IF I SHOULD SELL ME AMALGAMATERED SPINACH STOCK AN' HE IS WAGGIN' HIS TAIL ONCE FER "YES"!..QUICK, CASTOR, GET ME BROKER ON THE TELLYPHONE!
CLICK CLICK CLICK!
O.K. O.K.!
LONDON
SPROING!
THEY'RE NOT MAKING THESE THINGS LIKE THEY USED TO.
© 1987 King Features Syndicate, Inc. World rights reserved.

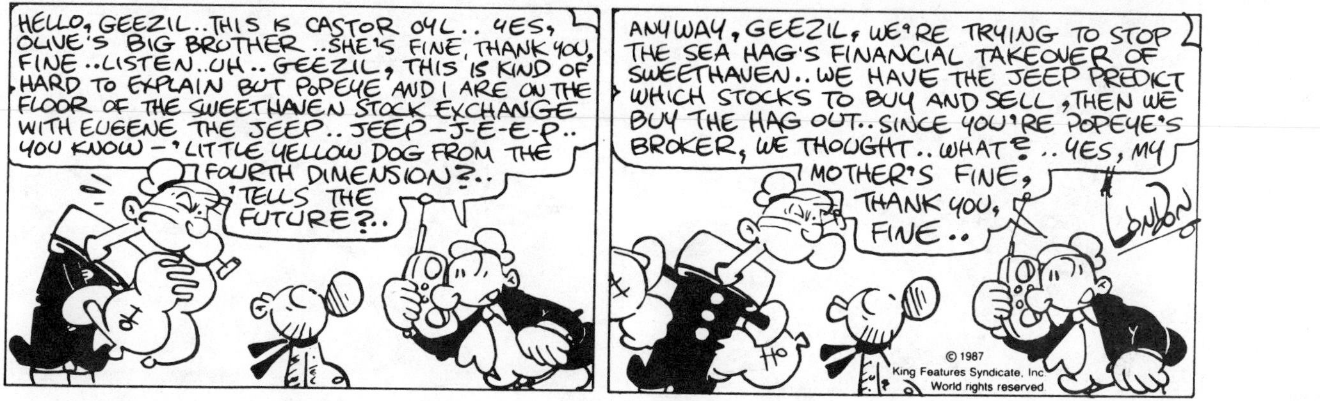
HELLO, GEEZIL..THIS IS CASTOR OYL.. YES, OLIVE'S BIG BROTHER..SHE'S FINE, THANK YOU, FINE..LISTEN..UH.. GEEZIL, THIS IS KIND OF HARD TO EXPLAIN BUT POPEYE AND I ARE ON THE FLOOR OF THE SWEETHAVEN STOCK EXCHANGE WITH EUGENE THE JEEP.. JEEP-J-E-E-P.. YOU KNOW-'LITTLE YELLOW DOG FROM THE FOURTH DIMENSION?..'TELLS THE FUTURE?..
ANYWAY, GEEZIL, WE'RE TRYING TO STOP THE SEA HAG'S FINANCIAL TAKEOVER OF SWEETHAVEN.. WE HAVE THE JEEP PREDICT WHICH STOCKS TO BUY AND SELL, THEN WE BUY THE HAG OUT..SINCE YOU'RE POPEYE'S BROKER, WE THOUGHT..WHAT?..YES, MY MOTHER'S FINE, THANK YOU, FINE..
LONDON
© 1987 King Features Syndicate, Inc. World rights reserved

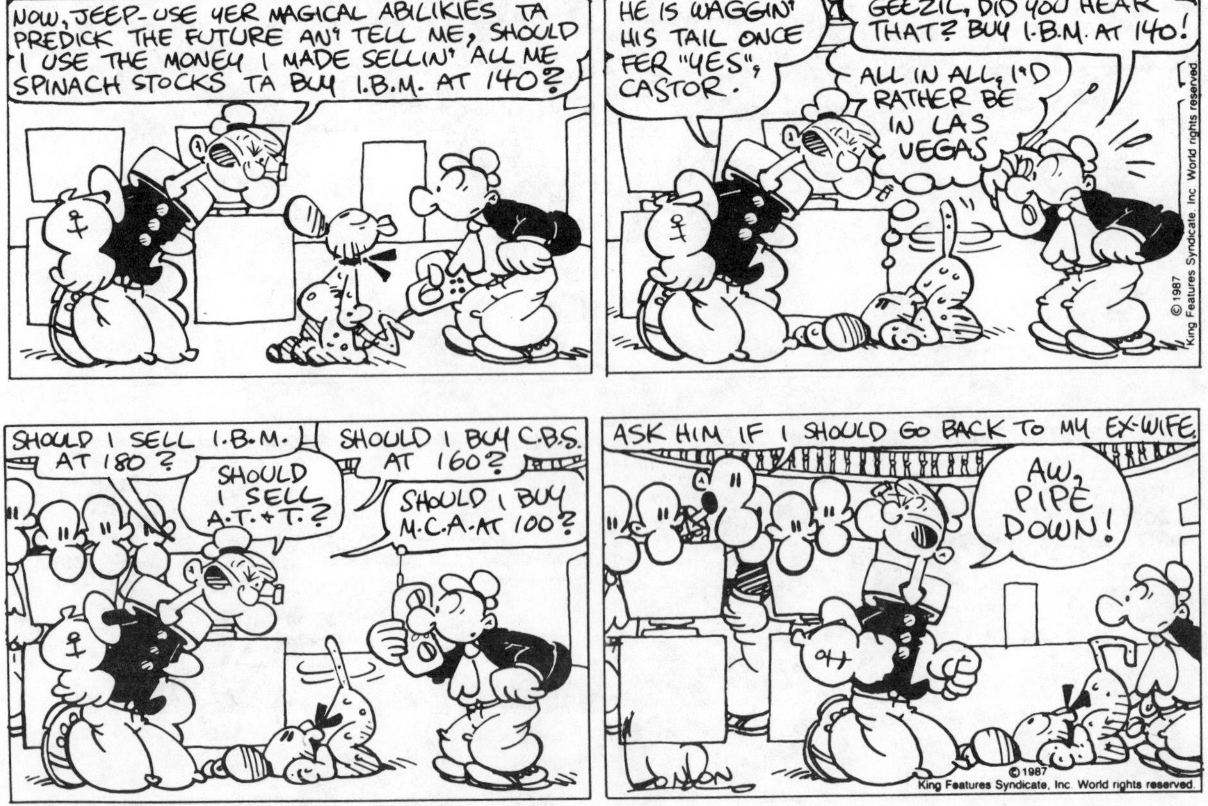

NOW, JEEP- USE YER MAGICAL ABILIKIES TA PREDICK THE FUTURE AN' TELL ME, SHOULD I USE THE MONEY I MADE SELLIN' ALL ME SPINACH STOCKS TA BUY I.B.M. AT 140?
HE IS WAGGIN' HIS TAIL ONCE FER "YES", CASTOR.
GEEZIL, DID YOU HEAR THAT? BUY I-B.M. AT 140!
ALL IN ALL, I'D RATHER BE IN LAS VEGAS
© 1987 King Features Syndicate, Inc. World rights reserved
SHOULD I SELL I-B-M. AT 180?
SHOULD I SELL A.T.&T.?
SHOULD I BUY C.B.S. AT 160?
SHOULD I BUY M.C.A. AT 100?
ASK HIM IF I SHOULD GO BACK TO MY EX-WIFE.
AW, PIPE DOWN!
© 1987 King Features Syndicate, Inc. World rights reserved.

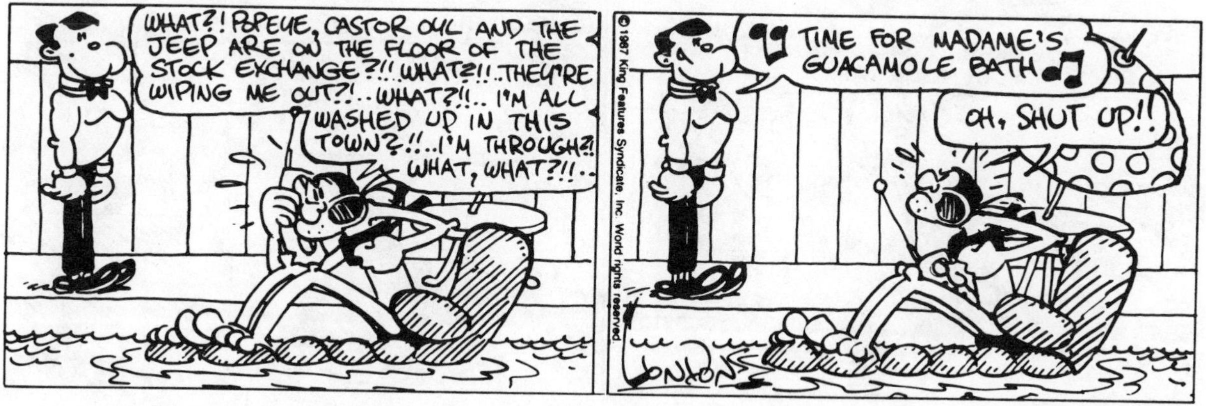
WHAT?! POPEYE, CASTOR OYL AND THE JEEP ARE ON THE FLOOR OF THE STOCK EXCHANGE?!!..WHAT?!!..THEY'RE WIPING ME OUT?!..WHAT?!!.. I'M ALL WASHED UP IN THIS TOWN?!!..I'M THROUGH?!! WHAT, WHAT?!!..
TIME FOR MADAME'S GUACAMOLE BATH
OH, SHUT UP!!
© 1987 King Features Syndicate, Inc. World rights reserved.

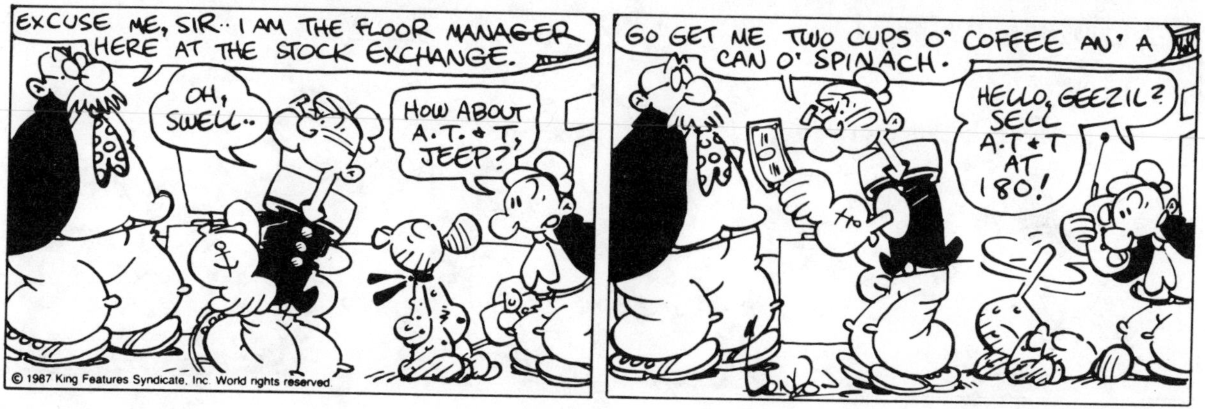
EXCUSE ME, SIR.. I AM THE FLOOR MANAGER HERE AT THE STOCK EXCHANGE.
OH, SWELL..
HOW ABOUT A.T.&T, JEEP?
GO GET ME TWO CUPS O' COFFEE AN' A CAN O' SPINACH.
HELLO, GEEZIL? SELL A.T&T AT 180!
© 1987 King Features Syndicate, Inc. World rights reserved.

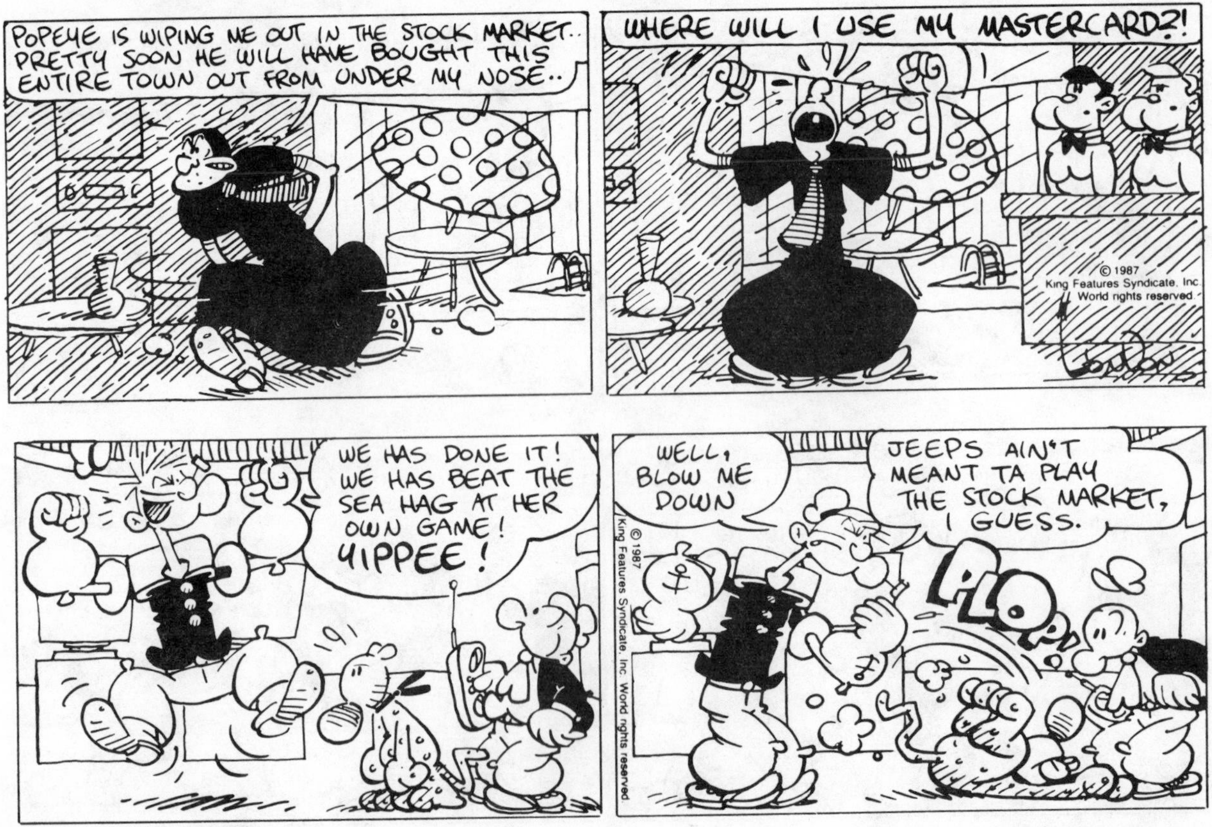
POPEYE IS WIPING ME OUT IN THE STOCK MARKET.. PRETTY SOON HE WILL HAVE BOUGHT THIS ENTIRE TOWN OUT FROM UNDER MY NOSE..
WHERE WILL I USE MY MASTERCARD?!
© 1987 King Features Syndicate, Inc. World rights reserved.
WE HAS DONE IT! WE HAS BEAT THE SEA HAG AT HER OWN GAME! YIPPEE!
© 1987 King Features Syndicate, Inc. World rights reserved.
WELL, BLOW ME DOWN
JEEPS AIN'T MEANT TA PLAY THE STOCK MARKET, I GUESS.
PLOP!

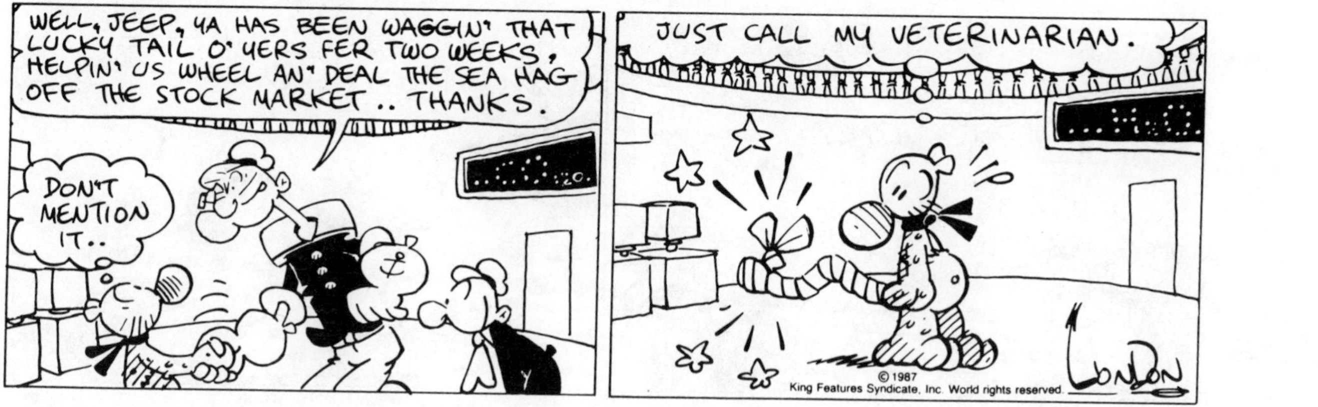
WELL, JEEP, YA HAS BEEN WAGGIN' THAT LUCKY TAIL O' YERS FER TWO WEEKS, HELPIN' US WHEEL AN' DEAL THE SEA HAG OFF THE STOCK MARKET .. THANKS.
DON'T MENTION IT..
JUST CALL MY VETERINARIAN.
© 1987 King Features Syndicate, Inc. World rights reserved.
LONDON

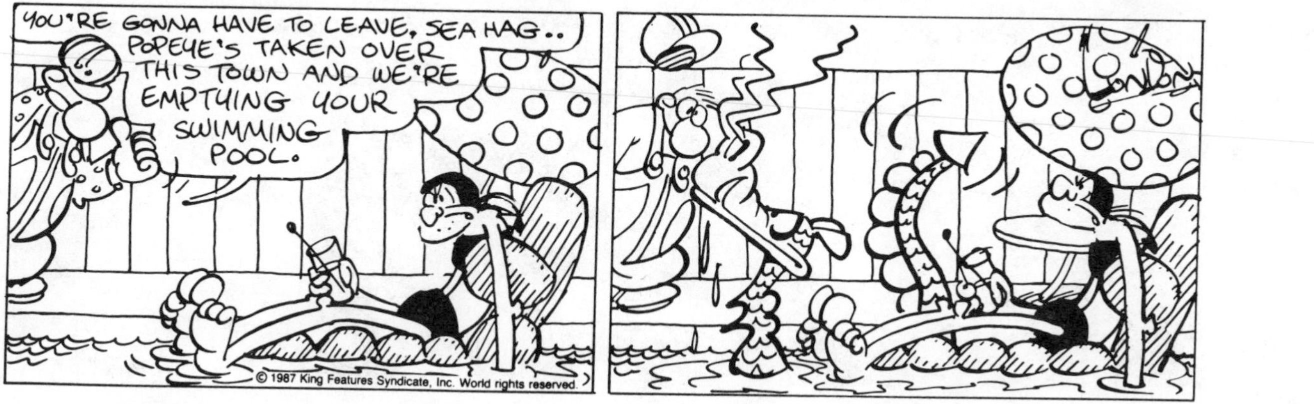
YOU'RE GONNA HAVE TO LEAVE, SEA HAG.. POPEYE'S TAKEN OVER THIS TOWN AND WE'RE EMPTYING YOUR SWIMMING POOL.
© 1987 King Features Syndicate, Inc. World rights reserved.
LONDON

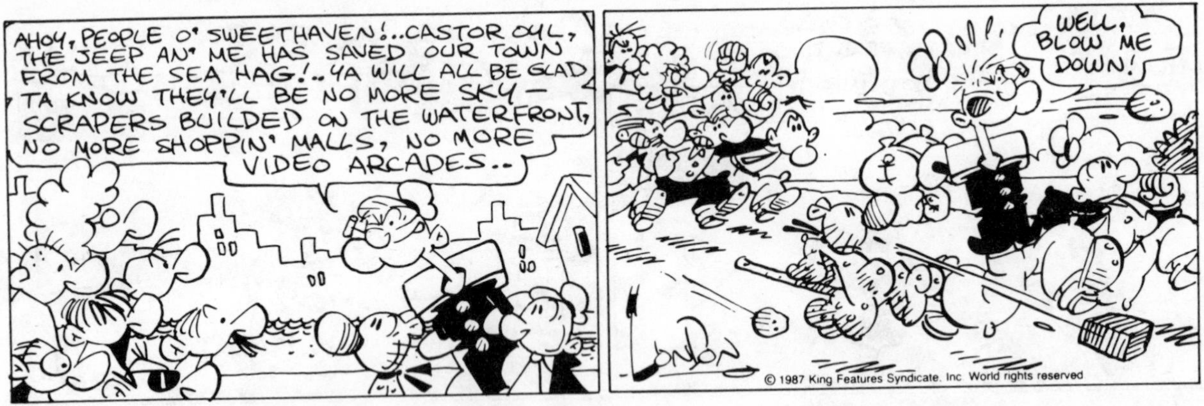
AHOY, PEOPLE O' SWEETHAVEN!..CASTOR OYL, THE JEEP AN' ME HAS SAVED OUR TOWN FROM THE SEA HAG!..YA WILL ALL BE GLAD TA KNOW THEY'LL BE NO MORE SKY-SCRAPERS BUILDED ON THE WATERFRONT, NO MORE SHOPPIN' MALLS, NO MORE VIDEO ARCADES..
WELL, BLOW ME DOWN!
LONDON
© 1987 King Features Syndicate, Inc. World rights reserved

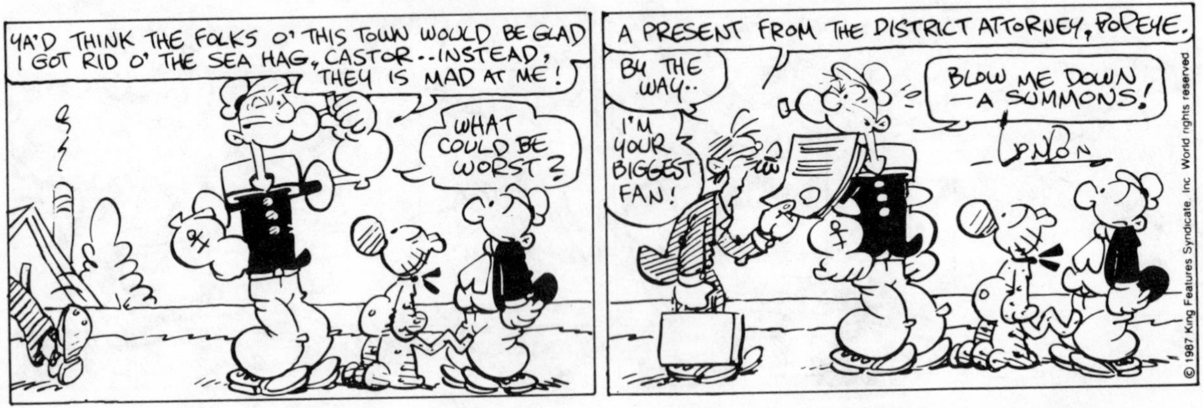
YA'D THINK THE FOLKS O' THIS TOWN WOULD BE GLAD I GOT RID O' THE SEA HAG, CASTOR..INSTEAD, THEY IS MAD AT ME!
WHAT COULD BE WORST?
A PRESENT FROM THE DISTRICT ATTORNEY, POPEYE.
BY THE WAY..
I'M YOUR BIGGEST FAN!
BLOW ME DOWN — A SUMMONS!
LONDON
© 1987 King Features Syndicate, Inc. World rights reserved

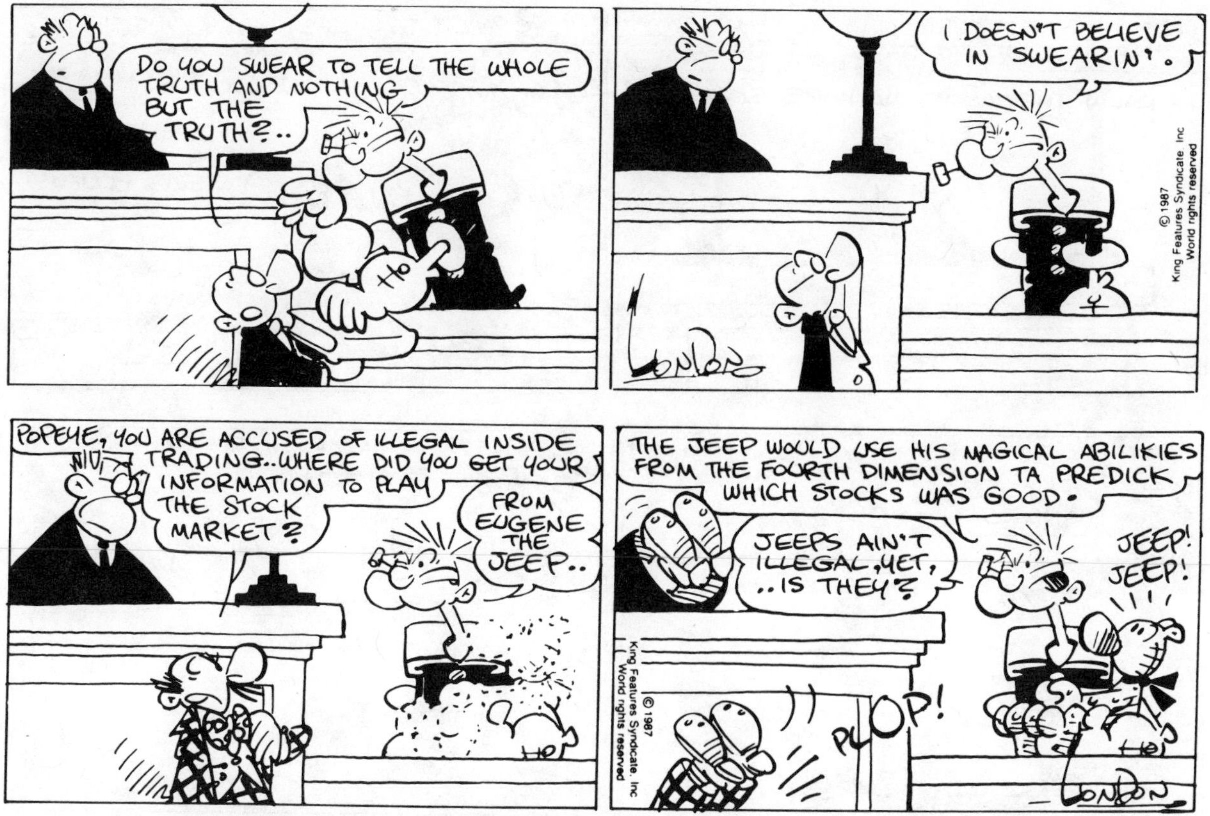
DO YOU SWEAR TO TELL THE WHOLE TRUTH AND NOTHING BUT THE TRUTH?..
I DOESN'T BELIEVE IN SWEARIN'.
LONDON
© 1987 King Features Syndicate, Inc World rights reserved
POPEYE, YOU ARE ACCUSED OF ILLEGAL INSIDE TRADING..WHERE DID YOU GET YOUR INFORMATION TO PLAY THE STOCK MARKET?
FROM EUGENE THE JEEP..
THE JEEP WOULD USE HIS MAGICAL ABILIKIES FROM THE FOURTH DIMENSION TA PREDICK WHICH STOCKS WAS GOOD.
JEEPS AIN'T ILLEGAL, YET, ..IS THEY?
JEEP! JEEP!
© 1987 King Features Syndicate, Inc World rights reserved
PLOP!
LONDON

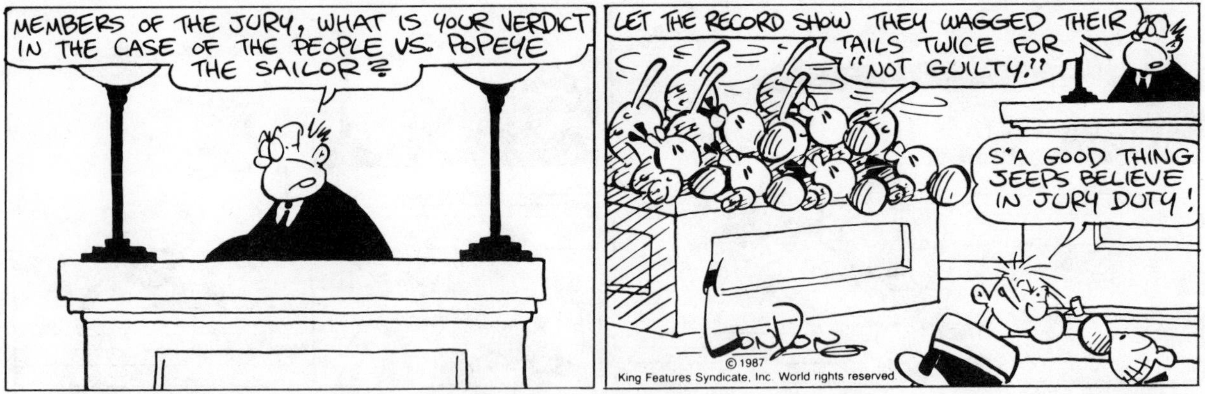
MEMBERS OF THE JURY, WHAT IS YOUR VERDICT IN THE CASE OF THE PEOPLE VS. POPEYE THE SAILOR?
LET THE RECORD SHOW THEY WAGGED THEIR TAILS TWICE FOR "NOT GUILTY."
S'A GOOD THING JEEPS BELIEVE IN JURY DUTY!
LONDON
© 1987
King Features Syndicate, Inc. World rights reserved.

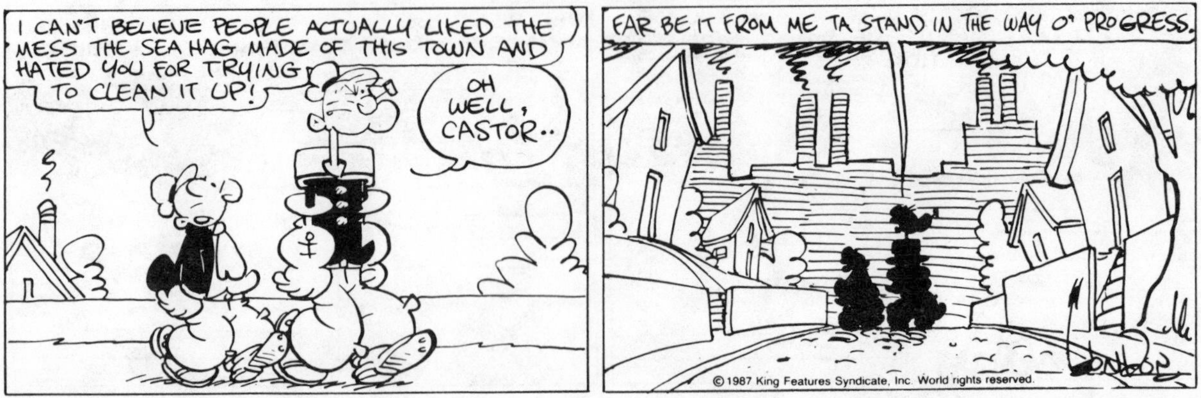
I CAN'T BELIEVE PEOPLE ACTUALLY LIKED THE MESS THE SEA HAG MADE OF THIS TOWN AND HATED YOU FOR TRYING TO CLEAN IT UP!
OH WELL, CASTOR..
FAR BE IT FROM ME TA STAND IN THE WAY O' PROGRESS.
LONDON
© 1987 King Features Syndicate, Inc. World rights reserved.

Born in New York City, Bobby London attended Adelphi University and had his first cartoons published in 1969, in the counterculture press of New York and Chicago. He moved to the West Coast in the early seventies. The *Los Angeles Free Press* began publishing his comic strip "Dirty Duck" in 1971; *National Lampoon* picked up the strip from 1972 to 1977, and it then appeared in *Playboy* from 1977 to 1987. London worked as a freelance artist for The Walt Disney Company in New York before becoming artist/writer of "Popeye," created by Elzie Segar in 1919, in February 1986.

London's illustrations have appeared in such publications as *Esquire, Rolling Stone, The New York Times,* the *New York Daily News,* the *Washington Post,* and the *Village Voice.* He has also contributed to "Saturday Night Live." Winner of the prestigious Yellow Kid Award at the 1978 International Salon of Comics, he currently lives in New York City.